This book is due for return on or before the last date shown below.

3/19

HORIZONS

The Life and Times of Edric Connor
1913–1968

An Autobiography
with *Foreward by George Lamming*
and *Introduction by Bridget Brereton and Gordon Rohlehr*

Edric Connor

Ian Randle Publishers

Kingston • Miami

First published in Jamaica, 2007 by
Ian Randle Publishers
11 Cunningham Avenue
Box 686
Kingston 6
www.ianrandlepublishers.com

National Library of Jamaica Cataloguing in Publication Data

Connor, Edric
'Horizons' : the life and times of Edric Connor, 1913-1968 : an autobiography with foreword by George Lamming and introduction by Gordon
Rohlehr and Bridget Brereton.
p. ;   cm.

ISBN 976-637-277-2 (pbk)

1. Connor, Edric, 1913-1968 – Autobiography.   2. Singers – Trinidad
and Tobago – Biography.   3. Actors, Black – Biography.   4. Music and
folklore.   5. West Indians – Great Britain.   6. Trinidad and Tobago –
Social conditions – 20th century.
I. Title
791.092   dc 21

Cover and book design by Ian Randle Publishers
Printed in Unites States of America

TO GERALDINE AND PETER

MY DEAR CHILDREN

TRINIDAD

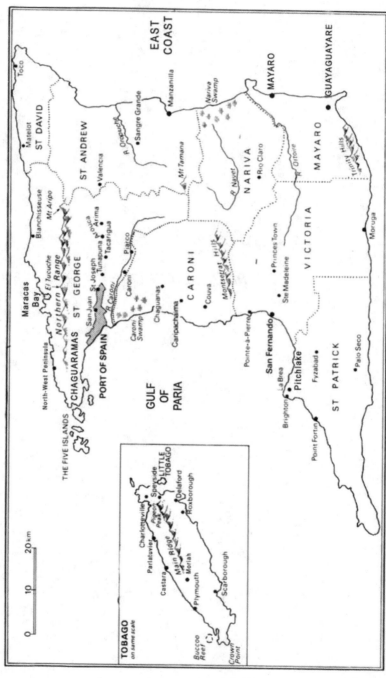

Map 1 Trinidad and Tobago

Source: Bridget Brereton, *A History of Modern Trinidad, 1783–1962* (Portsmouth, New Hampshire: Heinemann, 1981). Used with kind permission of author.

Contents

Foreword
The Artist As Ambassador
By George Lamming

The Moor is of a free and open Nature
That thinks men honest that but seem so.
(Shakespeare: *Othello*)

Edric was a great nationalist. He believed in the
independence of our country and the life of our people.
(Pearl Connor-Mogotsi)

She loved me for the dangers I had passed
And I loved her that she did pity them.
(Shakespeare: *Othello*)

Edric Connor, the Trinidad-born singer and actor, would be remembered by those who knew him in his London period as a man of singular generosity. The experience he has struggled to share, through illness and the painful awareness of an irreversible decline, is also the partial biography of an era. He belonged to that generation of emigrants from the Caribbean whose adventure is often recorded as part of the legendary arrival of the SS *Empire Windrush* at Tilbury Docks on June 21, 1948. He had come four years earlier, and his name had already acquired some resonance before the real migration story began.

England had known the black presence as far back as the reign of Elizabeth I. But the *Empire Windrush* was a different kind of story, and a startling revelation for those who thought they knew where they were going, as well as the native eyes which gazed in utter bewilderment, and wondered who these strangers were; why they came, and how long they would be allowed to loiter on England's green and pleasant land. Empire Windrush is now celebrated as a historic event because it initiated an unprecedented encounter between the English and the subjects of an empire which was being forced to witness its retirement from the prestige of imperial rule. Moreover, India and Pakistan had declared their independence in 1947. The fifth Pan-African Congress, convened in Manchester in 1945, had energized the forces of decolonization across all Africa south of the Sahara.

Edric Connor had the kind of sensibility which registered these changes, but he shared with his kith and kin a perplexing and almost tragic ambivalence which was the legacy of their historic formation. Some 20-odd years ago I tried to describe the nature of this experience and the source of that ambivalence.

> Migration was not a word I would have used to describe what I was doing when I sailed with other West Indians to England in 1950. We simply thought we were going to an England which had been planted in our childhood consciousness as a heritage and a place of welcome. It is the measure of our innocence that neither the claim of heritage nor the expectation of welcome would have been seriously doubted. England was not for us a country with classes and conflicts of interest like the islands we had left. It was the name of a responsibility whose origin may have coincided with the beginning of time...
>
> It had made us pupils to its language and its institutions; baptized us in the same religion; schooled boys in the same game of cricket, with its elaborate and meticulous etiquette of rivalry. Empire was not a very dirty word, and seemed to bear little relation to those forms of domination we now call imperialist...
>
> The English were not themselves aware of the role they had played in the formation of these black strangers. The ruling class were serenely confident that any role of theirs must have been an act of supreme generosity. The English working class were not aware they had played any role at all and deeply resented our arrival. It had come about without any warning. No one had consulted them. Occasionally I was asked: "Do you belong to us or the French?" I had been dissolved in the common view of worker and aristocrat. English workers could also see themselves as architects of Empire.
> (*Pleasures of Exile*)

But if Empire was in decline, London continued to be an important political capital for those who were negotiating postcolonial arrangements with the metropole. London also claimed, or was accorded the right to give a canonical validation to any cultural activity which originated in its colonial empire. And it is arguable to what extent this ethos of authority has been diminished by the new curriculum of concerns defined as postcolonial studies. The migration of artists had begun, many of whom would have started as a form of migrant labour before achieving recognition in some other field. Connor had some early training as an engineering student in Trinidad and Tobago and intended to continue study in England as an engineer. It was perhaps the rich tradition of folklore, originating in his native Mayaro village which had nurtured his essential gifts as a storyteller, that determined his future before his departure from Mayaro. It was the skill and integrity of commitment to this resource, the folk culture of Trinidad and Tobago, which distinguished him from the small enclave of black actors and singers who were then knocking desperately at a door that did not promise any easy entrance. It fashioned a particular trademark for him as actor and singer, and according to his own account, it was a major source of tutelage for his preparation of the role of Gower in the Stratford-upon-Avon production of Shakespeare's *Pericles* in 1958. There was a Connor voice; a Connor presence that was distinguishable from all others.

There is a register of significant names which will be found in Stephen Bourne's history of the period. Robert Adams and Cy Grant of Guyana, Pauline Henriquez, Nadia Catouse, Earl Cameron, and the renowned Nigerian Orlando Martins who had appeared with Paul Robeson in C.L.R. James's play, *Toussaint L'Ouverture*, in 1936.

When I met Edric Connor shortly after my arrival in 1950 I was very conscious of being in the presence of someone who mattered. I had heard him on the BBC programme 'Calling the West Indies', before I left Trinidad. Soon I would discover that the BBC was a royal gateway to national recognition. In this respect it was a unique institution, endowed with immense cultural authority and trusted without reservations by all layers of the society. Within two years of his arrival Edric Connor had become a familiar name in the British music world. The speed with which this career took off allows us to see the complexities of race in operation in a context where it was at once a veil of exclusion and a potential ticket of entry. In a sense, Connor had come armed with a certain kind of ticket, as his own narrative will relate, but it would never take him all the way.

Winnifred Atwell, the Trinidad pianist of meticulous classical training, who was the most successful female instrumentalist in the British pop charts in the 1950s, and whose hands were insured for £40,000 had always wanted to be a classical concert pianist. But in spite of the million and more sales of her records, and the BBC recognition of these gifts, they didn't allow the ticket to take her beyond the music of rag time and honky tonk. Permission was granted to enter, but there was no going beyond a fixed boundary. It was this boundary which the spirits of Mayaro persuaded Connor it was his duty to scale, transcend and confound by evidence of achievement whose horizons he himself had not defined. One was always conscious of the superb effort which he demanded of himself and the feverish conviction that no one, in similar circumstances, could have done better. He travelled always with the weight of Mayaro on his back, and it was both a liberating and a cumbersome sort of cargo to carry. It was Mayaro that had appointed him as their ambassador, and Mayaro, illuminated by his success, would become the jewel in Trinidad's crown, whether or not Trinidad chose to wear it. It was a religious and atavistic nationalism which gave a special dignity to the undervalued word, provincial. He would endow his province with honour.

This infectious zeal for a recognition that went beyond personal ambition, to embrace a country, a region and ultimately a whole people, would sometimes prove too rigorous an ordeal for those he tried to shepherd in the early stages of a career. The singer, Thomas Baptiste of Guyana, who appeared with Connor in the West End musical *Summer Song* in 1956, bore witness to this paradoxical gift which Connor bestowed:

> So when I worked with him I learnt a great deal. I also learnt something that has become important in my life. Edric always wanted to succeed to prove that he was as good as anybody else. But where he failed was not to realize he had a right to fail. I benefited from him because, for myself, I know I have a right to fail. But not Edric! He felt if he did anything which did not work out positively, it was a reflection on his people. Black people. And I don't think anybody should carry that burden or responsibility on their shoulders. But he was a great artist and should be remembered.

Some of the most rewarding moments of Connor's autobiography are his joyful evocation of the communal solidarity which defined Trinidad and Tobago rural life at the turn of the twentieth century.

> The day I left Mayaro Government School was a very important occasion in my life. Mr. Worme treated it almost like a speech day. All the children and many parents came to say farewell. I was on show by his table. I got up to make a speech. All my school memories came rushing back. The concerts, the cricket matches, athletic sports, the little loves and hates, the little fights. I looked at the whole school waiting to hear from me, and burst into tears. (*Horizons*).

After the caring and pastoral nursery of his Mayaro boyhood, Connor was soon exposed to a different kind of terrain. This internal migration from country to town occupies a significant chapter in Caribbean literature from deLisser to Selvon and beyond. Different codes of negotiating your survival apply. Each situation may require its appropriate mask; and it can be perilous to risk 'a free and open Nature'. In the midst of serial misfortunes Connor was enchanted by the novelty of special persons and important places, and could not always distinguish whether he was embraced for the purpose he might serve, or for what he was, and really wanted to become. An ungenerous historicism may find it easy to question his nationalist credentials and invite us to see him as a traditional impediment to the struggle for liberation from the colonial subjugation which shaped the consciousness of his time. But Connor is in very distinguished company when we come to examine the tragic ambivalence in all those combatants who contributed to the Caribbean collective will, even while they were celebrating themselves. Dr Eric Williams, presented with some bitterness of feeling in Connor's narrative, is a sparkling example of this crisis of the self. Nor is the issue an exclusively anglophone phenomenon.

The most blistering polemic in Caribbean literature is the Martiniquan poet, Aimé Césaire's *Discourse on Colonialism* written in 1950. He is merciless in his dissection of the anatomy of French racism, parading a galaxy of names which constitute a pinnacle of French intellectual and political life, and accuses:

> A civilization that proves incapable of solving the problems it creates is a decadent civilization.
> A civilization that chooses to close its eyes to its most crucial problems is a stricken civilization.
> A civilization that uses its principles for trickery and deceit is a dying civilization.
> Europe is indefensible.

Aimé Césaire, the Marxist and brilliant architect of the ideology of Négritude, was mayor of Fort-de-France in 1958 when André Malraux, the novelist and French Minister of Government, arrived as the imperial agent of General De Gaulle with a mission to persuade Martiniquans how they should vote in the upcoming referendum that would decide whether they chose independence or join with France in what was being constructed as the French Community. Here the loaded theme of that organic relation of politics to culture is revealed by the eloquence of Césaire's welcome of Malraux:

> In your person I salute the great French nation to which we are passionately attached. May you be the ambassador of our rediscovered hope. (Malraux: *Anti-memoirs*)

Under Césaire's loyal direction Martinique decided to stay with France.

In 1948 on a short return visit to Trinidad and Tobago, Edric Connor met Pearl Nunez for the first time. A few months later they were married in London. Celebrity had got entangled with youth and beauty in a whirlwind of mutual enchantment that swept them across the enormous social and spatial distances of their time. For the next ten years or more they created a partnership which had no parallel within the circles of Caribbean social and community life in London. The Connor residence became known as 'we going by Pearl and Edric': a self-evolving constituency of students, politicians, aspirants to political office, artists and the anonymous friend whom a friend had sent to seek assistance about jobs, accommodation, or advice about the best lawyer or doctor to consult. And once, to my amazement, there was a very quiet, unannounced wedding ceremony for a Trinidadian nurse and a Polish doctor whom I had never met before and who would be leaving for Nigeria the following week. It would appear they had no other connections in London. The Connor residence was home, embassy, an all-purpose bureau. It was a scenario created not only by the resonance of the name Connor, but also by the infinite charm and spontaneity of welcome of the man himself. In all her interviews, and long after his death, his wife Pearl insisted on bearing witness to these qualities. Her letters to me during 2004 and as late as December, less than two months before her death in South Africa, continued the urgency of this appeal:

> I feel Edric's contribution must be recognized. I witnessed and was part of his generosity to our Caribbean community, including Lord Kitchener who arrived in the UK on the *Empire Windrush* and headed straight for our home. There he met Edric who gave him his coat, and let him sleep on the living room floor the only available space then in the flat at Lancaster Gate about which Kitch wrote a calypso which goes as follows: "I took de train to Lancaster Gate, And de trouble dat I met is hard to relate."

In these circumstances it is beyond my knowledge or wish to speculate why Edric Connor retained such a stubborn silence about the vital role Pearl had played in their domestic and professional life; not even to concede:

> She loved me for the dangers I had passed
> And I loved her that she did pity them.

NOTE ON EDRIC CONNOR'S MISSING MANUSCRIPT

The history of the Connor manuscript and its mysterious burial for some 30-odd years is an exercise his biographers might want to excavate at some other time. I became aware of it during a visit to London in 2003 when Pearl, whom I always visited with her family on such occasions, sought my advice on its publication. Edric had submitted the manuscript to the distinguished writer and publisher, the late John La Rose of New Beacon Books for his consideration. John La Rose was in correspondence with the late Professor Errol Hill of Dartmouth College about the possibility of an American edition. These efforts did not materialize. When Edric died in November 1968 La Rose immediately informed Pearl of the status of these negotiations, and shortly afterwards returned the work to her. Pearl Connor moved house two or three times during the next few years, and could not remember exactly when she passed the pile of Edric's papers, including the manuscript, to their daughter, Geraldine. For a long time Geraldine was not aware of the contents of the box of papers which now travelled with her to and fro between London and Trinidad and Tobago.

During a visit to the Schomberg Library in New York Geraldine came across a catalogue with reference to Edric Connor and a letter to his daughter, Geraldine. It was this discovery which switched her attention seriously to the contents of the box. These migrations took place from house to house, and country to country during the 70s, 80s and 90s before the manuscript found its way back to its original source. But no one can be clear at this stage about the exact dates of transfer from person to person. It is just one episode in the continuing history of the Caribbean Archive. The miracle is that it survived and remained in the care of the woman who retained a passionate conviction about the significance of her former husband's life and career. In the last December (2004) letter to me she wrote:

> I see the light at the end of this tunnel and appreciate your confidence in the end result. More things are wrought by prayer than this world dreams of. And when I light a candle I pray: "Let this light rise like a fountain for me night and day. For are men better than sheep or goats who nourish a blind life within the brain, if knowing God they lift not hands of prayer, both for them and those who call them friend?"

I think she would have liked the project to end on that note.

G. L.

Introduction
Horizons:
The Autobiography of Edric Connor, 1913–1968

By Gordon Rohlehr and Bridget Brereton

*E*dric Connor's fascination with horizons began at Peter Hill, Mayaro, Trinidad, where he was born on August 2, 1913. From his bedroom window which opened out towards the east, Connor first gazed at three-quarters of a mile of coconut palms in the foreground, beyond which there was the Atlantic Ocean with its distant horizon behind which the sun rose every morning. The image of the horizon occurs six or seven times in Connor's autobiography and is explained towards the end. The horizon, Connor says, is a promise, not a boundary. 'The more it eludes your grasp, the further you go into the vast Unknown.'[132] He envisaged his life as a constant faring forward towards and beyond horizons, a Baudelairean journey 'into the Unknown to find the new'.[1] Often, having exhausted the possibilities of some phase of his life, he imagined the future as a new horizon to conquer, an unknown and challenging space into which he was determined to move.

Childhood was a dream, a reverie of anecdotes remembered against the background of an ocean of coconut palms, ferns, multicoloured crotons, flowering bougainvillea thornbushes and a Wilson Harrisian flock of peacocks. Connor depicts his community of folk in whom '[t]here was an underlying, unspoken concern for and interest in each other'. [2] His world was full of music. Workers habitually sang as they danced cocoa. His Aunt Dora singing 'Rock of Ages' in her 'beautiful baritone' was powerful enough to make everyone who heard her stop whatever it was they were doing and listen. His sister's contralto voice was, in Connor's opinion, as good as Marian Anderson's, the celebrated African and Native American singer of the first half of the twentieth century. His father, a shoemaker by trade as well as a small peasant farmer, played the guitar well and, even in that remote corner of Trinidad, studied and admired the styles of Segovia and Barrios.

The musical variety of Trinidad and Tobago was reflected in the range of songs and sounds available at the many festive moments of life in the village. String bands played Castilliane, Paseo, 'vie et quoix' (*Vieille Croix*) and Passé Doble, traditional Spanish and French Creole dances of old Trinidad, at a Sunday afternoon political meeting where Arthur Cipriani spoke. A singer, accompanying himself with a guitar, sang a calypso about a murder in the distant village of Fyzabad. 'The printed song was being sold at a penny a time'; [11–12] for, in 1920's Trinidad as in nineteenth-century England, the balladeer often bolstered his meagre income by selling song sheets from town to town. Connor learned from both Mr Mon Louis's band of flute, fiddle, bass, guitar and cuatro, and his Aunt Christine's phonograph records of Al Jolson, Rudy Vallee and Paul Whiteman. His informal musical education was rich and varied and provided the basis for his future interest in singing and performance.

Connor credits Mayaro as the source of his training as actor, singer and raconteur. The many religious sects were potential sources of theatre. 'Here was musical theatre in the raw and I didn't know it.' [8] Connor later realized that Mayaro was like an informal academy of folk culture in which he was receiving natural and organic training that, more than the refinements of RADA (Royal Academy of Dramatic Art) or anything he later learned from cinema or television theatre, determined his own style as singer and actor. He illustrated this observation by describing the lessons he received in storytelling on the Mayaro Savannah; lessons in movement, stillness, sensitivity and intensity. [8] He also learned to dance the Bongo. Connor would only later recognize in all this a distinct folk aesthetic; a series of principles and a viable way of doing: 'I carried this technique to the Shakespeare Memorial Theatre, Stratford-upon-Avon, and it worked perfectly.' [8]

Connor learned the principles of performance along with a repertoire of folk tales, folk songs and calypsoes, before he learned to read or write or, despite his mother's Moravian and Seventh Day Adventist rectitude and his father's Roman Catholicism, before he learned the Lord's Prayer! His grandfather John Jo, who was like a god to the young boy's eyes, did not believe in formal education, but rather recognized the power, wisdom and worth of ordinary working folk, and raised his family unconventionally to become 'extraordinary in their own particular ways'. Connor's formal education, including his learning to say the alphabet, began at age ten — five years later than was normal — when he realized that if he wanted to meet the challenge constantly posed by the horizon to the east, he would need to equip himself with more than the primal organic skills of the country boy. He would need to learn the skills of Ariel and Mi Jean, where before he had been content to be Caliban and to know thoroughly 'the qualities of the island'.[2]

Connor rapidly progressed in his formal education to become a monitor (a pupil teacher) by age 15. He then sat the Handicraft Exhibition Examination and at age 16 placed second out of over 350 candidates from all over the island — an amazing achievement for one who had learned to read only at age ten. He won a scholarship to the Royal Victoria Institute in Port of Spain, but received no encouragement from his father who, a product of grandfather John Jo's way of thinking, foresaw that further education would lead to his son's separation and future alienation from the cloistered and whole rural cocoon, and feared that the final outcome would be exile in England, marriage to a white woman and the development in his son of the supercilious airs of the educated and cultured élite.

It was the determination of Connor's mother, who was prepared to pawn her jewels in order to ensure her son's further education, that shamed the father into a reluctant acquiescence. The incident was paradigmatic, this movement that so many youths throughout the Caribbean were making out of the not-quite-edenic, but the wholesome and coherent rural village that Erna Brodber in her novel *Jane and Louisa Will Soon Come Home*[3] termed the kumbla, into the unknown world beyond the horizon. One sees in this episode simultaneously, the grace, the concern, the caring, and the limitation, bias, cloistered and even repressive nature of the world of the 'folk'. In Connor's case, as in that of Brodber's protagonist, Nellie Richmond, the problem and the test would be how to leave the kumbla and yet retain its organic naturalness, goodness and authenticity while encountering that other world that was signified by education, urbanism and for the most successful, élitism or at least the attainment of a petit bourgeois status.

It was the females, his mother and three sisters, who became the muses and spirit guides of Connor's crossing into the new world of Port of Spain. His self-sacrificing elder sister Germain told him, 'You don't belong to us. You belong to the world.' [24] This prophetic pronouncement endowed sixteen-year-old Connor with self-belief and a sense of destiny; of horizons to conquer, of a world beyond not only Mayaro, but Trinidad and Tobago, to which he belonged. Germain's 'prophecy' was echoed by Birdie, a vendor of bakes, accra and float, who during the first weeks of his apprenticeship virtually saved him from starvation by allowing him to eat whatever he wanted and pay whenever he could. Birdie told him 'You don't belong here. You are too big for this island'. [26] Reminiscing 35 years later, over his sister's prophecy Connor asked, 'How could she have known?' [24] He never ventured to answer his own question, but he did learn throughout his life to respect intuitive knowledge; non-rational ways of knowing or being, which he associated with both women's wisdom and folk intelligence.

It was his mother and sisters, too, who saved him from the clutches of Sister Murray, his Adventist landlady in Port of Spain who withheld from Connor the bags of ground provisions sent each week from Mayaro for his sustenance, and well-nigh starved him to death. They spent two months nursing him back to health after his surgery for tonsillitis, and teaching him to cook and take care of himself in the city. After their departure he seemed prepared for anything the city could devise: the starvation wages of sixteen cents per day for the first two years of apprenticeship; the poor housing conditions; the bizarre vagaries of street life; the rigours of the apprenticeship programme in which he was enrolled. Accepting Port of Spain as a version of the 'horizon', he installed himself after his mother's departure in the 'Ozanam Shelter', 'a place for ex-Borstal boys and young offenders, those who had been to the detention institute, ex-prisoners and old lags.'[27]

Why did he choose such a place, the very opposite of Sister Murray's puritanical and piratical lodgings? It may have been his young man's thrust towards independence, his signal that he no longer needed mothering after the superabundance of care lavished on him for three months by his mother and three sisters, Germain, Leonine and Elaine. He had broken free of Mayaro's kumbla and could now penetrate beyond his first horizon to fully embrace the different cries, fables and melodies of the streets of Port of Spain; the city's 'symphony' and 'concerto' of primal sounds. [27–28] Yet he never quite lost his Mayaro. He rather encountered 'home' on a symbolic level via the Charlotte Street market with its abundance of fruits and vegetables and the many famous 'characters' with which the city, like his rural village, was filled.

Some of these 'characters' have been celebrated in both prose fiction and calypsoes. 'Teacher' Nosegay, the street preacher who elects to die, like Christ, on a wooden cross in order to take away the sins of his people, but reneges when the stoning and scourging become too real, has entered fiction as Naipaul's Man Man and Lovelace's Taffy, and is the protagonist of the final stanza of calypsonian Wonder's 'Follow Me Children':[4]

> It had an old preacher by the name of Nosegay
> Once said he going to die as Christ to take our sins away
> He said, "Don't nail me; tie me to the cross
> Don't use no big stones; use pebbles, of course."
> Well, Peter hit him with a poui
> He bawl out, "Man have some sympathy!
> Help! Take me down!
> Help! I ain't do no wrong
> Every nigger man go bear their pain
> I ain't dying again!"

Connor tells this almost archetypal narrative of Port of Spain with such relish and fictional embellishment, that one might be inveigled into believing that he was there as witness to all of Nosegay's antics, and that he heard even those 'asides' that Nosegay whispered to his accomplices. [28-30]

Gombo Lai Lai, the man-of-words, another famous street character, is also immortalized in Lord Executor's 'Gombo Lai Lai Before the Court',[5] while the story of the man who, after murdering his sweetheart in Besson Street, blew his head off with a stick of dynamite, is recorded in Black Prince's ballad of 1934:

> Was it love, envy or jealousy
> That caused the dynamite tragedy?
> Such a solemn tragedy has exceeded all history
> In every part of this colony.[6]

There was another calypso, *Blow the Dynamite* (a duet by Lion and Atilla), which actually celebrated the incident in a vigorous up-tempo *lavway*,[7] indicating that in the carnivalesque consciousness of Port of Spain, tragedy could at times be regarded as just another phenomenon in a universe of bizarre happenings.

The voices of Port of Spain street criers selling plantain, fruit, fish or pork, that Connor heard in the thirties were later immortalized in *Ice Man* (1960), Lord Melody's memorable rendition of Pat Castagne's ballad. All of these voices, characters and narratives appealed to the storyteller and performer in Mayaro-trained Connor and led him to a conclusion that he repeated time and again, that Trinidadians loved 'drama'. [28] Playing mas' in 1948 after just over four years of absence in England, Connor concluded: 'It was then I discovered that the whole of Trinidad is one vast theatre'. [72] He had known this in fact two decades before. The appeal of the Spiritual Baptists, both those of his Mayaro boyhood and their counterparts in Port of Spain, was due to the dramatic and spectacular elements in that sect's public performance.

Connor lived at the Ozanam Shelter for three years (1929–1932), in which he seemed to be simultaneously immersed in and detached from the street-life that vigorously flowed all around him. He recognized, but claimed to have risen above, its capacity to corrupt. He learned to box, studied mechanical engineering, won the Stephens Gold Medal for his successful performance in the London City and Guilds examinations of 1934, and studied physics at night classes at Queen's Royal College, an institution where, he wryly observed, he would not have dared show his face in the day. Trinidad society, like most others in the West Indies, recognized a great divide between the sort of minds that were being shaped in grammar-school-type elitist educational institutions such as Queen's Royal College, and those being fashioned in schools for vocational training in practical life-skills, such as the Royal Victoria Institute.

The grammar schools produced your teachers, doctors and lawyers, the recognized intellectual leaders of an emerging nationalist movement; the technical institutes produced your artisans, lesser engineers, technicians, mechanics: essential trades people on whose intelligence and practical competence the new nation would have to be built. Yet such enlightened and trained workers were generally ranked lower in the public mind than their more prestigious grammar school manufactured compatriots. Connor moved with curious ease between the universes of the urban artisan, the middle-class intelligentsia and the proto-proletarian street people of preachers, men-of-words, market vendors, grotesques, tricksters and hustlers of all varieties.

During his five years of apprenticeship, he went through all aspects of railroad engineering, having been trained as a boiler-maker, fitter, blacksmith and worker in the foundry and machine-shop. The work was hard, the pay negligible. It required the most skilful management to stay above the level of starvation. Connor regarded the entire experience as a test, a sort of rite of passage towards manhood, in which hardship was simply a necessary part of the learning process. He did not sing for three years [27], though he developed an appreciation for the stage and the concert hall and occasionally absconded from classes to hear famous artistes perform at the concert hall of the Royal Victoria Institute. [30] He heard Menuhin, Barrios and Segovia; his father travelled to Port of Spain and sponsored his ticket for the Segovia concert. No one in particular seems to have introduced Connor to this new horizon: the concert hall and performance stage. He wanted to go there, into what was an alternative and perhaps parallel universe to the hard world of the machine shop and boiler room.

He first began to sing in resistance to the harshness of the industrial workplace.

> I suppose my voice really developed against the noise of the machines.... When Bansfield [his supervisor] gave me hell and I was sick at heart I would sing to soothe the pain, full-throated, drowning the noise. I set myself my first and only ambition: to sing in the Royal Victoria Institute choir. [30]

This he did, three months later (probably in 1933), when he appeared as lead singer with the Royal Victoria Institute choir, then as substitute for a visiting English baritone; though, he complained, he received no public credit for the latter achievement.

Eager for both performance experience and recognition, he acted in D.W. Rogers's play *Blue Blood and Black* and attracted the attention of two visiting English film-makers, Irene Nicholson and Brian Montagu, who felt that 'he would be great in any country' and insisted that a part be written for him in the *Trinidad Guardian* sponsored movie that they were currently filming. He acted in his first film which for some reason was never released.

Suddenly, a new horizon, the prospect of attaining greatness beyond Trinidad's shores had presented itself. The fact that the *Trinidad Guardian* had sponsored a film in which he had acted and performed well, made him feel that the *Trinidad Guardian* was an agency that might facilitate his movement into that imagined 'other world' where he longed to be. He therefore accepted the offer of becoming a reporter for the *Trinidad Guardian* in 1936, even though the salary was less than the survivalist wages he was earning at the railway. Manoeuvring well, Connor accompanied a senior reporter when he interviewed US President Franklin D. Roosevelt who passed through Trinidad on his way to the first Pan-American Conference in Rio de Janeiro. Roosevelt arrived in Trinidad on December 11, 1936 'to a rapturous welcome on the waterfront'.[8]

Connor, however, did not gain automatic admittance into the bourgeois world; he was rather, consigned to the magistrate's court and the 'real human drama pass[ing] in procession'. [32] As a reporter he covered industrial news, weddings, funerals and the people's theatre of the law courts, a traditional source of popular narrative. Famous murder trials in those days used to be reported as close to verbatim as possible and became, like today's 'reality TV', a sort of popular serial fiction that sometimes lasted for several weeks. Connor's new job awakened in him an old yearning to learn as much as he could about the lives of the people of Trinidad. His grandfather John Jo advised him that to do this he would need to consult not the teachers in the colleges or in the schools, but the old people of the villages.

> Go and talk to them. Live with them. Go to the cemeteries. Find the old cemeteries and read the tombstones. Then go to the libraries and look up the period. You will be lucky if you find any of the written history of the people . . . Son, if you truly want to get educated, walk. The whole of Trinidad is there. [35]

John Jo, redoubtable foe of formal academic education, knew that the people's history resided within the people's memory and oral tradition, and set Connor firmly on his journey towards what may be regarded as a new horizon, or as the original one in a new disguise: the true and authentic folk. Thus began Connor's pilgrimage as a self-taught folklorist, ethnomusicologist and organic intellectual — a quest that took him away from the superficiality of the emerging Creole middle class which he mistrusted, but towards which he had begun to drift. Following his grandfather's advice, Connor said, 'I walked the country. I found the cemeteries. I found the people and I found my roots.'[35]

He also found soon enough that it was impossible to live on his journalist's salary of $10.00 per month, $2.00 of which was withheld for the Sports and Superannuation funds. So he started the practice of giving concerts to raise funds to pay his rent. The first of these concerts took place early in 1937 and the names of those friends who supported him on that occasion — Hugh McShine, the judge and flautist; Umilta Mc Shine, his piano-playing sister; Myra Austin, Connor's accompanist on the piano; Beryl McBurnie, who donated an extra shilling towards Connor's rental debt; and Leslie Brunton, a newspaper editor who was Connor's 'great friend' and who gave the concert free publicity in the *Evening News*[35] — suggest that the twenty-three-year-old Connor had become securely ensconced in this niche of genteel Trinidad. In his other life, however, he was following the peregrinations of Spiritual Baptist Warner Woman[9] Sister Faith, who prophesied that a time would come when the fisherfolk of Carenage would be unable to fish in their accustomed fishing places, and the residents of Chaguaramas would be forced to leave their lands.

Connor, who seems to have taken Sister Faith more seriously than he'd previously taken Teacher Nosegay or the Spiritual Baptists of Mayaro, says that nobody believed this local Cassandra, who was jeered at and driven out of the village. He remembered her prophecy four years later when he became the facilitator of the Americans in their expulsion of Trinidadians from Chaguaramas and Teteron, prior to the building of the marine base. Connor also took seriously the preaching of Alupha Shekbawn and his Order of Melchisedek, who raged against Mussolini when he invaded Ethiopia in 1936, and later became the backbone of Butler's movement. Connor's account of the Butler Riots, [36-37] like his Nosegay narrative, is standard folk history in its description of Charlie King's immolation and Bradburn's murder, and in its focus on the role played by the Spiritual Baptists in sustaining the Black nationalist enthusiasm upon which the Butler protest fed.

After less than a year's employment at the *Trinidad Guardian*, Connor was declared redundant. He had learned much, both from his assignments as a reporter and from his 'pilgrimages' (his word) into the countryside, but he had gained little advancement towards his distant goal of being recognized as a superior artist by a worldwide audience. He applied to and joined the Police Force which, in a drive to modify their traditional profile of brute force and ignorance — a profile that had been terribly in evidence before, during and in the reprisals after the Butler Riots — had been making an effort to recruit better educated constables. He now was earning $24.00 per month, nearly two-and-a-half times his salary at the *Trinidad Guardian*. As Connor summarized: 'The railway had been hard, the Force was tougher, but the food was regular.'[38] He had entered Port of Spain at the beginning of the Great Depression, and had, during his eight years in the city, achieved all of his horizons and yet had never moved beyond the sufferers' level of bare survivalism.

After three months in the Force he was transferred to the Fire Brigade, then a department of the Police Force. He was also made a drum major and soon led the Police choir. Ironically he gained greater visibility and popularity as a drum major and singer with the Police Band than he had earlier performing with the Royal Victoria Institute choir, and in concerts with the musically accomplished gentry. Working with the Force kept him close to grass-roots situations; singing with the Force propelled him towards his other life on the concert stage. He remained in the Force for two years (1937–1939), resigning one month before the start of World War II and his twenty-sixth birthday. The reason Connor gave for his almost frantic and desperately resisted attempt to leave the Police Force, was its 'corruption'. He does not, however, say what form this corruption assumed; but it must have been some particular incident that had driven him from his best-paying job so far, back into the terrible no-man's land of unemployment.

Connor's reputation as a singer had grown, as an article published by poet (and eventually lawyer) A.M. Clarke just before his resignation[10] illustrates. Clarke began by complaining that with the mechanization of music and the popularity of the 'the talkies and radio', 'there has developed an Europeanising and Americanising influence on music locally, a distaste for anything but ultra-popular music and an increase in ear-playing'. He also complained that the Police Band which could have tried to maintain or set standards had also succumbed to the popular and played mainly music from films, light classical music, hymns and calypsoes, 'of which there are too many in every backroom of the slums'. He deplored a general tendency to descend to the level of the popular rather than to elevate the taste of the masses.

He advised local jazz combinations, which he considered hopeless, to desist from performing in public 'until the creative spirit and knowledge of music is more developed'. The country, he said, had no composer, few instrumentalists — he named only two — two cathedral choirs, the Training College Choir, and the Royal Victoria Institute Chorale which, along with its orchestral section, attempted 'serious work' such as a Beethoven Symphony and *Children of the Captivity*, an opera in three acts. Enthusiastic about both the choir and orchestra, Clarke commended the performance of Edric Connor, who evidently had not given up singing with the Royal Victoria Institute Chorale, although he sang with the Police Choir.

> In the solo-singing Edric Connor was outstanding in quality and natural dramatic interpretation: he sometimes used his voice in recitative fashion which was very effective.[11]

It is impossible to say what percentage of the genteel bourgeoisie towards which Connor partially aspired, shared Clarke's biases against popular music, calypsoes, film music and light classical European sounds, or his desire for the difficult, challenging and highly serious; but it is clear that by 1939, Connor had become a skilled negotiator between the clashing rocks of seriously antagonistic identities. It is significant that at this precise moment when, unemployed, he had rendered himself most vulnerable, he would try to manipulate members of this complacent but still powerless middle class, by whose grace he somehow survived the still hard times. Thus it was with a mixture of easy camaraderie and cautiously suspicious detachment that he began to talk about his 'friends': 'I numbered among my friends some of the people who were on the fringe of power. Were they really friends?'[39]

These 'friends' were Albert Gomes, Ralph de Boissière, Jimmy Bain, Bouch Bain, Carlton Comma and someone Connor referred to as 'Roast Corn'. Gomes, who in the early 1930s had published the groundbreaking literary journal *The Beacon*, would in the forties and fifties emerge as a journalist, trade unionist and considerable political figure. Connor casts doubt on the figure of Gomes who, he says, was supplied with a feasible public cause and political platform — scavengers' wages — by the above-named group of friends, because they thought this loud, large, energetic man would do less harm as a well-intentioned political charlatan than as a bad chemist preparing dubious concoctions in his father's Belmont drug store.

De Boissière, an emerging writer of fiction who had published in the *Beacon*, would later become famous with *Crown Jewel*,[12] a historical novel about the Butler Riots. Jimmy Bain in 1932 translated the first volume of Gustave Borde's seminal *The History of the Island of Trinidad Under the Spanish Government*[13] from the original French. This first volume had between 1876 and 1880 been translated by the redoubtable linguist, John Jacob Thomas, but that earlier translation had never been published.[14] Carlton Comma was a librarian who in the early 1950s facilitated the famous debate between intellectual stickfighters, Dom Basil Mathews and the recently returned Dr Eric Williams. 'Roast Corn' was the nickname of Harold Dupres, a popular footballer who eventually became Chief Engineer of the Port of Spain City Council, and was one of Eric Williams's chief advisers on strategies to contain the social disaffection that grew out of unemployment and urban overcrowding. Connor had fallen into the company of representatives of the multi-ethnic Creole community of 1930's Trinidad: Gomes was Portuguese; de Boissière and the Bains off-white and coloured versions of French Creoledom; Comma, like Connor himself, black.

Such members of the intelligentsia of the time sometimes had university degrees, sometimes not. They were generally concerned with public education, debates, youth clubs, drama, literary movements and the like, through which they endeavoured to raise the tone of cultural life in the nation. It was on the collective enthusiasms of such fascinating conglomerations as Connor and his friends that the nationalist movement of the post-World War II decade was based, though Connor could not know this in 1939 when, doubting their authenticity but needing their assistance, he stood simultaneously involved in but detached from their discourse. His pilgrimages in quest of living folklore continued, providing him with knowledge that reinforced his sense of worth as a man of the people and an organic, if starving, intellectual.

Connor was eventually rescued from his precarious situation by Aldwyn Beckles, one of his friends who was a successful building contractor. Beckles gave the desperate but stoical Connor a job as a time-keeper on a salary that Connor, who claimed to have mastered the art of living on nothing, could not recall. Resourceful as ever, Connor drew on his experience as a mechanical engineer and jack of all trades to adapt to the requirements of the construction industry and, in the short time that he generally took to learn anything, set himself up as foreman of his own building firm. By 1941 when the Americans began construction of the Chaguaramas Base, he was boss of a crew of 25 workmen.

Yet, what looked like success in the running of his own affairs was contradicted by a sense of having outgrown Trinidad. Connor continued his pilgrimages and research, his fund-raising concerts and his now insistent dreaming of fresh horizons. [40] Often seeking the sea's edge, the harbour, the jetty, he yearned to leave his now confining world. 'I dreamed of the day when I would conquer the horizons of the Atlantic that challenged me during my childhood.'[40]

The means to conquer these horizons became clearer when Connor took his 25-man work crew to Chaguaramas one Saturday morning and, by the following Monday, obtained the assignment to build the Naval Base. 'We formed the nucleus of the labour force that built Chaguaramas Naval Air Base.'[43] A nucleus can be, and in the case of Connor's 25 men, clearly was, a very small centre. The building of Chaguaramas was an enormous project which employed several thousands of workers. Connor seemed to have had little idea of how minute his core of workers was, and exaggerated the importance of his role in the greater scheme of things.

As 'expeditor' for the Americans, Connor liaised between his bosses and various local contractors. His knowledge of the people and the place was exploited by the Americans in their acquisition of land and removal of people, some of whose families had lived there for over a century. Connor also served as one of the Americans' chief consultants in the recruitment of local labour. The Local Government authorities ominously warned the Americans that 'the man who did the job [as "expeditor"] would commence it but might not complete it'. [43] So Connor had been commissioned to do a job that other prospective local intermediaries, fearful for their lives, might have been unprepared to do. Going well beyond his brief of overseeing the evacuation and demolition of family homes at Chaguaramas and Teteron, which he described as 'the most beautiful of the poor man's beaches near Port of Spain', [47] he also took charge of resettling the evacuees at Carenage, ensuring that they received materials from the demolished structures and that able-bodied men gained employment on the Base. Connor was concerned with and bargained for fair terms of compensation for the evacuees, and for better conditions for the workmen he helped recruit: 'sixty cents a day, two hours overtime and food.'[45] He also assisted displaced families in the reconstruction of their homes in Carenage.

Yet for all of that, the job was an ugly one and involved one of the oldest rituals of slave societies everywhere: that for one of the enslaved to move beyond his horizon, he needed to betray and at times annihilate a whole community of his brethren and sistren. It was a tragedy that Connor never quite acknowledges in his narrative. His power to demolish was absolute, his ability to assuage and compensate, limited. So though he was concerned about fairness of compensation, it was in fact the Trinidad Local Government authorities who were responsible for formulating compensation agreements, and their decisions were controlled by fixed rates specified in anachronistic statutes.

Connor, who considered those rates to be too low, feared for his life. Yet there is no doubt that he enjoyed the power and authority the job seemed to bestow, and was even tempted to believe that some of his American bosses who used him as their frontman, willing pawn and general factotum, were his friends. He claimed that he and J.P. Tiernan, Roosevelt's special envoy on land acquisition, 'became friends immediately', [49] and seemed to feel that the US owed him some special debt of gratitude for services he had rendered at Chaguaramas between 1941 and 1943. A disenchanted Ariel, he was deeply hurt in the fifties when Mc Carthyite US officialdom repeatedly refused him visas to visit and work in the USA, and grumbled that they seemed unaware of all he had done to help them in the building of Chaguaramas: 'I thought of the base I helped to build, the people whose lands I acquired for America, the people I evacuated from those lands.' [75]

Connor continued his research even while immersed in the

Chaguaramas project and by 1943 had become Trinidad's most knowledgeable folklorist and cultural theorist. The first sign of his competence as a commentator on folk culture was his participation in March 1943 in the debate in the press about the origins, quality and nature of indigenous music — especially the Calypso — in the Caribbean. This debate had started in 1940 (*Trinidad Guardian* January 21, 1940) in an article whose author speculated on the relative contributions of African, Spanish and French sources to the evolution of the Calypso. It arose anew in 1943 with a letter which Saint Lucia folklorist and painter, Harold Simmons, sent to the editor of the *Trinidad Guardian* entitled 'The Calypso and West Indian Music'.[15]

It had been suggested in England that the BBC should feature more West Indian music in its transmission to the Caribbean, and the BBC had sent Edward Evans CMG to find out what West Indian music was and whether the average West Indian listener, if such a person could be identified, wanted to hear it played. One Saint Lucian newspaper, the *West Indian Crusader,* had then criticized the suggestion that Calypso was adequate evidence that a West Indian music existed, arguing that the Calypso was a vestige of Latin American music that had survived in Trinidad, but not the music of the other islands where it was hardly ever played.

Simmons opposed this view and was writing to solicit the opinions of Trinidadian experts in the field. He enquired of the editor of the *Trinidad Guardian*:

> Do your readers consider the term "West Indian music" a misnomer? And if there is a music apart from the calypso, basically and generically West Indian, what would you cite as the best example of it? Has anyone in your island carried out research into the origins of the calypso?

Simmons stressed the need for such research because he felt that:

> A nation in the making should have its own music, art, literature and culture — a frank admission and self-criticism will dictate to the West Indian a true concept of himself, free from external influences.[16]

Ironically, at the very moment of Simmons's letter, Edric Connor, the person best qualified to answer Simmons's questions, was in one of his famous concerts illustrating the catholicity of his own and general West Indian musical taste. On the same day as Simmons's letter, the social events reporter of the *Trinidad Guardian* recorded that:

Mr. Edric Connor, the well-known baritone, held his audience spellbound at the smoking concert at the British and Allied Merchant Navy Club on Wednesday evening. Particularly appreciated were Handel's "Largo" and the "Volga Boatman." He was accompanied by Mrs. Pattison on the piano.[17]

Donning his ethnomusicologist's hat, Connor replied to Simmons the following week in a letter/article entitled: 'The Calypso and West Indian Music'.[18] Connor held that:

There is definitely a West Indian music. This W. I. music appears in WI Negro spirituals, e.g. "Joshua Walk round Jericho," "Death O Me Lawd," and West Indian Folk Songs e.g.: "See Me Nancy Comin' Down," "Pam pa nam Nak am pa nam." And "Lim Lim Lim." The above are but a few examples and are by no means taken from any one island. The West Indian spiritual is closely related to the American Negro spiritual, and so, too, the West Indian folk songs are somewhat similar to the plantation songs of America.

The calypso, which has its origin in these spirituals and folksongs is but an off-shoot. The calypso is typical to Trinidad because of its association with the Carnival celebrations. But this type of music which is indeed a corruption of the original folksongs and spirituals due to certain European influences, may be found not only in Trinidad, but also in the West Indian islands under different names.[19]

Connor then discussed the cultural impact of Haitian immigrants fleeing from the Haitian Revolution in the early nineteenth century; the competitive singing of spirituals and folksongs and stickfighting songs during the period of slavery; the changes that occurred in the music over time because of the interplay of French, English and African influences; the origin and historic importance of Canboulay and the significance of the change in the late 1840s from celebrating Canboulay on Emancipation Day, August 1, to incorporating it into the pre-lenten Carnival festival. Secularized in the Calypso, the spirituals 'lost their identity' and Calypso, like Canboulay, became 'attached to' and absorbed by Carnival.

Connor's theories of origin reflected his situation as an intermediary between classes, castes and cultures in Trinidad. Beginning with a task of theorizing the origins and nature of West Indian music, Connor arrives at and nonchalantly reconciles dichotomies of sacred (spirituals) and secular (Carnival); tradition and change; 'pure' and 'corrupted' forms; national and regional; African and European; and the overlap, seepage and transgression of adjacent cultures into each other's space. Most of these issues are still unresolved in the discourse about Trinidad's and the region's cultures. The quest of Connor and his generation was for a theory of ennoblement; one that would somehow reconcile the differences, even the ambiguities of their cultural tastes, their ambivalent swing between Eurocentricity and Afrocentricity. Connor needed to bridge whatever gap may have existed between Handel's *Largo*, the *Volga Boatman*, *Children of the Captivity* and other traditional concert favourites of genteel Eurocentric colonial Trinidad, with the folksongs of old Trinidad and other West Indian territories and the folk–urban barrack-yard ballads of the Calypso, which even then were undergoing radical transformation as calypsonians altered them to appeal to their new patrons: American marines.

The bridge between concert hall and barrack yard was what Connor termed the 'spiritual' music of an earlier time, whose high seriousness had become engulfed in the secular cynicism of the Calypso. The West Indian spiritual, according to Connor, was similar to its African-American counterpart. There was some truth in this assertion. Connor was familiar with Jamaican folk music where African-American influences had been deep since the advent of African-American Baptists in the 1780s and the Great Revival of the 1860s. Trinidad's Spiritual Baptists could also trace their ancestry to communities of African-American loyalists who, having fought on the side of the British, had been relocated in the 'Company' villages beyond Princes' Town after the 1812 war in which the British were finally expelled from America.

Connor's enthusiasm for the 'spiritual' as a sort of noble ancestor of the Calypso is, however, not due to these tangible historical linkages between African Americans and certain Caribbean communities, but to the roles that choral groups such as the famous Fisk Jubilee Singers, and individual artistes such as the contralto Marian Anderson and the bass baritone Paul Robeson, had played in enshrining the Negro Spiritual as an icon of the dignity and nobility of a race that had been both long-suffering and steadfast in their battle against oppression. It was natural for Connor to claim the spiritual in his quest for a worthy ancestor for all diasporan African New World musics. He was seeking dignity for the music and for himself.

Connor's reply to Simmons sparked off a lively discourse about the origin and nature of Calypso. Daphne Taylor wrote that Calypso was the 'national music of Trinidad and Tobago' and saw it as 'a blend of French, Spanish and Negro Folk songs'.[20] Eric Burger felt that calypsos had become too heavily intellectual and were now unable to do what was being asked of them. French 'chansonniers' were calypsonians.[21] Dom

Basil Mathews in January 1944 delivered four lectures on 'Folk Culture of Trinidad as revealed in folklore and folksong'.[22] These lectures came after Connor had stunned the society with two lectures on the same topic in July and December 1943. According to Mathews the folk culture of Trinidad came from four sources — Africans, Spaniards, French and English — whose mixture was peculiar to Trinidad. The novelist Alfred Mendes, recently returned to Trinidad, noted improvements in the Calypso[23] and felt that if Calypso was folksong, it should be encouraged.[24] This drew an angry rejoinder from Mc Donald Carpenter[25] and a dismissal from Edgar Mittleholzer, the Guyanese novelist then resident in Trinidad.[26] Both Carpenter and Mittelholzer felt that the Calypso was not 'art' and was a poor foundation on which to build a culture. Charles Espinet, who together with Harry Pitts had just written a book entitled *Trinidad, Land of Calypso*,[27] answered Carpenter[28] by arguing that today's crudity was often tomorrow's culture.

Connor's letter replying to Harold Simmons also led May Johnson, President of the Trinidad Music Association, to invite him to deliver a public lecture on West Indian Music on July 27, 1943. Connor curiously claims that lecture to have been the day that 'West Indian nationalism was born'. [53] This claim needs to be related to Simmons's assertion that 'a nation in the making should have its own music, art, literature and culture.' Connor not only lectured about the origins of West Indian music but illustrated his lecture by singing folk songs from Carenage and Teteron, accompanied by a chorus drawn from among the very people he had helped evacuate from those areas! The villagers sang the choruses to the folk songs and also demonstrated Limbo, Bongo and Belé dances to the stupefied audience, who did not leave until after midnight, and that in a time of curfew!

A correspondent for the *Sunday Guardian* wrote an extensive and enthusiastic account of the occasion on August 1, 1943.[29] The writer described the lecture/concert as a convincing illustration of the depth and breadth of Connor's years of research into 'the survival of African culture in the West Indies'. Connor had discovered nearly two hundred old songs, along with 'a comprehensive collection of Negro games, dances, customs, tales and proverbs'. For though Connor's chief concern was the music, 'music plays such an important part in the culture that folklore, dances and history slipped naturally into his discussion of the subject'.

Understanding fully the theatrical nature of his subject, Connor delivered not just a lecture, but a dramatic performance of his theme.

To demonstrate examples of the dances and songs he described, he brought along over 50 drummers, dancers and singers, who he has found, retain the most complete tradition of Negro music. In addition, the Jubilee Singers provided beautifully harmonized versions of three songs revived by Mr Connor, who is himself already known for his fine baritone. Mrs Robert Pattison has set many of the songs to music and she accompanied Mr Connor on several of them.

Mrs Pattison was the wife of Robert Pattison, Connor's chief instructor at the Royal Victoria Institute where, recognizing the need for self-improvement and certification after his work at the Base was completed, Connor had resumed night classes in Construction Engineering. [53] Together, the Pattisons proved to be two of the most genuine friends: muses who facilitated his mastery of the complementary universes of the workplace, the folk village and the concert stage. This concert/lecture/dramatic performance, which marked the end of his fourteenth year in the city, was a triumphant coalescence of the extremes of culture he carried within himself, between which he had always sought reconciliation. The lecture was Connor's identity in motion and illustrated how deeply — with a little help from his friends — he had penetrated beyond all the horizons that had so far challenged him.

Displaying a keen instinct for dramatic effect, Connor mesmerized his audience with his presentation. According to his reviewer:

> From the first word to the last, the audience was completely absorbed and entranced, and so, all one could see was Mr. Connor. He took the stage apparently alone, but in the semi-darkness behind him stood the drummers and singers, men from Gonzalez Place and Chaguaramas. Mr. Connor only had to break, unaccompanied, into the first tune of some folk song — usually quite unknown to his audience — and an answering chorus would reply, as if by magic from behind him. The major effect was one of absolute spontaneity: the performers were doing something they had done all their lives, and were surprised at the burst of applause which greeted each effort.[30]

The wonder of it was that Connor, one of the agents of the evacuation of Chaguaramas, had successfully required that the evacuees sing and dance and make response to his call at this climactic moment of his residence in Port of Spain. They danced Limbo, Bongo and Shango, though the latter two of these had long been prohibited by law. They played steelband, two years before the VJ Day celebrations of *Bitter Man, Pops and Battersby*,[31] and demonstrated how the tamboo-bamboo became the substitute for the banned Shango and other ritual drums. J.D. Elder's notion of the journey of the African drum from Congo drum to steelband[32] probably had its root in Connor's July 1943 lecture/concert. The evening ended with 'most of the spectators on their feet, swaying to the infectious rhythm of the tamboo-bamboo, even though many of the audience had never heard its name before'.[33]

Connor had become visible as never before, but was again unemployed — he doesn't say what happened to his crew of 25 workers after Chaguaramas. He was offered a job 'to teach Building Construction at Tuskegee Institute in Alabama'. [53] His resumption of night classes at the Royal Victoria Institute was clearly part of his preparation for that job. The British authorities in Trinidad, particularly Sir Edward Cunard, secretary to the Governor, thought otherwise. They wanted to involve Connor in their new programme of Social Welfare which the Moyne Commission had recommended after their enquiry into the causes of the West Indian-wide riots of 1937–38. They therefore blocked his application for a passage to the United States and virtually forced him to work as a Social Welfare Officer under Dora Ibberson. He did that job for ten weeks, during which time he continued his field studies into the folk life and lore of the areas he visited.

Connor was meanwhile requested to do a repeat performance of the lecture/demonstration for the benefit of those who had missed the July 27 occasion. Cunard, perhaps to soften the blow of having prevented Connor from taking up the job at Tuskegee, promised that he would get the Governor, Sir Bede Clifford, to attend the second lecture. [54] Connor related with obvious pride that his lecture of December 16, 1943 [56] 'was attended by Sir Bede Clifford, Sir Edward Cunard, Vincent Brown, the Chief Justice and other top people'. [55] Connor again brought the then much despised and harassed steelband on to the genteel city stage and savoured the impact that steelband rhythm made on the city's socialites. He also used the occasion to protest against anachronistic legislation prohibiting folk dancing (that is, the Bongo), drumming and the Shouters.

This time there was no review, but Canon M.E. Farquhar, in an article entitled 'Political Consciousness Is Born', commented on the Connor lecture while dealing with a meeting in Port of Spain of the West Indian National Party, which had recently won a sweeping victory in the San Fernando municipal election. Farquhar regretted that:

> when the Mayor called for the National Anthem, a number of
> people broke out into the fervent singing of the Internationale.[34]

As if this omen were not bad enough, Farquhar complained of an even more disturbing incident.

> Another incident which ought not to be ignored occurred at Mr. Edric Connor's lecture. When he referred to a song which commemorated a plot to murder all the Europeans in the Colony, there was instant and spontaneous applause to acclaim the plot.
>
> Many natives like myself were not a little embarrassed, and conscious of a sense of deep humiliation. It was unpardonably bad manners, and ill became the generous spirit which is the more natural heritage and instinct of the African race. Yet here again the incident furnishes more than an ordinary straw in the wind of public opinion.[35]

The song that occasioned such embarrassment was

Pain nous ka mangé	The bread we eat
C'est viande beké	Is white man's flesh
Di vin nous ka boué	The wine we drink
C'est sang beké	Is white man's blood
Hé St. Domingo	Hey St. Domingo
Songé St. Domingo	Remember St. Domingo

This song, cited in 1805 as evidence of a black plot to murder 'all the whites and free coloured inhabitants' of the island, according to historian E.L. Joseph, might have been little more than the battle-cry of one of the Convois, or Régiments, as the African Dance societies used to be called at the time. The Governor and planters believed otherwise and executed four slaves, tortured and mutilated others and flogged and banished the fortunate few.

Connor's resurrection of that song, with its sacrilegious jibing reference to the bread and wine of Christian Holy Communion and its allusion to the Haitian Revolution, needs to be viewed together with his equally pointed references to the bans on drums, Bongo, Shango and Shouter Baptist religious practices. One cannot but conclude that Connor, who considered the recent efforts to implement a programme of Social Welfare to be a means of masking decades of neglect, [53-54] had decided to use the privileged situation of the lecture to uncover the fierce and unjust pressures that the colonial élite had historically brought to bear on the cultural expressions of the island's black folk. In so doing, he was also revealing the real divergence between the colonial patronage implicit in Social Welfare, and the nationalist ambitions of the local intelligentsia, among whom he certainly numbered himself. If his first lecture was the beginning of West Indian nationalism, his second, disclosing as it had the stark divisions in the society and the age-old antagonism between contesting ethnicities and classes, was like a declaration of war.

Sir Edward Cunard acted immediately to bundle Connor out of Trinidad, not to Tuskegee, where he would have gained dangerously enlightening access to his diasporic, spiritual-chanting, African-American cousins in their dignified climb up from slavery, but to England, a scholarship to complete his City and Guilds degree, and easy access to the BBC radio network. Cunard recognized that there was a kind of politics implicit in the popular history and culture that Connor was researching. He seemed to sense that black cultural epiphany, the sort of illumination that came from the unearthing of buried histories and erased cultures, usually led to black rebellion. Something like Canboulay, reinterpreted and remembered, could be an explosive topic and precedent.

Cunard therefore yanked Connor out of Social Welfare as abruptly as he had ten weeks before installed him there. He explained the reasons for this second imperious/imperial action.

> I will not allow you to go to Tuskegee Institute, Alabama, to waste all your valuable talents. I cannot be party to such a crime . . . Why don't you go to England? You will be better appreciated there. Much better. [56]

This might be read as patriarchal benevolence or as a sudden revelation of the real rivalry that existed at this moment of the apparent waning of the British Empire, over who should exercise cultural hegemony over the colonized natives. Anglophiles in Trinidad resented what they regarded as a steady and insidious Americanization of West Indian minds. To send Connor to England was to save him from becoming Americanized and to deradicalize a potential rebel and natural leader. Connor grasped the opportunity to move towards this new horizon that had so suddenly opened out before him, but soon realized: 'I was a pawn in a very big game of chess being played on a board as big as the world.'[62] Two weeks after his second lecture, in the middle of winter, he was bound for England.

The journey to England, in that dangerous time when the Atlantic was infested with German U-boats, was made via New York, where Connor met Beryl McBurnie, his friend and colleague in Trinidad's cultural renaissance. McBurnie was dancing in New York and functioning as 'a stand in for Carmen Miranda'. [58] Connor also went to see Paul Robeson and José Ferrer perform in Shakespeare's *Othello*. Amidst typically impressionistic notes about New York's two extremes, of 'the stagnation of the slums' of Harlem, Greenwich Village and the Bronx, and 'the glamour and glitter' of Broadway and Radio City, Connor casually states that: 'I met Paul Robeson in his Council on African Affairs.'[58] Headed by W.E.B. Du Bois, Robeson and other prominent black militants, the Council on African Affairs

> encouraged independence movements in the British and French colonies. By the early fifties all such independence movements were regarded as tainted by Communist influence; consequently the Council was hauled before the Subversive Activities Control Board.[36]

Connor does not say what he and Robeson discussed — and this is one of the disappointing features of Connor's autobiography, this reticence about some of the most crucial issues. Connor had long admired Robeson with whom he had sometimes been compared, and, as Pearl Connor-Mogotsi testifies, considered Robeson as a role-model.

> Edric had his heroes and he was a great admirer of Paul Robeson. We all admired him, and thought he was one of the greatest artists, and a great man. We knew about his history. Edric hero-worshipped him. Paul was Edric's role model and Edric wanted to be like him.[37]

Robeson's career since the 1920s, whether as singer, actor or political activist, had contained an unwavering militancy. He had mercilessly unmasked America through the songs he sang which reflected the struggle, protest, sorrow or rage of both America's suppressed poor and black folk, and the workers and peasants of the world. He attacked racism and all other forms of discrimination, using his art as a tool in his struggle as an activist. He fought both within racist, segregationist America and, embarrassingly for the State Department, abroad wherever he visited: the UK, Russia, France, the Caribbean, Africa, China or Japan.

Connor, like Robeson, empathized with ordinary folk wherever he went. He also sang spirituals and made the spiritual central to his theory of how folk music and the Calypso developed in the West Indies. One of Connor's earliest appearances on BBC Radio (July 24, 1944) was as the character Joe from Jerome Kern's and Oscar Hammerstein II's *Show Boat*.[38] This was a role that Robeson had made famous, and Connor was following Robeson's lead when he performed the trademark song: 'Ol' Man River. Ol' Man River' had been written with Robeson in mind, and after he first performed it in London in 1928 he became a star overnight, 'with the English audiences waxing ecstatic over his performance' while the American Embassy 'ignored the event'.[39] Connor's 1944 revival of the song was for the British a revisitation of the Robeson moment of sixteen years earlier.

As actors Robeson and Connor shared a mission of bringing dignity to the black protagonist, though Connor, always on the verge of survival and eager for whatever work he could find, was less severe in his scrutiny of such roles as came his way than Robeson had been a generation earlier, when he turned down the starring role in Eugene O'Neill's *The Emperor Jones*.[40] Robeson was a black nationalist, a Pan-Africanist and a Marxist whose internationalism was rooted in his 'deep communion with his Afro-American heritage'.[41] Connor's ideology was altogether vaguer. It was humanist, maybe mildly socialist, sympathetic to workers' causes, yet sufficiently and pragmatically survivalist to enable Connor, with apparently few qualms of conscience, to function as 'expeditor' for the Americans when they were driving residents off their lands in Chaguaramas and Teteron.

Whatever anti-colonialist militancy might have been implicit in Connor's 1943 lectures, he was far more Ariel than Caliban and, as Connor himself came to realize, too completely a pawn of the colonial system to conduct the sort of outspoken and fearless campaign against it that Robeson did, both as a member of the Council on African Affairs and as an actor and singer inside and outside of America. So while Connor described himself and his unorthodox and independent-minded Mayaro family as being all 'rebels', as he manoeuvred himself along the twisted via media between folk-rooted 'Caribbeing'[42] and respectable Afro-Saxonism, he instinctively understood that there were limits beyond which his rebellious spirit should not proceed or even reveal itself.

Thus when at a luncheon 'some of the influential Negroes in New York City' offered Connor 'a rich contract' [58–59] to stay in America and/or to leave his research notes and songs in New York, Connor stoutly resisted both temptations and proceeded on his journey to England. For one brief moment, marvelling at the famous New York skyline, he had begun to view that city as 'the challenge of an horizon which was met by man: therefore an horizon for me to conquer'. [58] Put to the test, however, he chose Sir Edward Cunard's passage to England, an entirely different horizon and cultural and political challenge.

His first years in England (1944–1948) resembled the first years of his apprenticeship in Port of Spain (1929–1934). In England he displayed the same mixture of wonder and resourcefulness as he encountered new experiences. He exercised the same survivalist skills as he negotiated a passage between his studies at South East Essex Technical College, his radio programmes at the BBC, and his presence as a significant figure in the world of the Arts. He was successful in all of these domains, passing his City and Guilds of London examination in Structural Engineering; establishing through his radio programmes a popularity with British audiences similar to what he had earlier enjoyed with the concert-going Port of Spain élite; and most remarkably, becoming in 1944 a Vice-President of the Workers' Music Association. The Americans claimed that it was this last achievement that inspired their refusal to grant Connor a visa or work permit to visit and work in America for the greater part of two decades after 1944. 'They said,' Connor explained, 'the Association was used as a Communist front. They were highly suspicious of anyone connected with it.' [127]

Why such a position was offered to Connor, after less than a year's residence in England and at the bare start of his international career, is unexplained in Connor's autobiography and is as much a mystery today as it must have been during the years of hysterical McCarthyism. Why Connor accepted the post is somewhat clearer. He explains that the Workers' Music Association had included Ralph Vaughn-Williams and Benjamin Britten, Britain's most distinguished twentieth-century composers, among its Vice-Presidents. [127] Connor was evidently as pleased to be included in such prestigious company, as he had been to hob nob with the 'top people' of Port of Spain.

His broadcasts for the BBC — he is estimated to have made over 2,500 of them over the 25 years he lived in the UK — established his reputation as singer, folklorist and intellectual in both Britain and the West Indies. His 'Calling the Caribbean' programme preceded the later efforts of Henry Swanzy and Vidia Naipaul, whose focus was on the emerging West Indian literature of the later fifties and sixties. There was a difference, though, between Connor's impact as a remote radio voice and his mesmeric flesh-and-blood concerts/lectures/performances of 1943. Heard in the context of 'Calling the Caribbean', songs such as 'Pain nous ka mangé' or the Shouters' chorus 'A Little More Oil', which in 1937 had been the battle-cry of the Trinidad Oilfield Workers' Trade Union during its months of Butlerite militancy, separated now from their local political contexts, became harmless echoes of a distant and quaint folk culture, rather than the fuses for spontaneous rebellion that they had been in their original context.

Connor gained employment in a factory that manufactured breech blocks for three-inch guns, [62] which was the closest he got to the war. As in the earlier phase of his life, he balanced an industrial vocation with his other life as a singer. He recalls that his performance of 'Weepin' Mary' at the Palace Theatre in November 1944 moved the audience — some of whom had no doubt lost friends or relatives in the war — to tears. Connor was walking in the footsteps of Marian Anderson and Paul Robeson, who had both evoked similar reactions from audiences in the mid-twenties, setting high standards for future black artists in England and Europe. Connor's success with his BBC programmes was remarkable, with the 'Serenade in Sepia' series running for 45 weeks in 1948. Partnering Connor in that series was Evelyn Dove, a singer of West African descent. The 'brown', if not yet the 'black' presence had begun to find a distinctive space on the airways.

In the first five years in England, then, it was as a singer rather than an actor that Connor established his reputation. His repertoire of early recordings at the BBC indicates the thoroughness with which he drew on the folk songs of Trinidad and Tobago between 1944 and 1950. After 1952 he added songs derived from Tom Murray's *Folk Songs of Jamaica*[43] which, accompanied by 'the Caribbeans', he recorded for ARGO in 1954. It was from Connor's two ARGO long-playing records: *Folk Songs of Jamaica* (1954)[44] and *Songs from Trinidad* (1955),[45] along with Louise Bennett's seminal recording of Jamaican mentos,[46] that Harry Belafonte derived the core material for his best-selling *Calypso* LP[47] in 1956. Connor also sang songs associated with the southern plantations of the USA, such as the nostalgic 'Carry Me Back to Old Virginny', music-hall favourites such as the aforementioned 'Ol' Man River' and 'Water Boy', or worksongs like 'John Henry' that Robeson had made famous two decades earlier.

None of his renditions of European light operatic concert favourites is listed among the BBC's holdings on Connor,[48] though he certainly continued singing songs from that body of music at various concert appearances. His former wife, Pearl, testifies that Connor wanted desperately to sing opera, and practised by listening to and imitating Caruso records 'until he knew many operas by heart'. He also took lessons in voice both in England and later in America, even though he highly valued the natural raw ability he had brought with him from Port of Spain. But stereotyped as the black folk singer, he received very few offers to sing opera besides the role of Amanasro in Verdi's *Aida*, which required him to travel to Hungary. She does not state the year when this occurred, and Connor himself does not even mention one of the significant moments in his career, when he actually did cross the threshold into the 'high culture' space of opera. What Pearl Connor-Mogotsi does record is that Connor, simply by virtue of having performed in Hungary, awakened suspicion of being a communist when

> He was simply a black man originally from the colonies trying to sing Opera and getting no chance to do so in England.[49]

England had warmly embraced Connor as a folk singer, a sort of safe version of Robeson who was under attack for his socialist views. Pearl Connor-Mogotsi notes that

> it was the time when Paul Robeson was being scourged and demonized and attacked by the Press. Edric was compared with Robeson because he was the only high profile black singer/actor on the UK scene. They were both black men of African origin so they put them in the same bag.[50]

Connor's trip to Hungary, then, probably occurred around 1949, when the US denigration of Robeson commenced in earnest and spread to colonial outposts of the US like Britain. Before this, however, Connor had been to Europe at least two times. The first was a trip to Paris, when he hitch-hiked from Calais to Paris. This first trip, he says, whetted his appetite for travelling to Europe. He states that

> There was a so-called World Youth Congress in Prague and the Trinidad Youth Council asked me to represent them. I had never been acquainted with any of the isms — Fascism, Conservatism, Communism. Judging from the rumours coming my way it was time I got acquainted. [69]

Connor does not record anything about the Congress itself, or even explain why at age 34 (the Prague Congress was held in 1947) he had so suddenly been delegated by the Trinidad and Tobago Youth Council (TTYC) to represent them in Prague, at what was clearly a socialist affair. He distanced himself from the then current capitalism versus communism debate; chose a more comfortable (and probably more expensive) hotel in Old Prague than the wretched hostel that housed the British delegates; and gave to the committed the impression of having attended the Congress by fraud.

Connor denied any interest in ideology; yet he must have manifested some while in Trinidad to be chosen by the TTYC, which was formed seven months after his departure for England, to be their delegate to the Prague Congress. The TTYC was a confederation of many youth organizations which came together at a Congress held in July 1944. In 1945, the World Federation of Democratic Youth held its conference in Paris. Delegates from several West Indian islands attended and considered the prospect for a regional West Indian Youth Council. In March 1946 at its Annual Congress the TTYC, despite its penniless state, decided to host the first West Indian Youth Conference in 1947.

This conference was held over 15 days between August 12 and 27, 1947. There were delegates from Antigua, Barbados, British Guiana, Dominica, Grenada, Guadeloupe, Jamaica, Martinique, Puerto Rico, Surinam, Tobago, Trinidad, the Caribbean Association of Howard University, the West Indian Students' Association of McGill University and the West Indian Students' Union of London. It was a veritable cross section of the region's emerging Creole intelligentsia, and over a fortnight it deliberated the islands' future prospects with respect to their politics, economics, education, culture and the social scene. It designed and approved its constitution and passed numerous resolutions. Its zealous Chairman, solicitor Jack Kelshall, stressed in his keynote address the apocalyptic significance of Hiroshima which, he said, symbolized the end of an old and defective social order. The leaders of that old order had failed humanity, and it was the responsibility of the youth to establish

> a new social order based on the twin precepts of Justice and Truth — a social order in which all people regardless of race or colour or place of birth can live together in freedom and dignity bound not by the narrow bonds of outworn patriotisms, but by the newer greater concept of the brotherhood of man. Thus the world outside, like this small Island, needs a new and better economic system geared to production for the use of all and not for the profit of some, powered by the motive of public service and not by that of private gain.[51]

Kelshall's powerful speech was anticipated by that of the lanky Governor Sir John Shaw who, on opening the Conference, warned delegates against empty rhetoric, impracticable agendas based on unattainable ideals, and the desire to dismiss the experience of older generations without being clear about what was meant to replace the old imperfect system. Shaw also cautioned the delegates to speak only for those they were certain they represented. He clearly recognized that such delegates — Hector Wynter, Jack Kelshall, Errol Hill, Jacob Elder, Max Ifill, Lennox Pierre, Basil Pitt, Victor Forsythe et al. — were unrepresentative both of the masses of the people on whose behalf they sought to exercise a patriarchal caretakership, and the kaleidoscope ethnicities that existed and were politically active in the Caribbean.

There was no hint, for example, of the possibilities that had become manifest in the recent alliance of Butler and Rienzi in Trinidad, or of the emerging Indo-based movement of farmers, workers and small businessmen that, led by the recently returned dentist, Cheddi Jagan, was just one year away from manifesting its power in the 1948 General Elections in British Guiana. There was no Indo-Trinidadian or Indo-Guianese delegate to the Conference, though there must have existed eminently suitable representatives of that ethnicity, who shared in the broad ideals of Chairman Kelshall. Kelshall, indeed, would fifteen years later be chosen by Cheddi Jagan as a close adviser, after the People's Progressive Party won the 1961 elections in British Guiana: the two men shared the same basic ideology.

What then was the connection between the TTYC of 1947 and Edric Connor, singer, amateur actor, now celebrated BBC broadcaster of 'Calling the West Indies'? It could not have been shared ideology: Connor claimed to have been unconcerned about ideology up to that point and dissociated himself from British socialist youth while in Prague. Connor did believe in brotherhood, compassion and the fundamental oneness of the human race, though it is not certain that these concepts bore the same resonance when he used them as when Kelshall employed them. The choice of Connor as delegate to the Prague Congress probably had more to do with his close friendship with Lennox Pierre and Beryl McBurnie, both of whom were — along with Pearl Nunez, Connor's future wife whom, however, he had not yet met — organizers of the first West Indian Youth Conference.

When one considers the cultural dimension of the West Indian Youth Conference, the fortnight of entertainment concocted by the organizing committees burning to *zantay* — that is show off Trinidad to the fullest extent — one recognizes the centrality of Connor's vision to the embryonic new nation that was in the process of pristine self-inscription and self-identification. The 1947 West Indian Youth Conference became a showcase for Trinidadian hospitality and 'culture' as it was then perceived through the eyes of the emergent middle-class Creole intelligentsia. So while mornings were devoted to the ponderous themes of the Conference, evenings were the time of entertainment, which took the form of song recitals, plays, visits to places of note — the Pitch Lake, the Oilfields, Usine Sugar Factory, Lady Chancellor Hill, Gasparee, Maracas Bay — community singing, games, dances, a piano recital of classical European music, steelband and calypso lecture demonstrations by former Deputy Mayor of Port of Spain and current Member of Council for Laventille, Raymond Quevedo, the calypsonian; garden parties at Kelshall's home in the south and verna Crichlow's home in the north; tea dances, a beauty contest, demonstrations of the Bongo dance after the spirit of Connor's 1943 lecture/performances; a floor show by Beryl McBurnie's dance troupe; a comic operetta and of course, dinners. The emerging nation had simultaneously celebrated and identified a notion of itself that is still current into the twenty-first century.

It is because Connor fitted so well into this broader Creole construction of culture, that could simultaneously embrace Bach, Mozart, Atilla the Hun, Lord Invader, the formal ball and the Bongo dance, that he was both chosen to represent Trinidad in Prague 1947, and taken under the wing of Beryl McBurnie on his first return to Trinidad late in 1947 for the 1948 Carnival. McBurnie asked 23-year-old Pearl Nunez, and another member of the organizing committee of the West Indian Youth Conference, to accompany Connor, who knew Trinidad much better than they did, in his peregrinations around the islands. Homage of the highest sort was being paid to one who had brought honour to his country, class and caste.

Connor visited friends at the old working places and his sisters at Mayaro. He reacquainted himself with the calypso tents and played mas', as if for the first time, discovering 'that the whole of Trinidad is one vast theatre'. [72] More important than all of these activities was his filming of the 1948 Carnival in what was his first effort as a maker of films. Renewed and vitalized by his return to the source, Connor on his return to England and throughout the 1950s became the unofficial ambassador for Trinidadian and wider West Indian culture. It was he who arranged a programme of concerts for TASPO, the Trinidad All Steel Percussion Orchestra, when it toured England in 1951. His 'Caribbean Cabaret' television programme featured Lord Kitchener, and Boscoe Holder and his dance troupe in 1950. He became something of a godfather figure to Caribbean and Commonwealth artists trying to make their mark in the UK, even as he had in the fifties begun to find his own small niche as an actor in several movies.

Connor's autobiography becomes strangely amnesiac after 1948, as he attempts to exclude from his narrative 16 years (1948–1964) of marriage to Pearl Nunez, until their separation in 1964. This separation is referred to towards the end of the autobiography vaguely as 'some grave domestic problems'. [131] The marriage itself is never mentioned, the wife never named, though there are various references to 'my wife and baby daughter'; [88] 'my wife and two children'; [98] 'my wife and her relatives and friends'; [113] 'our children'; [125] 'my wife and children', 'my wife and I'. [126]

This nameless wife, mentioned most often in the company of the two children, Geraldine and Peter, she had borne Connor, was the young woman to whose care Beryl McBurnie had consigned Connor when he returned to Trinidad in 1948. Connor reciprocated some months later when Pearl Nunez, acting on his advice, arrived in England with the intention of studying law. She and Connor were married in June 1948, mere months after her arrival. When Connor says that he opened his house to West Indian students, [74] he declines mentioning that it was her presence that made possible this new dimension in his life. It is from her account of the relationship that we gain some idea of the variety of persons that enjoyed the Connors' hospitality: Kenyatta, Mboya, Odinga, Seretse Khama, Azikwe, Nkrumah, George Padmore, Grantley Adams, Norman Manley, Eric Williams, Errol Barrow and Forbes Burnham.[52]

Perhaps it is because Connor wrote his autobiography in 1964, soon after a painful separation and serious heart attack, that he prefers to treat 16 years of marriage as if they had never happened. The autobiography is the poorer for this erasure since Connor says nothing of the experiences that he shared with Pearl as he became acquainted with all those students, writers, artists and statesmen. Close friends like George Lamming, significant colleagues like the Guyanese actor Robert Adams, all those African and West Indian leaders with whose quests for independence Connor obviously sympathized are, like Pearl, rendered invisible in Connor's text. Even Robeson's visit to the Connor home in 1949 is barely mentioned, though it occurred after Connor had visited his great role model three times at his hotel. Connor provides no hint of what he and Robeson so earnestly discussed, though Pearl records that 'Edric wanted to hear about the civil rights struggle in America, and what Paul was doing.'[53]

Robeson was in transit through London on his way to Peace Conferences in Paris and Moscow. David Caute notes that at the time:

> The word "peace" signified in the [American] collective consciousness, not merely the absence of war, but also a particular conception of world order, the Weltanshauung of the Soviet Union, the Pax Sovetica.[54]

Speaking, he said, for 700 million non-Caucasian people, Robeson declared that coloured peoples worldwide, including African-Americans, were no longer prepared to fight and die in wars fomented by their oppressors. He 'thought it was healthy for Americans to consider whether

Negroes should fight for people who kick them around'.[55]

Robeson was pilloried in the mainstream American Press for his supposedly 'unpatriotic' and 'un-American' opinions and his advocacy of 'scientific socialism' which, like Jack Kelshall of the TTYC [1947], he believed would lead in time to a world order superior to the moribund one of capitalism and imperialism. W.E.B. Du Bois, who had attended the same Peace Conferences in Paris and Moscow was, in 1951, at age 83, 'hand-cuffed, finger-printed, baited and remanded for trial'.[56] Robeson's passport was confiscated in February 1952 and not returned until 1958. Connor, who had merely made contact with and spoken to the marked Robeson in 1949, but whose Pan-Africanist and socialist sentiments were mild in comparison, and who seemed always to operate within the limits that were imposed on him, suffered for years to get a US visa. Pearl Connor-Mogotsi remembers that after Robeson's visit in 1949, Edric Connor lost the easy access to the BBC he had up to that time enjoyed. He was, clearly, still a pawn in the international Anglo-Saxon game of chess.

In spite of strictures, Connor's career flourished as he discerned and pursued several horizons at the same time, experiencing a measure of both significant success and disappointment. His achievements as a movie actor were many and of varying significance. Most of his roles were small parts which he endeavoured to make memorable beyond the muscular dumbness to which he was at times consigned. It was as if — as with his ambition to sing opera — he had indeed crossed the frontier towards stardom, rubbing shoulders with the likes of Sidney Poitier, Gregory Peck, Tony Curtis, Rita Hayworth and Robert Mitchum, but having stardom constantly withheld from his grasp. So as an actor whose goal was to bring to the Western stage the 'new ideas and new cultural patterns' [114] that he believed it needed, to walk 'upon old streets with new feet', [86] he was often frustrated by the limitations set by the narrowness of the roles he was made to play.

There were, nevertheless, moments of fulfillment: *Moby Dick* (1954), *Fire Down Below* (1956), *Four for Texas* (1963). Yet in none of those films did he play a really important role. Connor takes ten pages (88–97) to narrate the story behind the making of *Moby Dick*, which is unusual for one who tends to present his memories impressionistically in fragments and splinters, very few of which extend beyond four or five pages. It is, however, the exciting ethos, the drama of the making of the movie in Youghal, Southern Ireland and Newport, Wales; filming in a storm with 50-foot waves; learning to sail, balance and throw a harpoon; befriending

50 children and leading them downhill, singing nursery rhymes with them, that make this *Moby Dick* episode memorable. Connor, who played Daggoo the African harpoonist, is not given any lines to speak, though he does lead the harpoonists in their pursuit of the whale singing the Jamaican folk-song, 'Hill and Gully Rider'. Connor ruefully complained that after the great effort expended by the cast in the making of *Moby Dick*, 'the public did not see the film we shot. They saw the film they were made to see, not the one we made.' [97]

Fire Down Below, too, was less memorable for itself than for the circumstances of its making. Connor was making only his second trip back home since his hugger-mugger departure in December 1943. On this 1956 return, he was very much the conquering hero. He received the freedom of Port of Spain in the presence of his wife and two children. There was also his friendship with Rita Hayworth, who seven years later reciprocated by extending to him hospitality and an easy avenue into the liberal Beverley Hills social and artistic set. Connor tells us little about the movie itself. Robert Mitchum emerged from *Fire Down Below* a temporary convert to Calypso and in 1957 sought to ride the crest of the wave created by Belafonte's late 1956 *Calypso* album[57] with his own version of then contemporary calypsoes: *Calypso is Like So*.[58] Mitchum included versions of 'Jean and Dinah', 'Ugly Woman', 'Mama Look a Boo Boo' and 'Mathilda', in his 14 tracks. Tiger's 'Take Me Down to Los Iros' becomes 'Take Me Down to Lovers' Row'. Connor does not comment either on Jeri Southern's rendition of the theme song 'Fire Down Below' which was at the time being touted as a calypso. Shirley Bassey also released a popular version of 'Fire Down Below'.

Four for Texas was significant as the first movie Connor made in the USA after finally obtaining a visa in 1963. He says nothing about the movie itself, but documents his impressions of Hollywood, and the social circle of 'rebels' [127–129] within which he moved during the several months he spent in the USA. He does not say who these 'rebels' were or what was the nature of their rebellion. Remembering the trouble caused for nearly 15 years by his association with Paul Robeson and his flirtation with post-World War II anti-imperialist doctrines, Connor in fact kept as far as he could from politics of any kind while in Hollywood. The Civil Rights Movement, about which he had been curious in 1949, was at its peak; the Black Muslims had become a prominent force in the African-American struggle for economic and political equality; Martin Luther King's march on Washington took place and Robeson had returned to America in 1963 after five years of self-imposed exile in Europe and

England; while Connor was dallying with the 'rebels' of Hollywood. He observed African-Americans erupting into visibility from the remote distance of the television screen in his living room, and accepted that the price of crossing the frontier into Hollywood was a necessary adoption of Mi Jean's wise and wordless neutrality.

Connor also acted in movies made in and about Africa, the experience of which brought the same ambiguous measure of fulfilment and dissatisfaction. In travelling to South Africa for the filming of *Cry the Beloved Country*, Connor, who since the days of Sister Faith had developed a respect for spiritualism, viewed himself as having fulfilled the predictions of a female spiritualist, who had told him that he would be acting in a movie and that he would visit South Africa. [76] *Cry the Beloved Country* (1952) enabled him to experience the weird reality of becoming an 'honorary white' in apartheid-ridden South Africa, which left such a negative impression on his mind that he began to view South Africa ('Lobengula's lands') [132] as the venue for World War III, a final apocalyptic encounter between the forces of good and evil.

Connor later played Ushingo, an African chief, in *West of Zanzibar* (1954) and Waitari, an African leader, in *The Roots of Heaven* (1958). These roles were both limited, and Connor does not say much about them in his autobiography. He does, however, describe his portrayal of Jomo Kenyatta in *The Snows of Kama*, an instalment of the British TV series *Espionage* (1964) as 'one of the most satisfying and worthwhile things I have done'. [131] Connor as actor in films, on television or on stage, was constantly victim of the dearth of roles for black actors and the consequent 'invisibility' of these actors in such roles as they managed to get. The answer to this problem was obviously for Africans in Africa and the African diaspora to command the means of creating and distributing their own films, and of controlling their own self-representation via the filmic medium.

This Connor sought to do when he started Edric Connor Films Ltd (1958). The first major undertaking of the film company was the filming of the MCC cricket tour to the West Indies (1959–1960). Connor, who was a friend of Learie Constantine with whom he shared a love of Calypso and cricket, was a keen cricketer himself, who turned out on weekends for his local club. The Connors hosted the victorious West Indies cricket team of 1950 and Edric instinctively recognized the link between West Indies cricket and the West Indian nationalist movement. The West Indian Federation was still alive in 1960 and Connor correctly felt that his over 30 hours of footage on West Indies cricket was an important mode of self-representation, and a celebration of emerging West Indian identity. The confirmation of Connor's opinion came soon afterwards with C.L.R. James's classic *Beyond a Boundary*[59] which located West Indian cricket in its socio-historical context, highlighting the respective roles of Constantine and Worrell in the early and latter days — the 1920s and the 1950s into the sixties — in establishing and forging the tradition, style and aesthetic of the West Indies. Connor recognized, as clearly as did James, that West Indian cricketers, like West Indian actors, singers and literary artists, were 'walking upon old streets with new feet' [86] and revitalizing the culture of the game in the very midst of celebrating and expressing their own and their region's unique presence and identity.

Connor seized the opportunity in 1960 to make a documentary of Trinidad's Carnival, the award-wining *Carnival Fantastique* (1960),[60] and to present on film the uniqueness of the Guianese landscape and people in another documentary entitled *Caribbean Honeymoon* (1960). Connor had prepared himself for this new 'horizon' — that of film-making — by training with the BBC to qualify as a television director and producer. [190] He received no assignments from the BBC. More frustratingly, neither the Trinidad and Tobago, nor the Jamaican governments, under Eric Williams and Norman Manley respectively, entertained Connor's plan to establish his film company on those islands, or offered him the tax holidays he requested. [107]

His cables to Norman Manley over the question of pioneer status for his company to make films in and for Jamaica [120] led, after considerable effort on Connor's part, to a meeting where Manley 'roughed' him up during their interview, but 'was the sweetest character and the most genteel on God's earth', seeing Connor out of his office. Connor seems to have considered these rebuffs from Williams, who ignored him, and Manley, who firmly rejected his proposals, as poor recompense for the courtesies he had extended to these and other West Indian leaders whenever they visited London. A self-appointed cultural ambassador for Trinidad and the West Indies, in the days before independence and embassies, Connor had chaperoned and organized programmes for the visiting TASPO in 1951. He had also assisted Ellie Mannette, Trinidad's brilliant pan-maker and innovator, in getting 'a scholarship with the Birmingham Symphony Orchestra, which changed his life'.[61] Having helped many others, Connor simply could not understand why he was receiving no encouragement in his attempt to promote the islands via films he had made and those he hoped to make.

Connor's misadventure with Manley awakens the possibility that some of the important people Connor knew, and tried to use, might have resented his efforts to advance on account of their power and influence. In the West Indies of the late 1950s or early 1960s, the question of Connor's seeking the patronage of either Williams or Manley might have involved a serious clash of similarly inflated egos. Connor's celebrity, based on his fame as singer, actor and BBC radio programme host, and on his achievement as a largely self-taught intellectual, might have proven a challenge to these two outstanding university-trained intellectuals and politicians, both of whom, Manley in particular, were patrician in demeanour and style, even though one had been to the manor born, and the other had, by his own account, had greatness, Trinidad-style, thrust upon him from the cradle.[62]

Connor's reaction to Manley's rebuff — the sneaky acquisition of copies of the Jamaican government's plans to establish their own film-making unit — was petulant. There was also a gloating tone in his voice when, with respect to the 1959–60 allegedly Rastafarian uprising, he commented:

> This must have been a shock to Manley and the middle class he was building with his so-called élite intelligentsia. [121]

Connor, a product of the feisty spirit of optimism and innocent idealism that only a decade earlier had informed the improbable coming-together of so many different ethnic, caste and class elements in the West Indian Youth Council of 1947, had been made painfully aware of the distance in caste that separated a man like himself from the bourgeois intelligentsia that had emerged at the head of the nationalist movement throughout the West Indies in the decade leading to the Federation and from Federation towards Independence. Connor later blamed Manley whose reluctance to lead had, in Connor's opinion, resulted in the collapse of the West Indian Federation.

Connor's effort to provide his notion of relevant film and television for a West Indies on the brink of nationhood, was scuttled first by the indifference or latent hostility of the islands' leaders; next, by the traumatic breakup of the Federation; and finally by the barriers that the new nations of Jamaica and Trinidad — who were aware of themselves as separate national entities even when they were part of the Federation — quite naturally erected against any homegrown 'outsider' riding in from 'foreign' to tell them what to do in such a crucial area as communications and what is today known as 'nation-branding'.

Connor's film-making enterprise was soon afterwards to sustain a crippling blow from an entirely unexpected source: Nigeria. Both Edric and Pearl Connor were invited by Nigerian President Dr Azikiwe to attend the Independence Celebrations in Nigeria in October 1960. Azikiwe, one of the dignitaries who had in the 1950s enjoyed the Connors' hospitality in London, was now reciprocating, as Connor had hoped Williams and Manley would. While Connor was in Nigeria, the government commissioned him to make a film celebrating the country's acquisition of Independence from Britain. Filming was plagued by a series of unfortunate circumstances: a sick cameraman who had to be replaced by a stranger; a local cast that daily demanded extra money; a series of events that forced Connor to flee Nigeria with his films safe, but his equipment abandoned. This depressing incident virtually marked the end of the Edric Connor Film Company. He was so deeply disappointed by this failure, that he completely omitted this Nigerian interlude from his autobiography. So it is to Pearl Connor-Mogotsi's valuable notes and interviews that one has to turn to get a fuller understanding of what had begun to transpire in Connor's life at the start of the 1960s.

The acme of Connor's parallel existence as a stage actor occurred in 1958 when the Shakespeare Memorial Theatre, Stratford-upon-Avon, offered him the role of Gower in their production of *Pericles*. This offer came at a particularly happy and productive time in his life. He had completed *Songs for Trinidad*, a book of folksongs assembled at the behest of Oxford University Press. 'The book was completed in a fortnight,' Connor enthuses. The record had been done since 1955. He had also launched Edric Connor Films Ltd, in the year of the inauguration of the West Indian Federation, whose leaders, as we have seen, he hoped would take an interest in his film-making endeavours. Now he was conquering Stratford-upon-Avon.

Curiously, this great moment also marked the point when he almost became a competitor with Paul Robeson for the part of Gower. Connor writes that he nearly refused the role — and this after weeks of preparation — when he learned that it had been offered first to Robeson, who had recently regained his passport and the right to travel outside the USA. Connor, eager to demonstrate that he was his own man now and nobody's second best, created a unique Gower whose chorus-like narrator's role was rendered in song, speech and at Connor's suggestion, dance. Connor boasts:

> I took all the storytellers of Mayaro taught me to Stratford. I reflected that, as a boy, those men were preparing me for Stratford. And I did not know it.
> [111]

Connor's Shakespearean moment was one of the pinnacles of his achievement. It was made even more memorable by the fact that his 45th birthday fell during the weeks of the play and was marked by a party thrown by the Connors for the entire cast and body of theatre workers involved in the play's production. Four hundred guests were regaled with rum and pelau. Boscoe Holder and his dancers, singers and drummers performed in a 45-minute cabaret; a steelband provided music for the occasion. As the West Indies cricket team and Lord Kitchener had blessed Lords in 1950 in celebration of the West Indies victory, Connor, Boscoe Holder and the steelband anointed the Shakespeare Memorial Theatre on the night of August 2, 1958. [113]

Another significant moment in Connor's artistic life was the ceremony of dedication of Coventry Cathedral, June 8, 1962. Connor played a major role in the designing of that ceremony, and later in the shaping of 'a new style service' for the Cathedral in August 1964, in which readings from the Bible were illustrated or augmented by readings from modern poetry and prose, and by song. This new style service was, to some extent, an amplification of the extremely popular 'Lift Up Your Hearts' 5-minute radio programmes that he had done for the BBC early in the 1950s. [80] A cathedral dedicated to the Arts, Coventry became for Connor's now troubled spirit a 'platform' [132] from which he seemed to gain extraordinary inspiration and, so he felt, clairvoyance.

Connor's many great achievements between 1956 and 1964 were paralleled, unfortunately, by the failure of his business ventures — the cinema in San Juan, Trinidad; the brick factory also in Trinidad, which he tried to run as an absentee landlord; the film production studio. These failures were accompanied by the failure of his health, which was itself the result of all these cumulative failures and the deepening depression that resulted from the failure of his marriage. The crisis of the early 1960s eventually cumulated in the double disaster of the separation that both ended and intensified the traumatic domestic situation, and secondly the massive heart attack that brought everything to a dreadful climax in 1964. Connor's autobiography, written while he was convalescing from that heart attack, served as therapy and partial recovery from both of these disasters.

How does one, given Pearl's short but telling account of her life with Edric Connor, and Connor's almost complete silence, attempt to construct a feasible version of what happened to make a relationship of sixteen years so totally disintegrate that one partner seeks to erase all memory of the other, even though the other, even after Connor's death and her remarriage, never abandons the surname of her first husband? Edric Connor, who hints from time to time that women were attracted to him, was no doubt dazzled by this vibrant, self-confident, politically committed, intelligent and beautiful young woman, 11 years his junior and a daughter of Trinidad and Tobago. Pearl speaks of the relationship as one based on mutual cultural, social and intellectual interests, almost an 'arranged' affair. But she too was drawn by Connor's charisma, celebrity, the circle in which he moved and the almost paternal way that he taught her and she learned from him about roots she never knew she had, given the coloured middle-class puritanical ethos in which she grew up.

But she would not forever remain his pupil or be content to be limited, as she is in his text, to the role of nameless wife and keeper of their two children. So she resisted his desire to close down the Edric Connor Agency, that bore his name indeed, but was being run by her. This Agency, which facilitated artists from the West Indies, Africa and Asia to find employment and in other related matters, began in 1956. By 1958 he had begun to feel that the agency was intruding too much into their domestic lives and should be closed down. She, however, argued that it had begun to do well and that to close it down would be to negate all the work that she had put into it.

Having abandoned her initial ambition to become a lawyer, in order to mother their children through their infant years, she now sent them home to be educated in Trinidad where they would connect with family and roots, an ideal clear and near to Connor's Mayaro-nurtured heart. But sending the children home to her parents in Trinidad also freed Pearl to move fully into her own space and to run her agency during those considerable periods in the late fifties and early sixties when Connor was away from home working on or acting in a variety of films in Africa, the West Indies and after he at last received his US visa, Hollywood.

A sick man with a bad heart and a multitude of woes, Connor became a jealous heart-sick man with a bitter spirit, one who now believed that the agency had become the enabling body for too many male actors. He could not bear her growing, which in his mind had become a challenge to his. So despite all of his marvellous and even monumental success, he chose to write her out of his text, cancelling thereby a substantial part of his life, and setting himself up for both heartbreak and heart attack. Was it a piece of dramatic irony that the first role he saw his double and role-model, Paul Robeson, perform early in 1944, was that of *Othello*? Or that he should in 1956 or 1957 weep at a performance of Verdi's *Othello*?

Or that the last role he might have seen Robeson perform was also that of Othello, when in 1959, the year after Connor's Gower, the Shakespeare Memorial Theatre at Stratford invited Robeson to play Othello?

Connor wrote his autobiography late in 1964 and so could not include the last four years of his life. There was, apparently, not much to tell. He could not sustain all of those parallel existences that had taxed his energies to the limit. As pathfinder for the score of actors who followed in his footsteps, his role had been the hardest, his road the most difficult. Being the man he was, he regarded everything as a challenge he needed to face, every obstacle as a frontier he must cross.

Pearl continued running the Edric Connor Agency that he had since 1958 wanted her to close down. Eventually the agency came to be known as the Afro-Asian Caribbean Agency. It continued to exist until 1976. The Negro Theatre Workshop, which both Edric and Pearl founded in 1963, under Pearl's inspiration produced Wole Soyinka's *The Road* at the Theatre Royal, Stratford, as part of the 1965 Commonwealth Arts Festival.[63] The next year the workshop produced its most challenging work, *The Dark Disciples*: a blues and jazz version of St. Luke's Passion, deriving its inspiration, perhaps, from a musical such as *Black Nativity*[64] or even from Edric Connor's radical experiments at Coventry Cathedral in 1962 and 1964. Duke Ellington had also performed *In the Beginning, God*,[65] one of his religious jazz suites, at Coventry Cathedral.

The Dark Disciples premiered in Easter 1966 at the World Festival of Black and African Arts in Senegal.[66] Understandably, but also regrettably, Connor was not featured in any of the productions of the Negro Theatre Workshop, even though the workshop was clearly the fruit of his pathfinding and pioneering efforts, and resonated with his spirit even as it showcased the talents of a score of younger West Indian singers, musicians, actors and dancers. Edric Connor's final appearances were not in African folk theatre of any sort, but in the movies *Only When I Larf* and the ominously named *Nobody Runs Forever* [1968]. His race, indeed, ended on October 16, 1968.

Connor was born in 1913, in the British Crown Colony of Trinidad and Tobago. These two islands were linked administratively in two stages in 1889 and 1898, but their historical trajectories had been very different. Tobago, the smaller island, had first been permanently settled by Europeans from the 1760s, following the cession of the island to Britain in 1763. It was then 'developed' as a monocultural sugar island, with British-owned plantations worked by enslaved Africans. After slave emancipation in the 1830s, the sugar estates declined and eventually collapsed altogether in the closing decades of the nineteenth century. Tobago became largely a peasant society, with African-Tobagonians cultivating the soil, shipping foodstuffs and livestock to Trinidad, and enjoying a sturdy, if cash-poor, independence on their holdings and in their cohesive village communities. This was the society that Connor's mother came from, and that he knew well from his childhood visits to his maternal relatives.[67]

Trinidad, the larger island, had been a sparsely settled Spanish colony since 1592, when the small, derelict 'town' of St. Joseph was formally settled. It had not been developed in the plantation production mode by the 1780s, when the Spanish government decided to open the island to foreign immigrants, in the hope that these would clear the virgin forest and establish flourishing estates. It was mainly people from the French, or former French, Caribbean colonies who came, most 'white' but some of mixed descent ('coloureds'); and these immigrants, who were encouraged to bring with them their enslaved labourers, were granted land and proceeded to develop sugar, cotton and cocoa estates, transforming the island into a slave society in the process. These French planters, and their 'French Creole' descendants, soon formed the island's new elite, and introduced the African-French 'creole' complex which became the core nucleus of Trinidadian culture.

With the establishment of prosperous sugar, cotton and cocoa estates in the 1780s and 1790s, and with all the security risks inherent in the revolutionary conflicts of that last decade, Trinidad became of interest to the leading imperial nation of the age, Britain. The island was seized by British forces in 1797, and formally ceded by treaty in 1802. This event, while making Trinidad a part of the British imperium, and introducing British modes of colonial government and legal forms, did not fundamentally dilute the significance of the French cultural and linguistic influence, and it accelerated the island's development as a plantation economy and a slave society.

But British rule had at least one major consequence: Trinidad became part of London's evolving policies on slavery. First the importation of enslaved Africans from Africa was prohibited to both Trinidad and Tobago in 1806; then admittedly feeble attempts to 'ameliorate' the slaves' treatment were made in the years between 1812 and 1834; in 1834, slavery was officially abolished throughout the British empire, but most of the ex-slaves were declared to be 'apprentices' still owing unpaid labour to their ex-owners; finally, in 1838, the former slaves and apprentices were given 'full free'. They were declared to be free British subjects, now to make their way with neither land nor money as compensation for their, and their ancestors' servitude.

Many ex-slaves, or their descendants, eventually became peasant farmers, as in Tobago, and in rural communities like Mayaro on the then remote southeast coast of Trinidad where Connor grew up. Others continued to work for wages on the sugar and cocoa estates, or practised craft skills in the rural villages and the towns. Despite the tradition of 'family land', and informal cooperative arrangements between families, both of which Connor describes in Mayaro and Tobago, the struggle to obtain, and keep, farming land was a hard one for the descendants of the enslaved in both islands.

The planter elite of Trinidad, anticipating correctly that many of the formerly enslaved would leave full-time wage labour on the estates, and quite unwilling to negotiate with them as free persons over wages and conditions of work, agitated for permission to bring in contract (indentured) labourers to replace them. Some came from captured slave ships (the 'Liberated Africans'), some were brought from Portuguese Madeira and China; but the great majority came from India, part of an empire-wide movement of indentured Indian immigrants to areas where European planters were in need of cheap, coerced labour. Around 144,000 Indians arrived in Trinidad (but not Tobago) between 1845 and 1917 under this scheme, and about two-thirds of them settled permanently, despite the free or subsidized repatriation to India which was part of the imperial arrangements.

Trinidad's demography and culture became extraordinarily diverse and complex; that of Tobago, however, remained simpler: a largely homogenous African population sharing an African-British cultural complex.

In Trinidad, a rich popular culture developed and flourished in the post-emancipation century (1830s–1930s), a 'creole' cultural complex which rested on a fusion of West African and French elements and cohered around dance, music, folklore and the pre-Lenten carnival. French Creole, or patois, was the lingua franca of this complex, and remained the majority language of Trinidad into the early twentieth century, by which time English, and English Creole, were beginning to eclipse the patois. The rural people in particular inhabited a world of folk figures, beliefs and stories, some described by Connor, often of clear African provenance; dance and musical forms were typically a creative fusion of West Africa and France, such as the *belair* or *belé*. The drum was central to the expressive culture, as everywhere among peoples of Africa and the Diaspora. Neo-African religions, such as the Orisha faith (Shango), and syncretic African-Christian groups such as the Shouters, or Spiritual Baptists, flourished despite official persecution.[68] Topical, witty, often risqué songs, the forerunners of the modern calypso, were sung especially at carnival time in patois, with English gradually coming into use after about 1900. Indeed, the carnival became increasingly central to the African-Trinidadian cultural complex, the occasion for masquerade, drumming and dancing, calypso and stickfighting. A key element between the 1840s and 1880s was the Canboulay, a noisy, boisterous street procession which took place on the Sunday night before the official start of Carnival early on the Monday morning. The authorities became increasingly nervous about the security risks of hundreds of men, armed with sticks and lighted torches, often drunk and looking out for rival bands to fight, on the streets of Port of Spain and the other towns. Canboulay was also (correctly) seen as an essentially 'African' celebration, as opposed to the more European-influenced masquerade bands, and was therefore a target for the elites bent on 'anglicization' of the colony. In 1881, the famous or infamous Captain Baker, chief of police, attempted to stop the Canboulay procession by force, and, though he was strongly resisted that year (the 'Carnival Riots'), he succeeded in banning Canboulay by 1884. Carnival continued to flourish nevertheless, and it never lost its anarchic, dangerous, 'African' elements even as some of the masquerade and the music became increasingly European-influenced in the twentieth century.

After the collapse of the estate-based sugar industry in Tobago, during the closing years of the nineteenth century, cocoa and coconuts replaced sugar as the estate crops; most Tobagonians eked out a living not so much from estate wages, but rather from peasant farming and livestock rearing. In many ways Mayaro, Connor's birthplace, and other areas on the northeast and eastern coast of Trinidad, were quite similar. Cocoa and coconuts also replaced the always small sugar estates, and peasant farming was the norm. The east coast was fairly remote at the time of Connor's birth in 1913; there was no paved road connecting the coastal villages to each other or to the capital, the beach was in effect the only road, and villagers depended heavily on boat transport, including the government coastal steamers serving both Tobago and Trinidad. Yet the people of this region participated in the 'cocoa boom' (c.1880–1920); many were small or medium landowners who cultivated cocoa as well as food crops, and a few black or mixed-race families became quite prosperous as a result. But many more families, who had borrowed heavily from local or (often) city-based cocoa dealers to buy land and establish cocoa cultivation, were forced to give up their holdings, often through foreclosure by these firms, such as Gordon Grant & Co, a situation vividly described by Connor.

At the start of the twentieth century, the commercial extraction of oil began in the southeast corner of the island, not far from Mayaro, when successful wells were drilled at Guayaguayare. The oil industry developed rapidly, and by the 1930s was the single largest revenue earner in the colonial economy (though it employed relatively few people). The oil workers, mostly African-Trinidadian, or immigrants from nearby islands like Grenada, emerged as the most militant, and best organized, sector of the colony's working class. Grievances specific to the industry, like the crude racism of South African or American supervisors (described by Connor), combined with the hardships suffered by nearly all ordinary islanders during the depression years of the 1930s, when many were retrenched by the sugar and cocoa estates, and most experienced underemployment or irregular employment and very low wages. The situation culminated in the widespread unrest of the second half of the 1930s.

Trinidad and Tobago was a crown colony; up to 1925, its Legislative Council had no elected members (Tobago's earlier, separate elected Assembly had been dismantled in 1876–78). All its members were officials, or private citizens from the elites nominated by the governor, with just one of the latter representing Tobago. Many groups ever since the 1840s had campaigned for the inclusion of elected members in the Council without success. But after World War I, Britain moved to permit 'mixed' Councils in her Caribbean colonies, with officials, nominated and elected members, albeit always on a very restricted gender, property and income franchise. This reform came into effect in Trinidad in 1925, with the first elections held that year. The only organized group contesting the elections was the Trinidad Workingmen's Association (TWA), then under the leadership of Captain A.A. Cipriani and William Howard-Bishop. The TWA was the dominant labour organization in Trinidad and Tobago in the 1920s and early 1930s, and Cipriani, who was from a white French Creole family, became an authentic popular hero. The TWA had branches all over the colony, including a remote rural village like Mayaro. But, as the depression intensified in the early 1930s, with thousands of people suffering unprecedented hardships from under- and unemployment, abysmal wages, rising cost of living and deplorable housing and health conditions, many became disillusioned with Cipriani's cautious Fabianism (though he never lost his personal popularity). Other leaders, notably T.U. 'Buzz' Butler, arose to organize the workers and the unemployed. Butler, a Grenadian immigrant who had worked in the oilfields until injured by a workplace accident, led several hunger marches in 1934–36, and organized the oil workers in the southern part of the island. Finally he called for a strike in June 1937, which escalated into islandwide strikes and riots, described briefly by Connor.

This unrest, which affected nearly every British Caribbean colony as well as Trinidad and (to a far lesser extent) Tobago, forced London to pay some attention to the widespread suffering and disillusionment with colonial rule. In addition to the popular protests, some influential middle-class spokesmen and members of the small intelligentsia raised their voices against the abject failure of crown colony rule in the region. In Trinidad, this group included Albert (Bertie) Gomes and his allies (see p.xxv). Britain appointed a Royal Commission — that time-honoured device of imperialism — to investigate the causes of the West Indian-wide unrest and to make recommendations. This time, perhaps to the surprise of the Colonial Office, the Commission chaired by Lord Moyne did a thorough job; the presence of Walter Citrine, Secretary of the British TUC, as well as (unusually) two women, one a noted public health expert, may have made the difference. The report, presented to the Colonial Office in 1939, was such a searing indictment of British colonialism in the region that London decided to suppress it until the end of the war, and it was not published until 1945. Some of its key recommendations, however, were published in 1940 and attempts were made to implement them during the war years. British money was voted for social welfare programmes (headed in Trinidad by the formidable Dora Ibberson, for whom Connor briefly worked), some aid was granted for public works and unemployment relief, and the process of constitutional decolonization was to be initiated.

But World War II intervened. This event had a profound impact on Trinidad and (again to a lesser extent) Tobago, mainly though not entirely because large naval and air bases were established by the USA in the larger island. In 1940, with Britain facing imminent invasion and the USA still neutral, Winston Churchill agreed to lease areas in the West Indian colonies for US naval and air bases in exchange for 50 old destroyers (the Lend-Lease agreement). Trinidad was chosen for major bases, and the US authorities decided on the northwest peninsula (Chaguaramas) and the Valencia area (Wallerfield) for their two biggest bases. The Bases Agreement was signed in 1941, over the protests of the governor, Hubert Young, who knew that the cession of Chaguaramas especially would be bitterly resented by the colonial population. All the residents of the peninsula and the small offshore islands were compulsorily evacuated (with Connor's assistance) and maritime activities in the surrounding coastal seas were prohibited. The bases were in full swing between 1942 and 1945, playing an important role in American wartime operations. Thousands of Trinidadians benefited by earning relatively decent wages in the base construction activities, and by supplying the US forces with all kinds of services. But the fishing and farming villagers of the northwest peninsula, very similar in many respects to those of Connor's childhood home of Mayaro, lost their homes and communities forever and were shabbily treated by the British and colonial authorities.

The effects of the war, the 1937 protests and the subsequent formation of trade unions, and the new, Moyne-inspired British policies, combined to push Trinidad and Tobago into a new era after the war's end. Constitutional change, recommended by the Commission, came into effect in 1946, when the number of elected members in the Council was increased and, most importantly, universal adult suffrage was inaugurated. Further reforms were introduced in the constitutions of 1950 and 1956. In 1950, a quasi-ministerial system was inaugurated, with elected Council members given ministerial responsibilities under the overall control of the governor; the most important, between 1950 and 1956, was Connor's old friend Bertie Gomes. Meanwhile the trade union movement developed and expanded, with Butler and other less orthodox leaders being squeezed out in favour of 'responsible', British-type unionists, often trained in Britain or, at least, deeply influenced by the TUC. The oil industry and the service, commercial and financial sectors enjoyed some prosperity in the post-war years as the agrarian colonial economy underwent modernization.

Until 1956, no well-organized political party had won a clear majority in the Council. But at the start of that year, the African-Trinidadian historian Eric Williams launched his People's National Movement (PNM) and embarked on an impressive campaign of public education and political agitation. Many of his speeches or public lectures were delivered in Port of Spain's main square, renamed by Williams as the University of Woodford Square. Unexpectedly to most, probably to the PNM itself, the party won a narrow victory in the elections in September 1956. It won 13 out of 24 elected seats in the Council; but it took the intervention of the British governor to insist that the PNM must be allowed to select two of the nominated members, and that the two official members would support it, giving the party 17 members out of a total of 31. Williams was thus enabled to form a genuine party government, with himself as the colony's first Chief Minister. From then until his death in 1981, his domination of local politics was near absolute. Not for nothing does Connor call him 'the don'.

A major issue which confronted the new Williams government, and those of the other British Caribbean colonies, was the establishment of the Federation of the West Indies. Since the end of the war, British authorities had urged this on the region's politicians, and there was considerable support from regional intellectuals and labour leaders. Williams supported a federation but disagreed with British plans for its constitutional arrangements. He soon saw an important political opportunity when the West Indian leaders — reversing a British recommendation — opted for Trinidad as the federal capital. The Federation was duly inaugurated early in 1958 with Trinidad as the capital, but Williams began to insist that Chaguaramas would be the ideal site. The northwest peninsula, however, was still in US hands, still closed off to Trinidadians, over a decade since the war's end. After consulting with Connor about the circumstances surrounding the evacuation of the area's residents, and learning of governor Young's protests in 1940–41, Williams embarked on a spirited campaign for the return of Chaguaramas, culminating in the famous 'March in the Rain' in April 1960. The outcome was a series of negotiations between the governments of the USA, Britain, the Federation, and Trinidad and Tobago, culminating in the return of nearly all of the peninsula to local control with a sweetener in the shape of modest US financial aid, a significant victory for the don.

Ironically, by the time the USA had agreed to yield up most of Chaguaramas, the Federation's days were numbered. It had faced huge political, economic and constitutional obstacles from the outset, worsened by the unfortunate fact that neither of the two leading regional politicians — Norman Manley of Jamaica and Williams — had agreed to leave local political office in order to serve as Prime Minister of the Federation. Grantley Adams of Barbados, who held this office, lacked the clout and, perhaps, the guile or ruthlessness of Manley and Williams. Manley himself was a supporter of the Federation, but the Jamaican public was lukewarm at best, and his political rival Alexander Bustamante exploited his opportunity by lending his great popularity to the anti-federal cause. Manley was pushed into calling a referendum on the issue in September 1961. A majority voted in favour of Jamaica's secession, and the Federation was doomed. Williams made it abundantly clear that he would not allow his country to remain within it and bear the sole burden of 'carrying' the smaller and poorer islands. 'One from ten leaves nought', he remarked, harshly if understandably. The British government, washing its hands of the whole mess, left the 'Little Eight' to their own devices, and signalled that it would speedily dissolve the Federation and facilitate independence for Jamaica and for Trinidad and Tobago whenever they wanted it. The Federation was wound up in early 1962, after only four years of troubled existence, and both countries became independent states within the British Commonwealth in August 1962. Manley lost the pre-independence election, and it was Bustamante who became the first Prime Minister of independent Jamaica. Williams, however, won the bitterly contested election in December 1961. The don was now Prime Minister of Trinidad and Tobago, an office he would hold until his death in 1981.

NOTE ON THE TEXT

Connor wrote his autobiography while recovering from his first heart attack in 1964; he died in 1968. The manuscript is a fairly clean typescript with a few small handwritten corrections or additions. The editors have rearranged portions of the text to provide a more coherent narrative and have supplied new chapter titles. We have also omitted the two last pages, and done light editing to remove obvious spelling or typographical errors. But there is no sentence in the autobiography as published here which was not written by Connor himself.

Annotations have been provided to explain possibly unfamiliar words, phrases, names and events, along with this Introduction which seeks to contextualise Connor and his times. The editors wish to thank Dr Susan Craig-James and Professor Lise Winer for help with the annotations, and Ms Michele Edwards for word-processing the text of the autobiography and the essay by Pearl Connor-Mogotsi.

The essay 'My life with Edric Connor' by Pearl Connor-Mogotsi (who, sadly, died in February 2005) has also been slightly rearranged and lightly edited.

The text of Connor's public lecture given in Port of Spain in December 1943 has been included as an appendix. It has been lightly edited. The editors wish to thank Dr John Cowley for providing this text, and Mrs Betty-Ann Rohlehr for word-processing it.

Readers will note that Connor uses the term 'Negro' throughout. This, of course, was acceptable terminology in the 1960s when he wrote his autobiography. We have chosen not to change it.

Bridget Brereton
Gordon Rohlehr
The University of the West Indies
St Augustine, Trinidad and Tobago
January 2006

Notes

1. Charles Baudelaire, 'Le voyage', in *The Flowers of Evil (Les Fleurs du Mal)* (New York: New Directions, 1955), 132–145 (First publication 1861). 'Le Voyage' ends with the protagonist's resolve to plunge into the gulf — 'Au fond de l'Inconnu pour trouver du noveau!' 'Beyond the known world to seek out the New!' Translator Roy Campbell.
2. Shakespeare, *The Tempest*, Act 1, Sc 11, 337.
3. Erna Brodber, *Jane and Louisa Will Soon Come Home* (London: New Beacon, 1980).
4. The Wonder, *Follow Me Children.*
5. Lord Executor, *Gombo Lai Lai Before the Court* (1939).
6. Black Prince, 'The Besson Street Murder', *Daily Mirror,* Sunday, January 14, 1934.
7. Lavway — a simple singalong chorus.
8. Michael Anthony, *The Making of Port of Spain: Vol 1 1757–1939* (Port of Spain: Key Publication, 1978), 191.
9. The Warner Woman was a prophet whose divine mission required her to traverse the countryside warning the nation of coming disasters she had foreseen.
10. A.M. Clarke, *Trinidad Guardian*, Sunday, January 8, 1939.
11. Ibid.
12. Ralph De Boissière, *Crown Jewel* (Australia 1953; reprint, London: Picador, 1981).
13. Gustave Borde, *The History of the Island of Trinidad Under the Spanish Government*, First Part 1498–1622 (Paris 1883; reprint, Port of Spain: Paria Publishing Co Ltd, 1982).
14. Olga Mavrogordato, 'Introduction' to Gustave Borde, *The History of the Island of Trinidad Under the Spanish Government*, First Part 1498–1622 (Port of Spain: Paria Publishing Co Ltd, 1982), x.
15. Harold Simmons, 'The Calypso and West Indian Music', Letter to the Editor, *Trinidad Guardian*, Saturday, February 27, 1943.
16. Ibid.
17. *Trinidad Guardian*, February 27, 1943.
18. Edric Connor, 'The Calypso and West Indian Music', *Trinidad Guardian*, Friday, March 5, 1943.
19. Ibid.
20. Daphne Taylor, *Trinidad Guardian*, Tuesday, March 9, 1943.
21. Eric Burger, 'Lovers of Calypso Need a Sense of Proportion', *Trinidad Guardian*, February 5, 1944.
22. Dom Basil Mathews, *Port of Spain Gazette*, February 1, 1944, 5.
23. Alfred Mendes, Letter to the Editor, *Trinidad Guardian,* Saturday, February 5, 1944.

24.   Alfred Mendes, 'If Calypso Is Folksong It Should Be Encouraged', *Trinidad Guardian*, Saturday, February 12, 1944.

25.   Mc Donald Carpenter, 'Calypso Sets Its Own Limitations', *Trinidad Guardian*, Tuesday, February 15, 1944.

26.   Edgar Mittleholzer, 'West Indian Culture Needs Firmer Basis Than Calypso', *Trinidad Guardian*, November 13, 1945.

27.   Charles Espinet and Harry Pitts, *Trinidad, Land of Calypso: The Origin and Development of Trinidad's Folksong* (Port of Spain: Guardian and Commercial Printery, 1944).

28.   Charles Espinet, 'Calypso Crudity: Tomorrow's Culture', *Trinidad Guardian*, Sunday, February 20, 1944.

29.   Sunday Guardian Correspondent, 'Limbo and Bongo Danced During Lecture', *Sunday Guardian*, August 1, 1943, 5.

30.   Ibid.

31.   Lord Kitchener (Aldwyn Roberts), *The Beat of the Steelband* (1946).

32.   J.D. Elder, *From Congo Drum to Steelband: a Socio-Historical Account of the Emergence and Evolution of the Trinidad Steel Orchestra* (Port of Spain: University of the West Indies, 1969).

33.   Sunday Guardian Correspondent, 'Limbo and Bongo Danced During Lecture', *Sunday Guardian*, December 19, 1943, 3.

34.   M.E. Farquhar, 'Political Consciousness Is Born', *Sunday Guardian*, December 19, 1943, 3.

35.   Ibid.

36.   David Caute, *The Great Fear: the Anti-Communist Purge Under Truman and Eisenhower* (New York: Simon and Schuster, 1978), 177.

37.   Pearl Connor-Mogotsi, interview with Stephen Bourne, in Stephen Bourne, 'Edric Connor: A Man for All Seasons', *Black in the British Frame: Black People in British Film and Television 1896–1966* (London: Continuum, 2001), 98, chapter 6.

38.   Ibid., 94.

39.   Amiri Baraka, 'Paul Robeson and the Theater', *Black Renaissance* 2, no. 1 (Fall–Winter 1998). See http://iupjournals.org/blackmen/brn2-1.html

40.   Ibid., 3.

41.   Lloyd Brown, 'Preface' to Paul Robeson, *Here I Stand* (Boston: Beacon Press, 1958), xix.

42.   'Caribbeing', a term coined by Trinidadian filmmaker Yao Ramesar.

43.   Tom Murray, *Folk Songs of Jamaica* (London: OUP, 1952).

44.   Edric Connor, *Edric Connor and the Caribbeans: Singing Songs from Jamaica*, collected and arranged by Tom Murray (London: Argo Record Company, RG 33, 1956).

45.   Edric Connor, *Edric Connor and the Southlanders: Songs from Trinidad* (London: Argo Record Company Ltd, RG 57, 1954).

46.   Louise Bennett, *Jamaican Folk Songs* (Folkways, F 6846, 1954).

47.   Harry Belafonte, *Calypso* (BMG Music, 1956).
48.   For the BBC's holdings on Edric Connor see list prepared by John Cowley.
49.   Pearl Connor-Mogotsi, in Bourne, 'Edric Connor: A Man for All Seasons'.
50.   Ibid.
51.   *Report on the West Indian Youth Conference, 1947* (Port of Spain, 1947), 31–32.
52.   Pearl Connor-Mogotsi, 'My Life with Edric Connor this volume.
53.   Pearl Connor-Mogotsi, in Bourne, 'Edric Connor', 91.
54.   Caute, *The Great Fear*, 176.
55.   Paul Robeson, *Here I Stand*, 42.
56.   Caute, *The Great Fear*, 217.
57.   Harry Belafonte, *Calypso* (BMG Music, 1956).
58.   Robert Mitchum, *Calypso is Like So* (New York: Scamp Records, SCP 9701 – 2, 1957).
59.   C.L.R. James, *Beyond a Boundary* (London: Hutchinson & Co Publishers Ltd, 1963).
60.   *Carnival Fantastique* was adjudged 'the best film from the Commonwealth' at the 1960 Edinburgh Film Festival.
61.   Pearl Connor-Mogotsi, 'My Life with Edric Connor'.
62.   Eric Williams, *Inward Hunger: The Education of a Prime Minister* (London: André Deutsch, 1969).
63.   Bourne, 'Edric Connor', 109.
64.   Langston Hughes, *Black Nativity* (directed by Mike Malone, 1961).
65.   Duke Ellington, *Duke Ellington's Concert of Sacred Music* (London: Decca, 1966), SF7811. Originally recorded by RCA, New York. This concert, first presented at the Grace Cathedral, San Francisco on September 16, 1965, was performed in February 1966 before the High Altar of Coventry Cathedral in England.
66.   Bourne, 'Edric Connor', 109.
67.   The following brief summary of Trinidad and Tobago's history between the 1780s and 1960s, but concentrating on the first half of the twentieth century, is mainly based on Bridget Brereton, *A History of Modern Trinidad, 1783–1962* (London: Heinemann, 1989), especially chapters 9 to 12.
68.   Harry Belafonte, Calypso (BMG Music, 1956).

Childhood in Mayaro

Yes. Yes. I was born on the second of August, 1913. I am Leo. They say a man died on the night I was born. This was in Pierresville, Mayaro, in Trinidad. In what was then the British West Indies. It is now Independent, you see.

"We lived on Peter Hill. Peter Hill is a lovely place — a beautiful place. There we looked over the tops of coconut trees for about three-quarters of a mile to the beach. We saw the Atlantic ocean reaching away to the East, even to Africa. We could imagine Africa was there. To the left, to the north, was a point, and we saw the tops of thirteen miles of coconut trees. A glorious sight. A wonderful horizon. It is one of the most beautiful parts of Trinidad."

As a child, I woke every morning in time to see the sun rise out of the Atlantic. It was the most golden and breath-taking sight one could ever hope to witness. It was a glorious lesson in faith. It was there every day. Even when there were dark clouds, the rays of the sun would come shooting up and over the sky, through the clouds, fan-like. Thirteen miles of coconut fronds. Five miles north and eight miles south. The trade winds wafted these like filigree and the devil grass kept the lawn low and good to sit upon. Bougainvillaea, bright poinsettia, croton, vied with each other to display their blooms, and the peacocks ran among them, mating. The Guinea birds and other fowls came and gulped their broken corn and went roaming. The day is six feet tall, and my shadow is twenty. There is singing in the cocoa houses while the workers are dancing on the beans. This is preparation for prosperity.

Little boys and little girls are fetching water from the pond in buckets. The shops have opened the grocery and haberdashery sections. The rum shops will open an hour later. The hunter is leaving for the woods. His dogs are eager. Aunt Dora will soon burst into song. Her favourite, Rock of Ages. You can't help singing in these surroundings. And if you knew

Aunt Dora's gifts, her glorious baritone, you would see how much we all blended with the beauty with which we were blessed. She could stop a cricket match in the Savannah any time she wished. It would be sacrilege to play against such singing.

In this village everybody knew each other. There was an underlying, unspoken concern for, and interest in, each other. My three sisters and my mother tended the family. My father and I were the men. My grandfather, John Jo, was the king. To me, he was a god, and looked one. His extraordinary wisdom was well known for miles around.

My aunts and uncles all shared the blessings of our heritage — a family secured by the land while others were breaking up. An unusual family, I suppose. My Uncle Anthony once horsewhipped a priest. His wife came home from confession crying. The power of the priest was shattered and he left the district. My father played the guitar beautifully. He was interested in Barrios and Segovia. My sister Germain was as good a contralto as Marian Anderson.[1] The others were extraordinary in their own particular ways. None of us had an orthodox education. That is why we are all rebels. My grandfather John Jo once told me: "No educated man ever started a revolution."

Colonial prejudice caused my parents to be out of the family fold after they met, fell in love and got married. My mother was from Moriah in Tobago. A small island. The prejudice against small islanders is still prevalent in the West Indies. To marry a small island girl seemed belittling to the family. To marry a Moravian was degrading. They ran away and lived with each other and my father taught himself the trade of shoemaking. He was ostracised from the family and excommunicated from his church. My mother was cut off from her family, on the other hand, for marrying a Roman Catholic. The Church of England rescued them.

It was five years before they were welcomed back into the fold of their families, at the height of the First World War. My umbilical cord was the peace offering of my parents to my mother's parents. The cord was planted on the family land and formed the manure for the roots of a small coconut tree. That tree is still standing. Legend and superstition have it that the fortunes of the individual are reflected in the way in which the tree grows and bears fruit. For many years I watched my tree grow, in great doubt and wonderment. It is planted on the side of a hill in a place where it is extremely difficult for a coconut tree to grow. However, the last time I saw it, it was standing tall against the wind and had three nuts.

My early years were shared equally between Tobago and Trinidad. The memory that stands out clearly from that period is the number of times I gave one of my shoes to children who had none. The consequent lickings were numerous.

The hills of Moriah are straw-brown and structured like a series of pyramids. To Castara — Runnymede — the sea.

The home of the Archer family looked out north into the blue waters of the Caribbean. There was a large soap-seed tree in the yard. The Adams family lived at the top of the hill. The Dukes perched precariously in their shack about a hundred yards below. The Dukes could not have a better home. They had too many children. Thirteen of them. The caterwauling and wailing that came from their home each night was everybody's business.

My childish memory barely managed to absorb the meaning of Armistice Day in 1918, in Tobago. We lived in a place facing the Moravian church. About a mile away on a hill. The cemetery was on the side of the hill. Everyone in the village contrived to put up some sort of token to represent his loyalty and joy at the cessation of hostilities in Europe. Tobago was too far away to have a Union Jack in normal family life. My grandparents contrived to use an embroidered tablecloth. White. The only relationship between the tablecloth and loyalty was that it was "Made in England".

It was run up to the top of a green bamboo pole. We were all assembled around the base of this flagpole, singing God Save the King and Land of Hope and Glory, songs I hardly knew. Effigies of Kaiser Wilhelm were dragged out of many homes, drawn through the streets, and mutilated. I remember feeling sorry for these effigies.[2]

A few weeks later I went to Parlatuvier with my grandfather to spend a fortnight in the garden.[3]

The main struggle in Tobago is for food. There was a time when the term 'rich as a Tobago planter' had its meaning. That was during the days of slavery. The descendants of these slaves never developed the habit of gaining or possessing riches. They went on planting sufficient food to store for the bad, hard days. My grandfather, Charles Archer, although he had a couple of horses that raced at Shirvan Park, was well and truly included in the gardening community. I was too small to help him till the land but I looked on, learning.

One afternoon, there was a screaming silence. Not a bird on the wing. Not a twitter. Not a rat. Not even an ant to be seen. They all seemed to have gone into hiding.

My grandfather collected me and took me up to the ajoupa — a small garden hut where we slept and ate during the time we were supposed to live in Parlatuvier.[4]

"It is going to blow," he said, "blow hard. When it is quiet like this, it will be very windy. Perhaps a hurricane."

I nodded, learning. There was a rustle of leaves outside, and — woouf! oouf! … It began to rain. Big drops. Painful, heavy drops. Then a sound came through as though hell had broken loose. Coming in the direction of our ajoupa! We were enveloped by this sound. The hut leaned with the first gusts and came back to its original position. Then trees. Big trees, little trees, banana trees, began to get uprooted. A tree, refusing to bend, screamed as it was torn painfully straight down the middle. I saw it a couple of days later. All it needed was blood to show that it had been murdered. Papa Charlie said "Pray! Pray!" He kneeled down and took me with him to pray. After a few hours he felt the ajoupa needed shoring. He tried to go out to get the necessary poles to be used as props. The poor man was blown back into the hut. He shed all his clothes and went out to shore up the ajoupa. It took him easily ten minutes to get back into the house, so strong was the wind. We could see sheets of galvanised iron sailing in the wind, leaves torn from their ribs, and branches also going. And the sea, a mile below, was white, grey, and terrible. Raindrops were running like missiles hurled at thieves. The thoughts of loved ones at Moriah beat on the brain. A hurricane seldom lasts for more than fourteen hours. Everything was primitive in those days. Registration of the people was hardly known, and many lives were literally lost — unaccounted for.

A calm descended and relaxed, like death. This is the time for finding your neighbours. This is the time for propping up. This is the time for the tragedies. Babies unattended, parents killed. Old people, limbs broken. Families homeless. Families roofless. Heaven be praised there is no winter, but these people will never know.

As the roads were impassable we went back to Moriah by boat to find the carpenters had already tackled the repairing of our home. The roof had been blown off completely. They formed a co-operative system whereby all the manpower was pooled. Together they tackled a house at a time. Repairing, sometimes rebuilding, a house in one day. This was called "a lending hand".[5] They pooled the food, cooked it, and fed the men while they worked. They also sang while they worked. Three days later the hurricane whipped back from the north. It came in from the Caribbean Sea and our home was again threatened. But it was in good repair and stood the test.

Back in Mayaro, in Trinidad, I was to find a remarkable man. I was a child at the time. Looking back through the years, I find this man's coming to Mayaro was the best thing that ever happened to that part of Trinidad.

The furthest one could have expected to reach in our village was to become a fisherman, a worker on the plantation or a monitor at the school.

Then came Charles Fitzgerald Worme, schoolmaster. He was sent there on promotion, because he disagreed with the ideas of the Board of Education in Port of Spain. When one was sent to Mayaro in those days, one was being virtually exiled. I suppose Mr. Worme did not mind. He believed in what he had to offer. He believed in his claim that the Board of Education was not going about the education of the people of Trinidad in the right way.

Many mortals would have gone to such a district and destroyed themselves with drink, but not Charlie Worme. He set about organising, reorganising, and planning the education as he felt it should be done. When we look back at the record we see the number of doctors, lawyers, economists, engineers and other technicians who came from the Mayaro Government School. Most of the security officers who run the police force are from Mayaro. And today many people in the Government have been at one time or other taught by Mr. Worme. This is his diploma and commendation.

The school faced the police station; the doctor's house looked down on it. If a child broke away from the establishment and showed brightness he could be put in gaol or certified — the position and interpretation I have always given to those two seats of authority. It is frightening to look back on, but it is true.

Here was a community of too many religions for too few people. The various ways in which they interpreted the Bible gave great entertainment. You became a member of a particular church but this did not prevent you from going to someone else's church. There were just over five hundred souls. They had to visit each other's churches in order to make up the numbers.

There were Roman Catholics, Church of England, Baptists, Wesleyans or Methodists, Seventh Day Adventists, Moravians, Jehovah's Witnesses — the lot.

To attract new members they all used the oldest and most successful method of propaganda: the procession. The Seventh Day Adventists were the newest in the district. My mother seemed to have a liking for this faith, and eventually she embraced it.

Despite the religious divisions in our home there was a great amount of love. I had to attend Sabbath with my mother on Saturdays and go to Mass with my father on Sundays. While other little boys had their weekends for play, I had to go to church.

The Seventh Day Adventist faith has overtones of the Jewish. They keep Saturday as the Sabbath. They do not eat pork. They do not eat fish without scales, considering them to be unclean. When I was a boy, they would not even drink coffee. They said the caffeine was poison. They did not smoke. I suppose they have relaxed that too.

The Sunday table of the poorest Trinidadian groaned with victuals. It carried everything — beef, pork, fish, freshly caught meat of wild animals, rice, Irish potatoes, sweet potatoes, English potatoes, corn meal. This came after the sacrifice of eating rough during the week. The dinner table of Edwin Connor's family was no exception. My father observed that pork was missing from his table and drew my mother's attention to it. She complained it was unclean meat and we could well do without it. My father, asserting his authority, called us all to the living room.

"Sit yourselves down, because I am going to tell you a story.

"Once upon a time, in the hinterlands of British Guiana, there was a Buck named Mungo. As you know, the Bucks are a nomadic tribe. Their main meal was wild hog, the meat of the beast they hunted for food. They followed the hunting wherever it took them. Mungo became Christianized by a missionary. He was taken to the river and plunged into the water. The missionary said 'Mungo, I baptise you in the name of the Father and of the Son and of the Holy Ghost. From today your name is John. You must not eat wild hog. It is unclean. God bless you!'

"Mungo returned to his home. The only food he had was wild hog. He felt hungry and tried to cut a piece of the meat. His wife stopped him, saying, 'No! The missionary said you must not eat wild hog. The good book said it is unclean.'

"Mungo went without his meal. The same thing happened later in the day. The woman was watching him like a hawk. She watched him even closer than God.

"The next day Mungo still had no food. There was nothing else. Only wild hog. Their staple diet.

"Later that day Mungo could bear it no longer. He called his wife, 'Woman. Take this calabash. Go to the river and bring me water.' When she returned, Mungo took a leg of the wild hog, plunged it in the calabash of water, and said, 'Wild Hog! I baptise you in the name of the Father and of the Son and of the Holy Ghost. From today your name is Fish.'"

My mother got the point. There was no longer a shortage of pork on our dinner table. I never asked Mother whether she baptised her hog. I am sure the missionaries would never give Mungo credit for the common sense he showed.

All around us blazed the fires of hell. Every one of those religions painted such a picture of hell, it was horrifying. Many were the times sinners would be groaning and crawling. Going up to the altar to present themselves to Jesus.

Pastor Wood was the greatest of these preachers. He painted such a picture of the birth and death of Christ that oceans of tears used to be shed. Many handkerchiefs needed drying in the afternoon sun.

The rivalry of the churches or religions had to be seen to be believed. The Roman Catholics were against the Adventists. The Shouters were very much more against them. All were against the Adventists because they were new in the district. Sister Townsend with the beautiful figure was of the Adventists. She preached under the shops and all the men turned out to see her. The women also attended to stake their claim. The women turned out in vast numbers to hear Pastor Wood. The men attended to protect their belongings and homes.

"Rasts bostchly sutchly!" shouted Sister Connor, and began to shake violently. "Sutchly, Amen, Sister!" repeated Brother Clarke and nuzzled up to the sister, who feigned she was in the Spirit.

"Let the Spirit move you, Sister."

The young woman stood up. "You lie, Brother Clarke! I did not catch the Spirit." And she walked out.

The gathering began chanting: "Something coming down. The angels sent me to tell you that something coming down."

Brother Clarke began to pray. He was so loud, he gave the impression his God was damned deaf.

"Send Gehazy leper down!"

The congregation responded, "Amen."

"The bud shall have a bitter taste but sweet shall be the flower!" They responded "Amen".

Sister Virtue rang the bell — b – a – l – a – n – g!! and all them sinners began to cower. Singing …

"When Joshua walk round Jericho he shout Hallelujah and the wall fall down. When Joshua walk round Jericho he shout Hallelujah and the wall fall down. In the morning. In the morning. He shout Hallelujah and the wall fall down."

This was the signal for 'Doption No. 5, which was "Kam ka mookoo moo, ka mookoo moo" repeated, and the place was jumping. Here was musical theatre in the raw and I didn't know it. I took so much for granted, like breathing the fresh air of the countryside.[6]

I was among five boys corralled by the storytellers of the village. We were taught all the folk tales and their songs. A mango tree was the proscenium and the Savannah the stage. The Savannah, or playing fields, was about fifteen acres in area. The teller had to act the story and each character in the story. If he wanted to show how a man walked or ran he had the whole Savannah in which to do it. Sometimes then he had to project his voice from across fifteen acres of ground.

Our teachers were not educated men so they expressed themselves in terms of their surroundings.

There were three basic lessons. All given at the same time.

- Walk like a cat. This means you must not be heard. Every movement should be like an illusion.
- Behave like a tiger. This doesn't mean you must rant and rage and tear up the stage, or eat up everything. No. It means you should listen. Listen with the back of your head. Listen with your toes, with your fingertips. Pay attention. Listen! Listen! Listen! I repeat:
- Behave like a tiger, which basically means you must be sensitive. You must throb. You must be alive.
- If you have to carry out any other movement or movements: dance.

I carried this technique to the Shakespeare Memorial Theatre, Stratford-upon-Avon, and it worked perfectly. We were asked to keep these three principles constantly in mind when telling our stories and: Voilà! The rest of our training was repertoire, the learning of the stories.

We jumped from heights and ran through shells and gravel without making a noise. We danced bongo, a dance which expresses the movements of birds in flight. This helped us to use our hands delicately. We practised diligently. All little boys like to be able to command attention. The best way to do this is the ability to tell a story well. I suppose that was one phase of my apprenticeship.

Although I knew all the folk tales, the latest songs and calypsos, I didn't know the Lord's Prayer or the alphabet. I didn't succeed in mastering these until I was ten years old.

At school I was a big boy among babies in kindergarten. One day I saw an East Indian boy, Rajcoomar, with a school satchel. I wanted one myself. I ran home to my mother, telling her I needed a satchel. She promptly asked, "What will you put in it?"

"Books, of course," I said.

"You do not even know the alphabet. You cannot say the Lord's Prayer. Do you want to grow up to be a transgressor? How can you carry an empty satchel to school?" I said, "Well, I will learn the alphabet this evening. By tomorrow you will have to get me a bag and the First Primer. Then I will take them to school with me." I kept my part of the deal and mother kept hers. Within four days I was moved from the infant grade to the classes upstairs. To Grade One. Something was ablaze in me and I never looked back.

The countryside echoed with the laughter of boys at play. We followed the old tracks and made new traces. We trapped doves and mongoose and the police gave us sixpence for each tail. The mongoose harried the chickens and had become a pest. I learned to stalk deer. To do this I had to know all its habits. I began to think like a deer. Like an animal. I had become wild and free as the air — wild and free and restless; and there was always my sunrise. Those eastern horizons challenged me every day.

Up to the age of twelve I had never seen a white man. Yves de Verteuil, the Warden of the district, was white, they said.[7] Probably he was not any different from the albino and the mulattoes. I anxiously awaited the coming of the white man. Most of the shopping done for our home was by mail order, from Oxendales in Lancashire. The white people I recognised were those I had seen in the catalogues.

Dr. Thwaites came and took up residence in the village. His wife was from England. She was white, just like the pictures of the catalogue. Price 50 shillings. At least that is what I thought he paid for her. I didn't change my mind about this until I was much older.

Another thing that worried me sick at the time came from American history. "The Pilgrim Fathers landed on Plymouth Rock in 1620."I wondered what would have happened to America and the world if Plymouth Rock had landed on the Pilgrim Fathers. Oh horror of horrors! A boyish mind with a boyish concern. I would take the goats and horses to pasture and fetch the coconut wood for baking. Mother had a lucrative arrangement to supply the shops with bread and cakes.

We would have family worship every morning. Although my father would not participate, mother would read the Bible loud enough for him to hear. In those days Roman Catholics were not allowed to read the

Bible. She would say, "Edwin, the Lord so wanted us to keep Saturday as the Sabbath. All the other Commandments commence 'Thou shalt not'. But when it comes to the Fourth Commandment, dealing with the Sabbath, the Lord says 'REMEMBER'." Father would reply: "If you were to die I want to see who would church you."

The Seventh Day Adventists at that time had no proper church in the district. Mother would reply testily, "If you don't want to bury me for shame, you would certainly have to bury me for my smell. Hymn number ..." And we would all break out laughing.

It was a Sunday afternoon and the pavilion was packed. There wasn't a cricket match on, but Mr. Monlouis still brought along his five piece band to play. This string band played Castillian and Passé Doble and Paseo. They also played *vie et quoix*.[8] People were dancing on the Savannah. The guest of honour was Captain Cipriani, political leader, accompanied by his lieutenant, Mr. Bishop.[9] They spoke about many things I did not understand. Bishop roused the audience and they cheered loudly. He had loose false teeth that rattled when he spoke.

It was at the height of the dry season. The earth was dry and hard. Water was scarce. Mr. Worme came over after a huddled conference and sent me for a glass of drinking water for the captain. At this time of the year all the barrels were empty, and drinking water was supplemented from the pond.

I faced the first real embarrassment of my life in a glass of water. It was opaque. You could not see through it.

Captain Cipriani took it from me and held it up. Amidst a mixture of laughter and angry shouts from the audience, he raised his voice and asked, "This is the water you drink?"

The crowd responded "Yes! Yes! ...", becoming wild with anger. "My friends, vote Bishop onto the Council, and you will get clean water."

Within a year there were large cisterns built at Mayaro to collect rainwater from the surplus rainfall we always had in this district at certain times of the year. We never had to go to the ponds or the springs in the cocoa fields again.

The incident turned out to be my introduction to politics.

The opening up of oilfields in Guayaguayare attracted my father's shoemaking business. "If you wish to spend your August holidays with me you must walk the sixteen miles to Guayaguayare.'[10]

This test my father set me was to reveal a new world and induce self-reliance. I studied the tides so I could get a reasonably wide beach for the long walk to Grand Lagoon. Choosing a morning when the tide would begin to fall about six o'clock, I said goodbye to my mother and sisters, and faced the journey from Plaisance.[11]

I used to watch the sunrise from Peter Hill, but to do so from the beach of an Atlantic coast is something out of this world. In a mass and maze of coconut trees singing in the high wind, the pounding surf, the splash and swish, is accompaniment.

I passed Lagoon Mahoe. Then St. Thomas and Radix. It was in the church here my parents got married. My uncle is buried in the cemetery. Quite a funeral it was. All his friends wanted to see him off gaily. The coffin was put on a cart bedecked with wreaths. The bearers were so sozzled they eventually had to be carried on the cart too. The cart was pulled by Boodoo, slowest bull in Mayaro, and driven by Abel.

The cortege got to the cemetery well after sundown. They unloaded the coffin at the gate as it was too late for burial. My uncle's friends decide to stay with him to the end, and fortified themselves with more liquor. It must have been a great shock to Mr. Worme to wake and find six men asleep under his window, surrounded by wreaths and hugging a coffin.

By the time I got to Lagoon Doux the tide was out. The beach was now a hundred yards wide, hard and firm and fit for playing and gambolling. Like a kid I did all these. I passed Grand Lagoon and took to the Inside Road. I was on my own. I no longer had the sea as company. No sounds to bear up my courage. All the ghost stories I had learned rushed to my memory. They were fighting with each other, struggling for supremacy. I walked as fast as I could. Sometimes I broke into a trot.

I got to the top of the hill, only to be greeted by an unending tape of red macadam leading out ahead of me for miles … This is it … This is it … Lush plantations. Cocoa and coconuts. Forests. Grassland. More forests. More cocoa. More coconuts … Coconuts … Coconuts. Then I got to Kalma Pass. I did not see a living soul until I got to Kalma Pass.

I had eaten my buttered bread and cakes miles ago. I got a cake at the shop and continued the last two hundred yards to the beach, Guayaguayare beach, sheltered and serene.

The map of Trinidad looks like a woman in a sitting posture. Well, Kalma Pass is the part she is sitting on. Mayaro is the base of the backbone. Guayaguayare is the other part of her thighs. What an area to hail from!

I arrived at my father's shop just before sundown. My first impressions were of an apprentice by the name of Eric King. A peg-legged shoemaker was his assistant, a Grenadian Negro, whose impeccable speech was a joy to hear. And a singer with a guitar. This minstrel was singing about a murder. The printed song was being sold at a penny a time. The man murdered was called Preito. The deed had taken place at Fyzabad, about ninety miles away.

My aunt Christina, Mrs. Levi Taylor, also lived here. Her husband was the overseer of a large plantation. They had a phonograph and all the latest records. Gene Austin, Rudy Vallee, Al Jolson, Paul Whiteman. I spent a lot of time with them. Learning.[12]

Guayaguayare is still unchanged. Still unspoilt. Still serene and crying out for visitors.

The oilfields are five miles from the beach. My father took me on one of his journeys. Perhaps it was the wrong day. I saw the big engines at work. I saw the derricks churning, digging, drilling. I saw the mud and the slime and was very much impressed.

Big Dennis trucks, red trucks and white trucks, crawling uphill with the heavy pipes, heavy loads, heavy cables. Skidding, sliding, wheezing, barking, baying, snorting.

There was too much oil and not enough storage tanks. Several gangs of men and unskilled labourers were hired to dig trenches, dug-outs, or ponds, whatever you may wish to call them. They called these men 'Tattoos', after the armadillo.

My father's business would be wherever the men were working. We stood a reasonable distance from the place where the Tattoos were digging. A white man used a horsewhip across the back of a Tattoo and a terrible fight started. The Tattoo waited for another blow and caught the whip. He pulled the white man to collision. After butting him with his head several times and being egged on by his fellow workers, he grabbed the whip and began to lambaste the white man with it. The man started to run, followed by the Tattoo, who was mercilessly whipping him. The other men were gleefully howling and cheering him on. They ran out of sight.

I later heard that the white man was the general manager. A Mister Cowan. He was from South Africa, where the use of the whip was prevalent. This incident assailed my senses, and will never leave me. On many occasions I enquired of my father about Mr. Cowan. He told me Mr. Cowan seldom left his office after that day.[13]

I had seen a lot of violence before. Mr. Mathew heated his ripsaw in the tropic sun to beat the buttocks of his son. Mrs. Duke hit Micheneau across the mouth with a pot spoon. Mr. Mitchell hit his daughter so hard, she screamed and evoked from my mother: "Ah! Hear how that child bawl! Backside and blows don't agree."

The stinging violence of the whip is a relic of slavery. It is a terrible scar. Somehow the opinion seems to be accepted that we cannot do anything right unless we are flogged. Beaten, bruised and humiliated. The fact will always remain: backside and blows do not agree. And there is nothing elevating or uplifting if they should clash.

The village at Guayaguayare was very peaceful during the week. On Saturdays and Sundays, particularly at night, this was the place for he-men. Gamblers, touts, prostitutes, card-sharpers, drunkards. Many times I saw my father fight and knock men cold in order to get at their pockets. To get the money for the work he had done for them — shoes sold or repaired. Not all sailors are seamen. So it was no surprise that the alleged murderer of Preito was arrested among the ruffians of Guayaguayare.

He was arrested by my mother's cousin, a detective sent from Port of Spain on horseback. He passed for a prospector and was closely associated with the minstrel who had gone into the interior and later returned to the village. This man, whose name I cannot remember, was arraigned with Marie Vidale and another man. Marie Vidale had previously been a teacher of the infant classes at Mayaro. The other man was the driver of the truck that took Preito to his death. Vidale and the truck driver were dismissed from the case. From that day a mentally defective man walked the roads of Trinidad. Like the Flying Dutchman, but with feet firmly planted on terra firma, he criss-crossed the entire island, driving an imaginary truck. His name was Mahal — short for Taj Mahal.

He parked his truck. Reversed his truck. Put it in gear. Moved forward. Second gear. Third gear, and away. This Mahal of the Fyzabad murder. Mahal, the demon of the road. Butt of village sport. Children and grown-ups do not know his roots. They see him and follow him, like the Pied Piper. To the edge of the village. To another tropic night.

I will tell of some of the people in our village. There was Mr. Assam of the lovely cakes. Mrs. Yeates, his mother-in-law. Mr. Aqui of the cinema, which we called Aqui Theatre. Mr. Mano Pierre, who had the vast estates which were taken over by Gordon Grant and Company.[14] The Misses Cuffie of the post office. The nurse, Mrs. Timothy, and her lovely daughter, Audrey, who wore glasses. Mohammed John of the trucks. For short, we called him Mama John. He had two sons, Abdul and Pampie. Mr. Budhoo, the solicitor's clerk; Mr. Dadden, the hunter. Miss Endora Williams, the Sunday school teacher; Ma King and her strapping sons, Tommy, James and Arthur. There was Uncle Lazarus. We all called him Zoas. Mr. Horne the tailor — he had a son named Hamilton. The Misses Lee Fook, who were the local Soong sisters. Oxley Eli, a very good batsman. He had a sister named Oxelia. Lois and Etrice were very good cricketers, very good stick players and bongo dancers; Cousin Favina and Cousin Alice Comfort; Mr. and Mrs. Eli, the parents of Etrice and Lois. Mr. Eli and his wife, who was called Mauricia, were both very old. Their age weighed heavily on the superstitious mind of the community.

When people live near the land it is easy to convince them of the magical properties of herbs and stones, beads and drums. A leaf swaying in the gentle breeze can strike terror in the hearts of half a nation. We do not feel the wind, but it is there. We do not know where it comes from, but it is there. The leaf shakes and sways. Pray tell us what causes it to move. We do not know.

Mauricia was different. She knew magic and we respected her for it. Rumour had it she was a *soucouyant*, otherwise called a vampire. They say her husband was a *lagahoo*, which is a male *soucouyant*. It seems that their abilities went beyond those mentioned.[15]

When King George V was ill in 1928–1929, Mauricia showed us a pink rose she picked from the garden at Buckingham Palace. How she got there nobody knows, but she had much to say. She assured us then the King would live. But after he died in the years to come there would be only one more King of England. I remember the rose and the prophecy. It was always too dry in our village to grow such a flower. There is always history.

After Mr. Mano Pierre lost his estates to Gordon Grant, he had a job as overseer at Quesnel's estates at St. Joseph, three miles from our school. After a few months on the job he fell ill. The doctors came and went. They got paid. He went to Port of Spain and saw the specialists. Returned. Still a sick man. Mr. Mano Pierre then turned to the obeah-man in desperation. As a last resort. He was taught to look after himself.

What he did is still a secret. But one morning he woke to find the naked figure. On a galvanised iron tank of water outside his window at the back of the house. It was Mauricia, naked, pleading. Begging him to let her go free and she would see to it that he got better.

She was put on a cart and with a crocos bag thrown around her, driven slowly south along the Manzanilla Road.[16] Past the school, where all the children gazed. She was taken up to the police station. She was put in a car eventually and driven away, out of Mayaro. Not another word was spoken of Mauricia. We never heard of her again.

George and Philip, two men from China, owned the shops at Pierresville. Women came here to buy their clothes and hats and cretonne from England. To make curtains for their houses and shirts for their men. Children were sent to buy 'message', which consisted of rice and sugar, and lard and butter, and pig's feet or salted fish, pig-tail and smoked herrings. Sometimes we would break up the message into three sections.

Philip and George and, for that matter, all the Chinese shopkeepers, were very generous to children. It might be a biscuit with a dash of butter, a sweet or just plain sugar, after each purchase. No one knows how they managed to make a profit.

Starvation Wall was the name of a concrete culvert that spans a ravine that runs between the two shops.

On Saturday afternoons the village swains would take their place at the wall to admire the belles as they sought their bargains. The marchandes would be under the shops, selling fried float and accra and Bajan cake and butter bread.[17] Sweet potatoes, plantains and pineapple would be on view for sale. Also beef, pork and mutton. Everybody would be preparing for Sunday.

Even as a child I found great affluence at Mayaro. Mr. Aqui had the Theatre. Mr. Dasent was the overseer for Mano Pierre's estate. Mr. Budhoo, the solicitor's clerk. Here was a thriving community. Coconuts and cocoa had long replaced sugar cane. World prices were very good. The Tangs, Bovells, Quesnels and de Meillacs had also joined us. Slicked field boots and gaiters glistened in the tropic sun. Silk shirts and cream flannels and garbadine trousers greeted and soothed the eyes. There was no poverty here. Even the estate workers were contractors at certain times of the year.[18] The mail was collected from the Post Office in a landau and at times on horseback. We received the *Port of Spain Gazette* every other day. It was as old as *The Times* of London. The *Trinidad Guardian* was unheard of in the district.[19] People did not die here. They just faded away. My uncle was the only exception. That is the reason there was no hearse to take him to the cemetery. We were not prepared for anything like death.

The SS *Belize* came to Mayaro once a week and made two calls, one at Plaisance, the other at Lagoon Doux. Then she sailed to Tobago. Oh, to watch the strong black men straining and tearing the Atlantic breakers with the oars! The white boats filled with freight! Standing almost on end now, and disappearing later behind a wave. The wind, driving spume to shore to keep the company of man o' wars.[20]

Christmas is here, and all the women of the Connor family gather at Peter Hill to bake, roast and cook. The men are out serenading. There is no sleep on Christmas Eve. With the first light of Christmas Day the serenaders wend their way home with their friends and others they may have picked up during their carousing. Instead of the usual breakfast of boiled chocolate, bread and bul-jol, there is split-peas soup trimmed thick with pig's tails and dumplings. There is also a side dish of souse and an array of beverages ranging from ginger beer for the children to rum and whisky for the men, and Carupano wine for the women. The soup settled the stomach and absorbed the potency of the strong drinks.[21]

Waterfall curtains trimmed with hibiscus, bougainvillea and croton leaves spread the message of peace, plenty and goodwill. Come! Welcome! Come! Every home in the district is visited throughout the day. All the little fractures are healed. "Neighbour, you too damned deceitful." "Fire one, neighbour, fire one." And the singing could be heard at Mafeking, where almost the same thing was going on. Talk about fete! By sundown all the men of the village will have visited, eaten and drunk to the glory of God and the other god, Bacchus. They return home to change into top hat, tie and frock coat. They spread out among the bushes in one last desperate attempt to prevent Christmas Day from coming to a close. They shout instructions to each other: "Hold him!" "I got him!" "Don't let him pass!" and so on. Then, as the dark descends, they gather at the house. Some muddy, bruised and battered. Some with an array of sticking foliage. Others with their neighbours' daughters for dancing belair and storytelling.[22]

The rum shops are open. I stand at a reasonably safe distance. Watch the men go into the rum shop, and wait until they come out. You study them as they stagger up the road. I go away and practise being a drunk. You must be very sober to do it well.

The Foresters' lodge is decorated because there will be a dance tonight. The windows and doors are embroidered with the fronds of coconut palms, with bouquets of bougainvillea and hibiscus hanging from the middle. It will be Mr. Monlouis' band, with flute and fiddle, bass and guitar, and cuatro.[23]

All the people dancing tonight will be at the cricket match tomorrow. They needn't go home. They could look at the game from the lodge or from the shops.

Etrice and Lois, the sons of Mauricia, are picked to play in the game on Sunday afternoon. Nobody looked down upon them or segregated them for what happened to their mother. The one thing inevitable is death. We might as well make as much as we can of our lives. That is the way things are. A fact of life has passed out of this community. Mauricia has gone. Cricket must go on.

The hunter comes home from the woods. He walks at a brisk pace down the hill from the old road, his gait one of triumph. The dogs are ahead of him, prancing. Waving semaphore with their tails and barking morse. Signalling the success of the hunt.

"Mister Dadden, how much you catch?"

"I catch foh!"

"What kind?"

"Three him and one he!"

And the whole village knows that there is fresh wild meat for the pots on Sunday.

All of Sunday morning the groundsmen watered and rolled the cricket pitch. The matting was laid, the stumps set up. An air of jousting and tournaments pervaded the scene. Images of King Arthur and his courtiers and the Black Prince raced through the mind; coats of mail and shingles and scales. Instead, they were all dressed in white, the cricketers, the only protection white leggings. My father made them out of canvas. Instead of spears they had bats. And a ball was bowled at them.

Mr. Monlouis' band is over at the pavilion, scraping and plucking away, as only country musicians can play.

A strong team had been sent from the oilfields at Tabaquite. They had five white men who wore cricket caps. A sure sign they belonged to some club we read about in the papers.

Many truckloads of visitors came in from Tabaquite and Rio Claro, Nine Miles, Mitan, Tamboo Laytay and Kan Kay. Some also came from Guayaguayare.

The shops were not open. Whatever drinking there was came from leftovers from Saturday.

The boundaries are marked with flags and sticks, tall enough to protrude out of the bush so that they can be seen by the umpire.

The short grass grows quickly in the Savannah. To score two runs the ball must roll past the end of the grassy patch. To hit a four the ball must go straight over the grassy patch but not beyond the flagpoles. To hit a six the ball must go clear over the pavilion and over the flagpoles, or a similar distance all around the ground, or over the mainroad past Mr. Leonard's house.

Visiting teams called the ground 'The Gallows'. The best of them from all over Trinidad got beaten there. The umpiring was always fair, but the ground had the edge. Making seventy-five at Mayaro is as good as scoring two hundred and fifty at Lords.

Laughter and music are to the surface, and the wit is always ripe. The eager faces of grown-ups and the children alike are a joy to behold. Everyone had been well fed at his Sunday lunch.

Mayaro has won the toss and Uncle Nathaniel as captain has graciously invited Tabaquite to bat. The players take the field and Etrice will open the bowling from Mr. Leonard's end. Two white men, with fancy leg-guards, cricket gloves and caps, and flannel trousers and white shirts, opened.

Etrice starts his run from the bank of the ravine and up the hill he bounds. He leaps into the air and comes down at the wicket. The ball leaves his hand with the speed of lightning. Crashes down on the matting. Rises sharply. The ball edges off the player's bat and goes pelting to the slips, straight to Lois.

"How's that?"

"No! Oh God, he dropped it!"

The groans could be heard in Mafeking.

The batsman looks at the edge of his bat. Surveys the matting and removes an imaginary piece of straw.

Etrice retrieves the ball and walks back to the edge of the ravine.

The batsman nods and Etrice starts his run again. He delivers a round arm at the wicket; and before the player can barely raise his bat, the ball slices past the leg stump, almost touching it. Daddy Worme, keeping wicket between the bush and the crease, was so sure he was out that he had to stretch full out at the last moment to stop the ball from going for four byes.

This world of excitement was in complete isolation from any other part of the universe. The only thing that mattered was the next ball. The speed of the bowling filled the batsman with terror. What is he thinking? What will the bowler do next? It was obvious the batsman had never experienced anything like this before.

The next ball was short of a length from over-arm. The batsman was going forward. He changed his mind and before he could withdraw his bat got a touch. Big, burly Uncle Nat, at third man a safe catch, made no mistake!

The place erupted. The string band began to play louder. The spectators began to dance. Some got branches from trees and waved them. Little boys hugged each other and danced. The girls pranced like kids. We watched the batsman come in and another take his place. Another cap. The board read one wicket for no run, and Tabaquite was in trouble.

They made a good score, 116, and were the first visiting team to go past the hundred.

Oxley opened for Mayaro, partnered by Mr. Mitchell, a Negro but almost albino. The psychology of this, he said, nearing white, would strike fear into the hearts of the visitors; but he didn't have a cricket cap.

Oxley played himself in and began to find the little path through the grass which was made by players going to and from the wicket. He found it so often they put a fieldsman near the pavilion to cut off the twos.

When Dr. Mahabir went in he crashed the first ball he received over Mr. Leonard's house. Six!

The place went wild. The band played. The people laughed. The little boys jumped in the air. The women danced and waved their branches.

Quiet, for the bowler to deliver.

Next ball, and crash! Over the old road. Over the hill and all the way down to Mr. Austin's house. It was the biggest six ever seen at Mayaro. We lost sight of the ball because it had gone over the top of the coconut tree at the top of the hill behind Mr. Leonard's house.

While they were searching for the ball there was time for comments and dancing. The white visitors seemed very amused at this type of cricket and the villagers seemed to lay it on for their benefit.

At sundown the match was won by two wickets. We went home spreading joy through the hills and under the coconut trees. Some of us were singing, "If you follow Mayaro boys you will get fever, and the fever will never recover." The visitors went their way, defeated, but only after having enjoyed a grand game of cricket.

Next morning the conch shells blew. Fishermen were summoned to the sea. Labourers went on to work on the plantations. The post office and the shops opened as usual. Children walked to school, barefooted, from Five Miles, Mafeking, Cedar Grove and Lagoon Doux. They carried their lunch in skillets and their books in bags of assorted shapes, sizes, colours and materials.

Rajcoomar, of Five Miles, came in every day with his mother, Maharajin, who sold the milk. It turned to butter many times when she used the pail to fend off little dogs that teased her. Cousin Alice continued to comfort the whole village with her philosophy. Poonsie gave her sweets to all the nice young men. Emelda was nearly always jealous and became her rival. She took up religion seriously after biting off a piece of Poonsie's ear.

The day Natisse Sylvan died was a warning. He killed himself. Poison. Took it in his coffee. He was found with his head resting on the open book of the estate accounts. Natisse had been away working in the oilfields to make extra money to pay the interest on the mortgage that encumbered the family estate. He had come home the night before wearied and worried at the encumbrances.²⁴ He saw no other way out of it. Natisse was young. Only twenty-five. He was handsome. And the best cricketer in the village of Mayaro. He always went in first wicket down. His family had a big estate but he never wore cream flannel pants for cricket. He didn't wear cricket boots. He wore a black hat with a broad brim like a Spanish matador, white shirt, and white drill trousers, pressed so neatly the seam would cut you. He also wore white watchicongs.²⁵ He and Oxley, Etrice, and Lois were our heroes at cricket.

It was sad when we lost Natisse to the oilfields. But a great shock when we heard he had died. We did not even know he had returned home. I was a little boy in shirt-tails then, like all little boys in the country districts of the West Indies. Shirt-tails are functional. I was sucking a piece of sugar-cane at the side of the house when Ma Laffy came up the little hill to discuss the situation with my grandfather. She was about fifty, dressed in a *douillette* and a tartan (madras) headscarf, tied to show that she was past it.²⁶ Two little goats were mating in front of her. She chased them away with the forked stick she carried.

She continued slowly up the hill picking her way with the forked stick in all the queenly glory of the country landlady. She played her age to the hilt of the forked stick. Especially when the peacocks greeted her with their presence. At the almond tree she straightened up. I stood up in respect. My grandfather came forward.

"Ah, John Jo! How are you today?" "Bien, bien, Ma Laffy," my grandfather replied. "You hear about Natisse? I come to talk to you about him. What is life, eh? You come today, you gone tomorrow. Heigh, in the midst of life we are in death."

My grandfather said, "Yes. Natisse was in a lot of debt. But he was a very proud young man. Do you want to come inside?"

"No, man, it is a nice day. Let us sit down in the air, under this almond tree. Go boy, go 'way. We don't want you to hear what old people saying," Ma Laffy cordially shouted at me. I went to the kitchen, and then wandered away. They talked for a long time. On the other side of the house the sea, the horizon, and the coconut trees stretched away in front of me. Those thirteen miles of coconut trees were once sugar-cane. The coconut oil factories were once sugar mills. They were bought by a primitive co-operative system which came out of the abolition of slavery. The Apprenticeship the masters clamoured for was to have lasted six years, but the insurrections were too many. It was abruptly terminated after four years. The barrack rooms on cocoa plantation and sugar estate are the last remaining relics of this abominable Apprenticeship.[27]

The ex-slaves were paid sixpence per day for their work on the plantation. They pooled all the money they earned into a primitive kitty, or co-operative. And simultaneously with the dramatic fall of the price of sugar they began buying out their masters. Within the three years from 1838 to 1841 they made such inroads into the land and economy of the island that a Committee was set up to investigate. It found that the ex-slaves no longer wished to work the land of the Europeans. They had their own. The Committee recommended that East Indian indentured labour be introduced.

To work the lands my ancestors resorted to a simple cultural tradition. In the days of slavery, when there was a fire on one of the plantations conch-shells were blown to summon the slaves of the neighbouring plantation. With lighted torches they would sing songs of bravery while they marched to put out the fire. This custom was known as Canboulay; a corruption of the French "cannes brulées". The day slavery was abolished, August 1st, 1834, Canboulay was used to celebrate abolition. Some of the ex-slaves broke down and cried. Some just sat there, speechless. Others stood on the beach of the east coast of the island. They just looked out to sea. Beating their drums and calabashes. There was nothing lewd or discordant about the celebrations. Needless to say, the ex-masters were afraid and concerned about Britain giving freedom. Slavery was abolished, but the plantations remained. Freedom was here, but the cane-flowers beckoned. And they all went back to the plantation to do an Apprenticeship. To learn to work in freedom. Each year on August 1st, Canboulay was used to celebrate the anniversary of abolition. When the co-operative began, Canboulay was used to till the land. To summon the ex-slaves and to reap the harvest. The ex-slaves grew prosperous. The co-operatives enlarged in different districts in proportion to the number of estates they were able to appropriate. The Europeans now found it extremely difficult to compete. East Indian indentured labour was introduced in 1845. Canboulay continued annually and became a political force. More and more Indians came into the island. So many that the authorities shifted Canboulay from August 1st to the two days before Ash Wednesday, making it a Roman carnival. Nobody complained about this. The ex-slaves could not read. They had just begun sending their children to study in Edinburgh and Glasgow and Dublin. They returned home as doctors, lawyers or engineers. Canboulay continued to be used to express political aspirations. August 1st was now Discovery Day, because Christopher Columbus discovered Trinidad on July 31st, 1498.

More lands were added to the co-operatives and a very Victorian but affluent society was being built. Communications were not good. However this helped the co-operatives to be built up as separate units. It took one week from Mayaro to Port of Spain on horseback — a journey of 56 miles. Canboulay was intensified when news came to Trinidad of the uprising of Paul Bogle in Jamaica. This was subdued by his horrible execution ordered by Eyre, the Governor who had given his illustrious name to Lake Eyre in Australia. This was in 1865. It coincided with the ending of the American Civil War, when the slaves of that country were supposed to get their freedom.[28]

London was unhappy about all these things. The experiment of freedom was taking some unfortunate turns. Canboulay continued until the so-called Canboulay Riots of 1881. They were a minor affair. They took place in the middle of Charlotte Street between Park and Duke Streets, Port of Spain. Captain Baker, Chief of Police, ambushed a Canboulay band which was headed by Robert Myler and his brother. From Belmont. Nobody was killed, only a few policemen beaten up. Myler and his brother had a mule cart in the middle of the band, which was about 1000 strong. When the police attacked, the band opened and the mule cart jumped forward at speed under a hail of blows — splitting the police in two and isolating them in sections. To be dealt with by the members of the band. But nobody was killed. This was a sufficient excuse to send in a Commission to investigate Canboulay and the "riots". All sorts of evidence was given about the fire hazards of Canboulay, the lewdness and the dangers. But the main reasons were omitted.

When the Commission tabled its Report, some of its recommendations automatically became law. The torches were removed. The beating of drums was restricted. These were basic items of the culture reflected in the prosperity of the co-operatives. Without them it would be difficult to keep the people together. A wedge was driven between the people, and the Do's and Don'ts of Calvinism whipped the population into class-consciousness. Canboulay now became Carnival. The drum was replaced by lengths of bamboo called Tamboo Bamboo. The co-operatives were split and the share-out became legal only when the land was registered under individual family names: The Pierres. The Laffys. The Sylvans. The Connors and the Elis. The Lemessys. The Borelles, and so on. They now had to hire labourers to work on their plantations.

Banks moved in to lend their money. The Sylvans, the Pierres, the Elis. My great-grandfather registered our lands as minors' property to keep the family together. It cannot be sold. Every member of the family, though unborn, has a right to it. We cannot borrow money on it. No bank would lend to us because it is not good collateral and cannot be seized.[29]

The day Natisse Sylvan died was a warning. The banks and money-lenders were about to come to Mayaro. The Sylvan estate was first to go. Then Mano Pierre's. Mano Pierre of the cork hat, of the breeches and shining brown gaiters. Yes, the day Natisse Sylvan died was a warning. No more the building of a house to music. No longer the sowing of corn to the drums. But the harvest moon we can always share and the music we can still hum.

Days and weeks, months and years of sunrises passed. I stalked the grey deer and chased the wild birds. Mongoose was good revenue for boys. I saved and bought a Meccano set. Apart from Mr. Worme, my teachers were Mr. St. Louis, Mr. Hackett and Mr. Albert Mark. They called me the big-head boy.

This big-head boy must have been a sight, skinny and lanky in shorts. He was made a monitor and taught the lower classes when he himself was not studying.[30] Then he was sent to San Fernando on his own to sit an examination called the Handicraft Exhibition. The examination had nothing to do with handicrafts.

It took place at a school in Paradise Pasture near a rum shop owned by a man named Jesus. I was terribly amused by this while answering the papers, and it must have relieved whatever tensions I might have had in me. The examination was for boys under sixteen throughout the islands of Trinidad and Tobago. The results came out on my birthday, August 2nd, 1929. I came second out of over 350 boys.

If I accepted the bursary I would have to leave Mayaro.[31]

My mother wanted me to become a doctor. My father wished me to continue in his trade and carry on the business of shoemaking. A lot of money would have had to be found to send me to college. We could not afford it. Mother said I should do the next best thing and take up the bursary. My father was angry and snorted. "Whenever he gets that college education he will give it to himself. Too many college boys win scholarships and go to England and come back here with white wives and break up their families."

Here was the first quarrel I had ever seen in our home and my future was the cause of it. My sisters and I huddled together silently, just awaiting the outcome. My mother, a very strong woman, went calmly to her chest of drawers, opened it, and began taking out her jewels. Gold this, gold that, and gold the other. She came back to the front of the house and quietly said, "You will be going to Port of Spain. Never mind your father." Father eventually capitulated when Mr. Worme spoke to him seriously a few days later. If I did not take up the bursary by a certain date it would be given to another boy. Over 350 boys were fighting for four places.

The day I left Mayaro Government School was a very important occasion in my life. Mr. Worme treated it almost like a speech day. All the children and many parents came to say farewell. I was on show by his table. I got up to make a speech. All my school memories came rushing back. The concerts, the cricket matches, athletic sports, the little loves and hates, the little fights. I looked at the whole school waiting to hear from me, and burst into tears.

Daddy Worme pulled me into his arms. By now I was weeping bitterly and I think they all understood.

I woke early to do the last bits of packing and to see my sunrise for the last time. A bedroom had been built for me at the house and the windows opened to its full view and glory. I said my goodbyes to the neighbours and the family. John Jo was at Cascadura tilling the land. He knew I would come back.

We took the bus by the shops, my mother and I. The people had turned out to say goodbye. I kissed my sisters and we were all crying. On the trip I remembered my sisters and the sacrifices they made to get me where I am. They completely effaced themselves. They were just the silent helpers. My sister Germain had once said, "You don't belong to us. You belong to the world." How could she have known? She too was very tender in years. I have never been able to repay them.

I sat on the back seat so that I could see as much of Mayaro as possible as we moved away. When it was gone I turned and found my immediate travel companions were two pigs. They lay there silently with their legs tied.

Young Man in the City

We travelled all day and arrived in Port of Spain at eight o'clock that Thursday evening. We stayed with Sister Murray, a friend of my mother's. A Sister in Christ. A Seventh Day Adventist. At 28 Jerningham Avenue, Belmont, Port of Spain.

The following morning my mother took me to the Royal Victoria Institute. We reported to Miss La Forest, who was just writing a letter cancelling my scholarship. She ushered us in to Mr. D.M. Hahn, Director of the Board of Industrial Training. He said, "This is a damned bad beginning," and scrapped the letter. He dictated another and sent me to Mr. Carmichael of the Trinidad Government Railways.[32]

Port of Spain was not a big city then. We took the tramcar that passed in front of the Institute and rode down to the railways. We were lucky to find Mr. Carmichael in his office. Mr. Carmichael was the Superintendant of Railways. A fine English gentleman. He ushered my mother out of his office and sat me down so we could talk like two men. It was to be an apprenticeship of three months' probation and five years if accepted. The first three months you worked for nothing. The first two years at 16 cents, or 8d. per day. In the third year, 24 cents, or 1/- per day. In the fourth year, 32 cents per day, and on the fifth and final year, 40 cents per day.[33]

"Do you understand the meaning of this?" he said.

I nodded in assent.

He stood up and shook me by the hand, and said, "Welcome to the Railways, sir! You start on Monday."

He took me out to my mother and told her, "He will be all right, Mrs. Connor."

She thanked him and we left.

"You know what, Titty? He called me Sir! He called me Sir!" It was the first time anybody called me Sir.

We looked round Port of Spain that weekend, purchasing overalls and books I would need at the Institute. I began on 21st October in the boilermaking department. The foreman was a Scotsman named Begg. Another Scotsman, named Robert Dick, was the works manager. I was put under Lio Bon. Apart from boiler-making, Lio Bon used to train boxers. As evidence of his ability, all the champions of the West Indies came from his stable.

Here I found noise, nicknames, and a broad humour. It was extremely heavy work. Everybody was friendly and I learned quickly. Clermonte Rogers, the boy who had come third in the examination, was also studying there as a bench fitter. Mr. Bansfield was the foreman of the machine shop.

Every week my parents sent to Port of Spain two bags of ground provisions, clean laundry and money for my upkeep. The goods arrived on Saturday. Owing to Sister Murray's religious teaching, they could not be taken out of the station or brought into the house before Monday. Between Monday and Wednesday she would send gifts of ground provisions to all her friends.

The word 'confused' has made an indelible impression upon my mind. Whenever Sister Murray said she was 'confused' on a Wednesday I knew I had no food for Thursday, Friday, Saturday, and sometimes Sunday. She insisted on reading all the letters I wrote to my mother. In fact Mother would have it no other way.

At the railways my tummy was empty, my lips white, and the work hard. A fat woman named Birdie came to the workshops every day with fried muffins, floats and accras, bread, butter, tea and mauby to sell as refreshment and lunch to the workmen.[34] Birdie must have noticed how I was wasting away. She called me to her stall when it was private and said, "You see you, you don't belong here. You are too big for this island. Come! Eat! Eat as much as you like. When you get your money pay me."

I was from the country, from the land, and I was proud; but one should not refuse benevolence when in need. It is insulting God.

Remembering that my first pay would be at the rate of 8d a day I ate very sparingly, and only when I was extremely hungry. But it was too late. My health broke. I had to have my tonsils removed. I told my mother and she had to come into town. She could not recognise me, I was so thin and wasted. The unchristian attitude of her Sister in Christ was what hurt her most. She immediately got rooms at Lodge Place, and I left Sister Murray that night. My parents and sisters were all in Port of Spain to be near to me when I had the operation.

My parents, my sisters, Dr. Francis, Dr. McKechnie, and three nurses were there when I came round from the anaesthetic. Dr. Francis told me in later years they had to be nearby because of the things I said while I was under chloroform. He said he and McKechnie thought they were remarkable for a boy of sixteen.

Trinidad became a different place. Port of Spain was now my home. My mother and sisters nursed me back to health over a period of three months. I begged them to return to Mayaro to look after my father. They insisted on teaching me to cook, mend and wash my clothes. When the lessons seemed never-ending, I bought them railway tickets for Rio Claro and installed myself in the Ozanam shelter.[35]

This is a place for ex-Borstal boys and young offenders, those who had been to the detention institute, ex-prisoners, and old lags. The moment you entered your attention was drawn to the sign, "God will provide".

Mr. Peschier was the warden. A smooth-skinned black man with white hair. He might have stepped out of the pages of history — the Haitian Revolution, or Danton of the French Revolution, but black. He ran a small printery as a sideline. The Angelus tolling from the Cathedral daily reminded us of our poverty.

I lived at the Ozanam shelter for three years. The things the inmates taught me could have turned me into a great crook and a criminal. Instead, I learned to box and studied engineering. I went to Queen's Royal College at night to study physics. I suppose it is the only way I could have gone to Q.R.C. I didn't dare show my face there in the daylight. I was a 'Mayaro boy' with a common B. I took the City and Guilds of London examinations and in 1934 won the Stephens Gold Medal for mechanical engineering.[36]

In all these years since I had my tonsils removed I did no singing. I continued to work at the railways at 40 cents per day. I still lived in Duncan Street. There was something fascinating there. Life was raw. The market place was just around the corner on Nelson Street. The little girls teased and the little boys played pranks on each other. There was nothing offensive here but poverty. The men played whe whe and loved the women; there was nothing else to do. It was at the height of the depression. I had seen men hold their hands to their heads and holler like animals because they made a mistake in the work and might get dismissed.[37]

It was a tough district. On Besson Street, near the police station, a man smoked a stick of dynamite and blew his head off to prove his love for a woman. Family life here was never a private affair. The streets rang with the cries of the vendors. The whistle of scavengers and the clip-clopping of mules. The exultant cries of sex. Dogs barked and cockerels crowed proudly. These noises were the Symphony of Life. The Concerto was played over and over at the market.

The market place had the smell of the countryside. Strong, fresh and blooming. The honeycomb man was singing his wares: "One cent a honeycomb." The chocolate vendor said, "Madam, my cocoa got fat." "Oranges", "Pomerac", "Pomme cythere", "Avocado", "Sapodillas", and "Plantain to fry and boil".[38] "Wake up, wake up! Get your nice pork pudding. Fine and dandy in due time. Ma Ma, look pork!"

Amidst the cacophony, a shrill nasal sound would come from a "Baptist" preacher in the distance regaling the multitudes. It is 'Nosegay' of the flamboyant personality, giving vent to his feelings about the Bible. Regaling us poor mortals about the wages of sin. With perfect timing a little boy shouts "Nosegay!" and bolts. Nosegay would put down the Bible. Turn to his followers and say calmly, "Brothers and sisters, excuse me." Then he'd turn in the direction from which the call came and hurl the most obscene invectives at the boy and the crowd. When he had said enough, a member of his followers would say, "Amen!" He would then return to the business of preaching the Word.

When times are hard in Trinidad there are two avenues open to the local man for making money easily. You may set yourself up as an obeah-man, or form a new church and become a "Baptist" preacher. You don't have to build any edifice. All you have to do is get a flambeau and a Bible. You are not bound to be able to read well. Somebody will help you out in that department. Follow the wayside and the hedges, and the money will come. Man, you can grow fat on free fried chicken and rice.

I once asked a wayside preacher what were the requirements for becoming a "good wayside preacher". His reply was very frank and without shame. "You must have a good voice, a fair knowledge of the Bible, and the ability to make the bed creak." Like Nosegay, the wayside preacher always plays for drama and spectacle. This is very attractive to the people of Trinidad. They do not get it in the orthodox churches. There is a sense of theatre in the Roman Catholic church with the exits and entrances well-timed. The bell chimes to raise the Host and that is the end of the drama. Not so with the Shouters.

For several weeks in advance, Nosegay was telling his congregation that he would die like Jesus Christ upon the cross on Good Friday.

Custom has it that the market is opened from five o'clock to nine o'clock on Good Friday morning. Nosegay arrayed himself in long white robes and the heavy cross he intended to carry to Piccadilly Street. He and his followers preached and sang for four hours. At nine o'clock sharp, Nosegay shouldered his cross and crawled along Nelson Street. Then across Prince Street. Over Duncan Street. Past the bridge, and right into Piccadilly Street.

Not far from the school there is a bit of open ground near the Dry River. The hole was already dug for the foot of the cross. A piece of half-inch manilla rope took the place of the crown of thorns. People from Rose Hill, Besson Street and Duke Street were running, converging on the spot, to witness the spectacle of a real crucifixion.

Nosegay turned to his congregation and said: "Today I am going to die like Jesus Christ on the cross. Today I shall be crucified as they crucified our Lord."

He was disrobed and displayed the body of a well-fed, well-built man, clad in an oversized bikini. He lay down on the rough cedar post and stretched his arms wide on the four-by-two plank. He clutched two large nails that were driven at each end of the plank. Then he called upon his followers, "Nail me! Nail me to the cross! Like they nailed our Lord!" Then he said quietly, "Not too close me fingers, but make sure your hammer sound as if you nailing. Use rope and tie me."

His wrists and ankles were tied. After making sure he was comfortable, his followers hoisted the cross aloft and erect. The singing grew louder. Nosegay screamed, "Eli! Eli! Lama Sabachthani! And for those of you who don't understand what I mean: My God! My God! Why hast Thou forsaken me? Spit on me! Spit on me!" he shouted. "Spit on me as they spat on our Lord!" Then, in a more modulated tone, he said "Brother Braveboy, I notice you have a bad cold. Be careful." "Stone me! Stone me! As they stoned our Lord!" he shouted. And to his followers he said, "But wid little pebbles."

It was coming up to the hot midday sun and Nosegay had had enough. He thought it was time he should come down, and called upon his followers. They had taken him at his word. It would be embarrassing to do such a thing before the entire congregation. Nosegay would have none of this. He cried out, "Take me down! You sons of bitches! What the hell, you all think, I'se Jesus Christ? Take me down, I say!"

Much to the amusement of the crowd, and because of the violent protestations of Nosegay, the cross was eventually uprooted. After he was released, he rubbed his wrists and ankles to get the blood flowing again. He was very belligerent, despite the success of his ordeal. He turned on Brother Braveboy: "Half a chance and you'd put me in a tomb." The crowd drifted away to the hills with perhaps a better understanding of Easter, but certainly very amused and well entertained.[39]

After my apprenticeship was over I continued to work at Trinidad Government Railways, still at 40 cents per day. I had gone through all the shops. Boiler, fitting, blacksmith, foundry, machine shop, I did my turn.

Mr. Bansfield was very hard on me. It was all for my good. The greater the test, the greater the hardships, the more I learned. The more I learned with practical experience.

There were times when famous artistes passed through Port of Spain on their way to and from Rio de Janeiro and Buenos Aires. They would give concerts at the Royal Victoria Institute, the De Luxe Cinema, and at the Princes Building just across the way.[40] I used to sneak away from classes. Cyril, the janitor, would let me in through a steel door to the side of the stage. There I would rub shoulders with Menuhin, Elman, Zinka Milanov and others.[41]

I remember Barrios giving a full recital, dressed in his native Mexican Indian costume. Complete with banded plume sticking out at the back of his head and multicoloured beads adorning a broad chest. Sometimes they rolled on to the box of the guitar and gave dramatic colour to the music. Steamships were the means of travel then. My father came to town to hear Segovia. He booked tickets for both of us at the Empire Theatre. The boat was late arriving and Segovia did not get on to the stage until ten o'clock that evening. He was worth waiting for.

I suppose my voice really developed against the noise of the machines and engines of the Trinidad Government Railway workshop. When Bansfield gave me hell and I was sick at heart I would sing to soothe the pain, full-throated, drowning the noise.

I set myself my first and only ambition: to sing in the Royal Victoria Institute choir.

It was realised three months later. I felt a fool. What does one do after he has realised an ambition? Shoot himself? I promised never to set myself another ambition. I engaged in amateur dramatics.

After many years singing with the choir as baritone lead and soloist, an unusual opportunity came my way: to deputise at an important concert for an English singer who had suddenly been taken ill. Next day the press reviews talked only about the singer who was ill. Not a word, not even a mention, about the person who deputised for him. My singing that evening was very good.

About this time there came to Trinidad to run the *Trinidad Guardian* a Canadian named Major C.L. Harrington. He was the man who saw the possibilities of the Loch Ness monster story and gave out to the world that it was seen in Trinidad. Harrington felt Trinidad needed more publicity and the best way to do this was through a film. He also discovered that there was no tuberculosis sanatorium in Trinidad. Through the press he established a public subscription towards such a sanatorium. After collecting over $50,000 he called upon the *Trinidad Guardian* to run a competition to get artistes to play in a film about the island.

The requirements were: two leads, one villain, two underdogs and the villain's girl. All you had to do was send in a photograph and state the category under which you would like to act. I sent in my photograph and asked to play the 'male underdog'. It was promptly returned without comment. Then a panel of judges chose a dozen photographs from each section. The public was asked to vote for the prettiest by a coupon attached to the paper.[42]

Sales of the *Trinidad Guardian* rocketed. It seems everybody wanted to get into films. Island-wide canvassing was done.

The people who won the competition knew little about acting. I, at least, was taught to tell Anansi stories.[43] Many people saw themselves as little Greta Garbos and Jean Harlows, Clark Gables and William Powells.[44] I stuck my tail firmly between my legs and got on with my job of work at the railway. We enjoyed ourselves at the Royal Victoria Institute, and rehearsed a new play called *Blue Blood and Black*, by D.W. Rogers.[45]

The *Guardian* brought in two young people from England to make the film, Irene Nicholson and Brian Montagu. The play had its first and only performance at St. Anne's Hall, Oxford Street. Irene and Brian were sent to review it. They said, "Two things emerged from the play, important to Trinidad. The play and the author; and Edric Connor, who played 'Thrasher'. He would be great in any country." The only copy of the play was lost in a fire at Freeport. We still have the songs. I composed them.

Irene and Brian told the *Guardian* they'd have nothing to do with the film if I couldn't be in it. A part was written in for me.

The *Guardian* gave me a job as a reporter so that I could be on hand whenever needed for filming. They also gave me a cheap serge suit as wardrobe. I supplied the shirt, shoes, and other paraphernalia. I became very valuable to them, because they had no reporter with a knowledge of engineering. I was their industrial correspondent. I was worse off than at the railway. They only paid me $2.50 per week. I also covered funerals, weddings, and the magistrates' courts.

An assignment I eavesdropped upon was when US President F.D. Roosevelt was on his way to Rio de Janeiro to the first Pan-American Conference, late in 1936. An Indian reporter named Singh was assigned to cover the story. He had to go out to the Bocas where Roosevelt was fishing. I popped a lift so I could be within close view of the great man. He was sitting in the stern of a heavy launch, with rod and line overboard.

Singh went aboard and I sneaked a glance now and then. I wasn't too happy with what Singh had to say when he returned to our launch. All we had to do was wait and see. Singh showed me the autograph he received from Roosevelt.

The depression in America was solved by Roosevelt with the New Deal. He had taken away real profits from the moguls of Wall Street. They called upon him to replace those profits and he was going to South America for the first Pan-American Conference. Let us wait and see. South America at the time had thriving industries. They were viable and expanding. Brazil, Uruguay, Peru, Argentina and Chile. Tariffs were lifted in all the territories. They became flooded with American goods. Many factories closed down and bankruptcy was a common affair. This was six months — only six months — after Roosevelt headed the Pan-American Conference in Rio de Janeiro.

Only recently (1958) Vice-President Nixon of the United States had to run from South America. In every country he went he was stoned and booed, even shot at. President Eisenhower followed. It was a different matter. There was good security and great respect shown to him. The simple reason is, the South Americans respect a President. But they would shoot a Vice-President. They will not forget the raw deal they had for the New Deal. I waited and I saw.

I had never been in court until I became a reporter. I watched real human drama pass in procession. The fights. The beatings. The thefts and even arson.

My copy for the *Trinidad Guardian* was good. Sometimes I would put a dash of the atmosphere of a folk tale to press home the point of a real human need.

One morning in the Magistrates' Court, three cases in quick succession showed the remarkable place Trinidad was at the time. My story did not make good copy. The reader would not have believed the happenings were true.

"Once upon a time there were two Gumbos: Gumbo Lai Lai and Gumbo Glise. The two were well-known to the police and even better known in jail where Glise did 45 of his 60 years on earth for stealing. Lai Lai went there mainly for being drunk and disorderly, or assaulting the police. They were both very ugly men. This was not because of their criminal record. They were characters in their own right.

"It would appear that Gumbo Lai Lai took Gumbo Glise into a rum shop for a drink. Lai Lai, as always, would become noisy after having had a few.

"A policeman was attracted to the noise and entered the bar. Somebody whispered, 'Sandy', and Gumbo Lai Lai knew at once the policeman had come from Tobago — the only place from which all the Sandys in the Force came. Gumbo had another drink and made a little more noise. Sandy put the King's hand on his shoulder. Gumbo disdainfully looked at the hand, and with great sarcasm spoke: 'Now. Now. Now. You son of Tobago. Forsake your Mother's country and come into happy mine, Trinidad. With your ten commandments bare.[46] Not even a Sacrament to control them. Now you are wearing the best of black. Let go, my man. Don't you know that I am a citizen living in P.O.S.?'

"Gumbo Glise laughed at this and Sandy nabbed him too. Next day, all sobered up, they appeared in Court before Mr. Boland, who was well acquainted with them individually. He never bargained to have two of them together.

"He looked at them hard, then turning to the Court Prosecutor he asked:

"'Do you want these two men here, Captain Powers?'

"'I don't know, sir,' was the Prosecutor's reply.

"Then Mr. Boland lowered his reading spectacles to the tip of his nose and smacked his lips, as if he tasted something good but wasn't sure what it was. Everybody had known the beauty of Gumbo Lai Lai's invective. Mr. Boland did not want this Court turned into a comedy theatre.

"'The line of least resistance, Sandy, is to let them go,' the Magistrate said. 'It is true you're from Tobago. I am not so sure about the Ten Commandments. Perhaps we had better send them to hell — out of this Court. Go away, you two! Go and spoil some other place! You might despoil even a quarry.'

"Gumbo Lai Lai turned to Gumbo Glise. 'You see what I tell you! I only had to look at my friends, Mr. Boland and Captain Powers, and justice is done. Come, I buy you another drink.'"

The next case before Mr. Boland was history. The first case of bigamy in Trinidad.

Most young men in the island ran away from the responsibilities of wedlock, but not Armstrong. He was Casanova and Don Juan rolled into one.

It was hot in court but Armstrong was dressed in the finest three piece Harris tweed suit with spats and all that goes with being the best dressed man in the island. The only thing missing was the bicycle he left outside — a Raleigh, made in England.

The charge was read. Armstrong stood to attention as though on military parade. Mr. Boland smacked his lips, but this time as if he tasted trouble. Then he beamed over his spectacles, and Armstrong wilted visibly.

Regret, pain, remorse and thanksgiving all combined to bow his head and he said, "Guilty, Sah," in the tiniest squeak of a voice.

Mr. Boland said nothing for a little while, as if waiting for something more to come from Armstrong. Armstrong's forehead raised very slightly, with pleats.

Mr. Boland said, "Armstrong, why you do dat?"

Armstrong's right shoulder twitched as if to raise his hand to wipe a tear.

"Armstrong, one is bad enough — but two!"

Half crying, but mustering all his courage, Armstrong said, "Sah, I like the ceremony, but it is the jail I 'fraid."

It is difficult to keep a straight face under such provocation but Mr. Boland kept his. More in sympathy than anything, "All right, I will send you up for thirty days. How many days in the month? Thirty-one. Yes. Do thirty-one days. No labour. Just enough exercise every day. I am putting you away from these two women. I feel if they were to catch you, they'd tear you apart. Go on, now. Enjoy yourself."

Mr. Boland put his head in his hands. Not in despair. Even a Magistrate must laugh sometime.

The next case met a smiling Mr. Boland. The last one concerned two 'wives' but this one was a paternity affair involving two fathers. It wasn't long before Mr. Boland was serious again. He smacked his lips and the upper one was jutting out above the other. Both men had sworn they never touched the girl. Solomon had to deal with two mothers who wanted the child. But he never tangled with two Trinidadian fathers who wanted to escape paying five shillings a week. The spectacles left the tip of Mr. Boland's nose and settled themselves in their right place. Then, as if brushing imaginary fluff from his case book, he said, "Go! All of you!"

They were leaving. One, catlike. The other, in a hurry. When they reached the door, with perfect timing Mr. Boland called: "Childfather!"

The one who had protested the most looked back and said "Eh?"

"I catch you!" Mr. Boland said. "You pay five shillings a week for the maintenance of that child."

From hurrying away, the father walked out as quietly as a cat.

"Next case."

Even Mahal came up for vagrancy on a couple of occasions. But the most pathetic were the people who came charged with violating laws that were against their cultural heritage. The Shouters and the Shangos for breaking the law by practising their religion.[47]

My contact with the Court threw me in to the Registry where I examined old deeds, old laws, and old papers.

I had already found that the young people of Port of Spain seemed careless and undecided about their direction.

I went home to my grandfather and complained about this. He said decisively, "You will not get any answers from the teachers in the colleges, or in the schools. You might get it in the libraries. The best way to get it is to go to the old people of the villages. Go and talk to them. Live with them. Go to the cemeteries. Find the old cemeteries and read the tombstones. Then go to the libraries and look up the period. You will be lucky if you find any of the written history of the people."

Then he looked me straight in the eye. "Son, if you truly want to get educated, walk. The whole of Trinidad is there."

I walked the country. I found the cemeteries. I found the people and I found my roots.

Two dollars and fifty cents a week is not much of a salary to live on. It is not even wages. But as they took out 25 cents for Sports Fund and another 25 cents for Superannuation Fund, I suppose they had a right to call it a salary. The balance of two dollars was only eight shillings and fourpence with which to feed, clothe and house myself for the week. It was no surprise that my rent arrears built up in two months to ten dollars. The only way to get this, short of stealing, was to give a concert and to let my friends know that it was in aid of myself.

It took place at a home for blind girls on Fraser Street. Hugh McShine, the judge, played the flute. His sister Umilta played the piano. Myra Austin accompanied me at the piano. I got the chairs free. Leslie Brunton, my great friend, who saw me through the *Guardian*, gave me publicity in the *Evening News*. We charged one shilling and sixpence at the door.

We gave a very good concert. In spite of all our efforts we were still one shilling short. Beryl McBurnie made the adjustment. I still owe that shilling to Beryl. I will never be able to finish paying it back.[48]

During my apprenticeship, in February 1934, my friend at the railways, Cleremonte Rogers, died suddenly. He was drowned the day after a man and a little boy came to St. Rose Street and predicted — we should say 'prophesied'— a sudden death in the area. Cleremonte was there too. We were both in the full bloom of twenty and death was remote from our thoughts.

"It might be old man Nanton, Frankie's father, who is always paralysed with gout. He is about eighty. Perhaps Freddie Blackman, the old cuatro player."

The next day Cleremonte was drowned in the Blue Basin, a beauty spot at Diego Martin.

The mystery of the prophecy aroused my curiosity. I began to investigate the rites and powers of the Shouters' faith.

I followed a woman named Sister Faith whenever I had the time. Two prophecies she made in my presence involved me in later years.

One was at Hart's Cut Canal near Chaguaramas. She stood up under the shop and told the people the time would come when they would see "the fish beating in the bay and wouldn't be able to cast a net to catch them." The livelihood of the people there was fishing. They chased us out of the village.

Five miles away at Mount Pleasant she told the people a time would come when they would be "glad to get out of the area".[49]

The police had to protect Sister Faith. I myself thought it was far-fetched and a lot of mumbo jumbo. Sister Faith just wagged her finger at me and threateningly said, "All right! You'll see!"

One of her colleagues was a man named Alupha Shekbewn. A ubiquitous man and slippery as an eel. I had seen his power when he marched his Order of Melchisedek in support of Ethiopia during the Italian war.[50] He was at work again, this time in support of a political leader named T. Uriah Buzz Butler.

Alupha Shekbewn would send out his telepathic thoughts and call all Shouters to Fyzabad, the oilfields where Butler was waging his campaign for better conditions.[51]

Sunday after Sunday the Shouters would come and give him support. The procession is the most potent form of propaganda. The Shouters attracted the masses: workers in the oilfields. The meetings echoed in Port of Spain and in London. The Governor, Sir Claude Hollis, took no action. The shareholders and the boardrooms of London had to be satisfied. There was a hunger march to Government House. Butler, Alupha Shekbewn and various Shouters, working people, many of them unemployed. Many of them hungry. They marched from Fyzabad, Point Fortin, La Brea, San Fernando, Pointe-à-Pierre, all the way to Port of Spain. Sir Claude Hollis saw the delegations. The people turned away, still hungry.

Another Governor came. Fletcher was his name.[52] He was a kind man. A good man. But he met a system that enmeshed his livelihood and therefore had to carry out his duties as Governor. The police were called upon to take action at the next Sunday's meeting. A famous detective named Charlie King, notorious for his rough manhandling of people, was detailed to break up the meetings. Charlie King was big and he was bad. To the full view of everyone he let Fyzabad know that he was there and meetings on that day would be forbidden.

The procession wended its way to the main gate of the oilfields. Peaceful. Orderly. They were singing that hymn again: "Oh God, our help in ages past, Our hope for years to come, Our shelter from the stormy blast, and our eternal home."

Over this, like a descant, with more staccato, Butler spoke.

Three things stood out in Butler. A limp. A beard. And sincerity. You could see it in his eyes.

Captain Cipriani, great leader though he was, could not muster the crowd. Could not muster the fervour. Could not touch the devil in the people as Butler did. He was the spark that set the oil and the oilfields ablaze.

Then Charlie King made the wrong move: he attempted to arrest Butler. He was immediately seized by a hundred men. They threw him in the gutter, where he wallowed in crude oil. He got up and tried to escape. They set the oil alight and a human torch ran through the oilfields.

That was not all. The officer in charge, Major Powers, was hit on the head with an axe. Shots were fired. More officers were killed, and the riots broke.

Butler was taken away by Alupha Shekbewn and his friends.

The news spread quickly and disturbances started in all the neighbouring oilfields. It spread to the sugar plantations and the cocoa estates throughout the island.

There was no trouble at Mayaro. From every other part of the island the news was of bloodshed.

Civil servants and young office workers were put in trucks, given rifles with ammunition, and sent to the front. Some of them made very unfortunate comments. But times have changed, thanks to Butler. The Sherwood Foresters were sent in. Peace came once more. Butler was eventually arrested with Alupha Shekbewn and about six of his lieutenants.[53]

Irene Nicholson and Bryan Montagu had already returned to London and the axe, the cold axe of redundancy, fell on me at the *Guardian*. I could have easily volunteered to be a mercenary. To fight the workers. My last salary was two dollars and fifty cents a week. Now, nil. If I had volunteered and been paid danger money, it couldn't last all the time. I did not like the tone of events. The whole thing was very ugly.

Colonel Mavrogordato, the Chief of Police during the riots, put out a call for a better policeman. A better citizen. And a group of young men who achieved good standards in schools and their apprenticeships volunteered to be examined for the Police Force.

I had the background of the Courts, the Registry, the *Guardian*, the railways, and an enquiring mind. The railways had been hard, the Force was tougher, but the food was regular. We were the best platoon of policemen the Force had seen. We broke all records.

Apart from normal duties, they made me Drum Major, at no extra salary. Twenty-four dollars per month. It was high by the standards to which I had been accustomed and worked out at six dollars a week.

Three months after arriving at Police Headquarters, I was transferred to the Fire Brigade where I could be more readily available for singing and leading the band. There I met men like Drax and Mead, one Williams, Boland, and a tyrant of a sergeant major who liked cricket. His name was Cox.

I left the Fire Brigade and the Force after two years.

Adrian Cola Rienzi defended Butler unsuccessfully and they all went to prison. However, Rienzi and Butler put the case of the workers and the people of Trinidad before the Royal Commission sent out to investigate. This Commission was headed by Lord Moyne who was later assassinated in Cairo.[54]

Walter Citrine was on the Commission. We never saw that report until after the war was over. The war gave Britain an opportunity to put her colonial house in order. Trinidad came in for a good spring-cleaning.[55]

I became disenchanted with the Force. There was a lot of petty corruption. It was difficult to be incorruptible on twenty-four dollars a month. You looked outside and saw that clerks in offices, and shop assistants, were getting six shillings a week, and ran back to the shelter of the uniform. Several times I asked to go. In the end I stayed home after weekend leave. For five days I did not return to duty. After midnight of the fifth day they sent my batch — De Four — and two other constables to pick me up.

"I am not going without an ambulance," I told De Four.

He gave the two constables an order. They left. He came back to sit down and have a chat.

We had a hell of a laugh in my rooms. "Can you imagine? You want to give them back their damned uniform and they don't want to take it."

"I am going just as I am," I said. "In my pyjamas. Without drawers, and without the blasted uniform."

De Four put his head back and roared with laughter.

Next day the Commissioner of Police sent me to be examined to see if I was right in my head. To see if I was mentally sound. I asked the doctor kindly to release me. I said, "I want to go, doctor, I have had enough."

It was Dr. MacLean, and he replied, "I don't blame you." It was just around my birthday. One month before the war broke out in Europe.

I handed in my kit and went home. I slept for three days non-stop. Yes: the only way to get it out of my system was to sleep it out.

When waking out of deep sleep one remembers only the deepest impressions. Pack drill and the fines. The poetic filthiness of Sergeant Dash's cursings when I was a recruit. Springer's untidiness as a policeman. And an ugly batch of mine who rejoiced in the name of Dove. His girlfriend came to keep sentry with him one night. He showed her how to load a rifle, got a round in the breech, and panicked. Forgetting how to get it out, he pulled the trigger and nearly killed the girl with fright.

As Drum Major and singer with the Police Band, I had become very popular and well known. There were people I met on my pilgrimage of the island and those with whom I lived on my journeying. They all remembered. I love them all for it and we never changed. I numbered among my friends some of the people who were on the fringe of power. Were they really friends? They became a very eloquent part of my education. We would ride to Point Cumana in the late afternoon and swim in the sea.

The Gang consisted of Albert Gomes, Ralph de Boissière, Jimmie Bain, Bouch Bain, sometimes Carlton Comma, and Roast Corn.[56] This strata of the society run the rum shops and the pharmacies. Also the groceries and sundry public utilities. Some of them were civil servants. They all looked very affluent on hire purchase. They would claim the sympathy and following of the masses, but the masses must know their place.

We thought Bertie Gomes was a damned bad chemist. We feared he would poison somebody. So we took him from behind the counter and put him to run for the City Council elections. It was easy. We got him on the Council. The next step was to find a cause. Ah! The scavengers.

These men would start at twelve o'clock at night. Following mule-driven carts they would sweep and clean the streets and pick up rubbish all over Port of Spain. They'd wash down and polish Port of Spain come rain, come shine. At thirty cents a day. Most of them were thin and undernourished. The mules were better fed and cared for. Yet they were all better off than I was. I lived like Mrs. Howard's cat. A bite of food at Banda's. Bertie's mother. Or a cup of tea at the Beckles family. A sandwich from Myra Austin, with whom I rehearsed. Sometimes lunch with Elsie Richards. When these benefactions failed, mangoes and bananas were cheap.

The call for better conditions for the scavengers went on for nearly two years. Other just claims were put forward for the cleaning up of Port of Spain. The City Council was throbbing and Bertie Gomes made a lot of noise.

Here was a man who had every right to be a politician. He was big and fat and had a lot of children. While giving his daughters a piggy-back ride I realised I was an engineer, and should at least be participating in the amount of new building that was going on.

I saw Aldwyn Beckles who had a thriving building business. He gave me a job as a timekeeper.

I would start the day at seven and return home at midnight. I never remember how much he paid me. What does it matter? I had already learned to live on nothing at all. I was learning the slight differences between building construction and mechanical engineering. It wasn't long before I was applying real engineering to Aldwyn's business. He did not know I had done engineering until I took him to the Royal Victoria Institute and showed him the roll of honour.

All this time I continued to sing. Whenever I was in need of cash — desperately in need of cash — I gave a recital. Never very profitable, but it helped.

I went around collecting folksongs and did research into West Indian history. I dreamed of the day when I would conquer the horizons of the Atlantic that had challenged me during my childhood. I was confident it was just a matter of time. Soon the war would be over and people would start to travel again. Just a matter of time.

When I wanted to take stock I would go and sit on the huge piles of timber unloaded on the edge of the harbour from ships that came from abroad. The raw smell of pine and ozone would tickle my senses.

I had seen Lindbergh land in the harbour, blazing his trail for the air routes to South America.[57]

The St. Patrick floats hard by the lighthouse jetty.[58] That boat needs a new boiler. A new engine. Perhaps a new boat. The sloops and yawls from small islands display their tall masts and bob up and down in the water, beckoning. Their captains prouder than Drake and Nelson; their crew, motley.

I will not go now. This method is too hackneyed. But I will. In a big ship. When the time comes. When the time comes, I will go with pride, and my friends will know. I would then spit in the sea and walk home, because it would be too late to catch the tramcar. Follow the scavengers, who whistle as they urge on their mules and scrape up the refuse into boxes.

Port of Spain is asleep now. A chat with the friendly policeman doing ghost duty would bring back memories of old times.

"Whatever happened to that film?" he would ask.

"Oh, that? A rough copy was sent back from England. They held a special showing at the Globe for the board of the *Trinidad Guardian,* the artistes, and their friends.

"I did well in it. Man! I had on a jacket that stole the show. It was a blazer I used to wear when I played cricket for the railways. It had broad sky-blue stripes on a dark blue background. You could see me a mile off in it. I used to call it my 'go to hell' coat. In the film you didn't have to know my name. You only had to see the jacket."

We laughed quietly.

"When do you think they are going to show it to us?"

"The last I heard, the *Guardian* Board said it was costing too much, and they ought to scrap it. But a close friend of mine, who has a knowledge of what goes on behind the scenes, says it is because I nearly 'stole' the film. If any of the white ones had come near to my standard, they certainly would have completed it."

It is all right when an ordinary mortal says it, but when a policeman, in the King's uniform, says "Oh God!", the implication is as serious as Lincoln's Gettysburg speech. "Oh God! Boy! It is a hell of a thing to be black."

I would put a philosophical air on it and wend my way into the night.

Trinidad at War

*A*ldwyn Beckles was building two houses. One at Oxford Street for Dr. Inniss, the other at Petit Valley for Dr. Farrell. I commuted between the two as Timekeeper and Ideas Man. I also assisted the labourers and the masons when required.

Dr. Inniss invited me to his home at Woodford Street in Woodbrook, Port of Spain. He showed me a broken down galvanised iron fence. The sheets were sixteen feet tall. They caught the full blast of the wind that came down from the Grand Savannah. He complained of having lost count of the number of times the fence had been repaired. He induced me to put it right, persuading me to take it on as my own contract. I told him yes, on condition that he gave me the time, men, and materials I required. He agreed.

I set about testing the soil, designed special footings and concrete posts to take the fence. I completed the job and made a profit of sixpence. The fence is still standing and will last a hundred years.

Dr. Inniss was very pleased. He told all his friends and the word went round. More contracts came my way. I built roads and new houses on Lady Chancellor Hill. I built new foundations and blasted rock with gelignite. Men liked to work for me: I paid them well. Better than the normal rates. They worked harder and faster. We always made a profit. Instead of a car I bought a bicycle.

German U boats were marauding in the Caribbean and took a heavy toll of British shipping.[59] Building materials and food were at the bottom of the sea. By the time my last contract was ended the United States government sent their contractors to build two large military bases in Trinidad. A Naval Air Base at Chaguaramas and an Army Air Base at Cumuto (Wallerfield).[60]

J.P. Connelly was the owner of James Stewart and Co., the contractors for the Naval Air Base. I marched to him with my twenty-five men on a

Saturday afternoon. We formed the nucleus of the labour force that built Chaguaramas Naval Air Base. We started work the following Monday. Mark Segal was the Chief Field Engineer. He showed me his plans and I became Expeditor. I knew the place and the people. This was at Hart's Cut. Last time I was there I made an undignified exit. I was with Sister Faith. They were throwing stones at us.

One week later, Lt. Arthur Roy Thompson, Civil Engineer, and Lt. Geiger arrived to represent the United States Government. Frank Ferro came as Chief Carpenter and Foreman for the contractors. I was put to liaise between contractors and Navy. Old man John Sweeney was general manager for the contractors. J.P. Connelly set the ball rolling and returned to Washington.

Technicians arrived in large numbers. Sweeney and Lt. Thompson called for a conference. They wanted me to take over acquisition of lands and to evacuate the people whose lands were acquired. The Local Government informed them that the man who did the job would commence it but might not complete it. Thompson was very frank. I remembered Sister Faith's prophecy. I remembered the way she wagged her finger at me and said "You'll see!"

"Yes, I will do it on condition that you give me certain facilities."

"What are the conditions?" Sweeney asked.

"Three months rehabilitation rent for every family removed. All the building material from the broken-down houses. Transport for these materials and all personal effects."

Thompson said "You can have these. Just give me a list of all the families."

"When do I start?"

He and Sweeney stood up. Then Sweeney said, "Come. We will take you to your office."

I spent the remainder of the afternoon going round to the various families telling them of the acquisition. It was a compulsory acquisition. They need not have been told.

Families had owned land there (Chaguaramas) for over a hundred years. It is hard to move people when their roots are so deep. I arranged for all the able-bodied men to get work on the Base, then got in contact with my friends who were estate agents in Port of Spain and secured accommodation for scores of families who would be homeless. I got Thompson to have the Local Government mark off new building lots at Carenage so that the evacuees could rebuild their houses. They were extremely slow about this.

Some of the people had lands and friends in districts nearby – outside of the Base area. I tackled these people first, and got moving. I threatened to send in a tractor with a bulldozer to clear Carenage. St. George's County Council jumped to it. Hart's Cut was cleared within a week. Chaguaramas and Stauble's Bay were next.

Everything was moving quite smoothly. I got them to apply the Lend-Hand system to building their houses in Carenage. Many evenings after leaving work on the Base I'd stop over and help them in the construction of their homes. I spent only two hours a day in the office.

There were now three thousand men working on the Base but the population of Port of Spain was vastly increased with men who were unemployed. They left the sugar plantations, the oilfields and cocoa estates in the hope of getting work with the Americans. Owing to the recent disturbances and the Royal Commission inquiry, the minimum wage increased to sixty cents per day. They believed the Americans would pay them more.

Those who were already working on the Base had peculiar hardships. They left their homes in the morning before the shops opened and returned after they were closed at night. They had great difficulty in getting food. The Medical Department of the Base had already discovered how widespread was the incidence of malnutrition. They found some of the men could hardly do a full day's work.

Naval and contractors' personnel also increased. The men I continued to deal with were John Sweeney and Lt. Thompson, now assisted by Lt. Robert D. Powers, Legal Officer. Sweeney was anxious to know what to do about this question of malnutrition. I suggested simply, "Feed 'em."

Seemed there were no two ways about it. He set up soup kitchens and hired a battalion of Chinese cooks. As the workmen were better fed I suggested they should do two hours overtime each day, to augment their sixty cents a day minimum. In the majority of cases they didn't have to work, just stay on the job.

Came a day of gold braid, red velvet tabs, Sam Brownes and chichi men from Washington.[61] Among them was a news cameraman. I remembered seeing his picture in *Life* magazine. He had lost his pants on the Yangtse Kiang in China. The Japanese shot up the Panay.[62]

They were having a meeting in Sweeney's office. I was told not to go out. Sweeney might want to refer to some files or need information. After an hour I was called. I faced a horseshoe of faces. Lt. Thompson introduced me but didn't tell me who they were. They threw questions at me. The first came from a hooknosed naval officer.

"Well, er, I don't know, sir – it's going on in Europe. We are building a base here."

A khaki-clad American asked, "What are conditions like here?"

"Better than most, sir."

"What is the pay like?" asked the first naval officer.

"Sixty cents a day, rising, sir; and they get two hours overtime and food."

Then Sweeney asked, "Where does Britain stand in this?"

"Sir?" I fumbled. One of the officers with red velvet tabs on his collar and Sam Browne leaned forward, his eyes piercing me. Sweeney asked again, "What do you think is going to happen in Britain?"

"I don't think she will be the same after the war, sir." We had already heard of the retreat from Dunkirk. Lowell Thomas described a blazing picture of the scene on radio.[63] Many of us in Trinidad were ready to volunteer. We were told the war did not concern us.

"What do you mean – not the same?" said the officer with piercing eyes.

"Well sir, I mean that America will be more powerful than Britain, sir." There was silence. The man who had lost his pants in China said: "You say conditions are better than most here. The people are fed."

"Yes."

"But are they satisfied?"

"They seem to be." Then, turning to Sweeney, I asked, "Are you prepared for a strike, sir?"

"Why do you ask?"

All the heads craned forward.

"There are thousands of unemployed men in Port of Spain. Many of them have nowhere to live and are sleeping out of doors. It is possible disturbances will start to get them recognition."

"Thank you very much, Edric," said Lt. Thompson. He showed me out. Later that day he brought the man who lost his trousers in China to film some of the work I was doing.

The base area is not an isolated place. It is well known in British military and literary history. It was inside these Bocas that Apodoca lost his ships. Sir Ralph Abercromby mustered his forces here before marching on Port of Spain in 1797. Some of his men stayed on and married. Their descendants were the people being moved out of the area. Charles Kingsley, the famous English author, after holidaying in Trinidad in 1869, referred to the area in his book *At Last*; it was the biggest and best natural harbour in the world and could hold all the ships of Her Majesty's navy.

It only needed the drainage of a few acres of swamp land. The drainage of the swamp and reclamation of the harbour were in progress.[64]

Mark Segal would point a finger reaching from the end of his outstretched arm and a road was built. This was not fast enough. Sweeney sent me to Cocorite to organise employment and transport services.

"We want fifteen thousand men. We only have three thousand. Ask for anything you want but let us have another twelve thousand men." As an afterthought he said, "You have three months to do it."

At last the scavengers' case had come to a head and they were on strike. Port of Spain was putrid. Sometimes on evenings after work I would collect the underprivileged children on my street and take them to my home, No. 10, Gallus Street, Woodbrook. There were eight of them. We would sit and listen to the radio. Then each one would say in his own words what he heard. This helped them to develop self-reliance and the simple ability to explain themselves. As our street had gone dirty we went out and swept it. Dr. Marcano, the Medical Officer of Health, had set an example by sweeping the street in front of the City Council. Who knows, I might be Mayor of Port of Spain one day so I might as well start cleaning it up.

The task Sweeney gave me concerned transport and men. I watched the job for a few days while Port of Spain was stinking. There were many quarrels on the Council. Albert Gomes was lifted bodily from the Council Chamber and put on his behind on the pavement outside. He was still fighting for the scavengers. Owing to the strike the mules were unemployed. They grazed daily in the pasture just outside Mucurapo cemetery. I travelled the buses to see what transport was available. On one such trip, while passing the cemetery, a ragged man who was among my travel companions pointed to the frolicking mules and simply said, "Look, the Councillors!"

Local transport was inadequate. I asked Sweeney to provide fifty trucks. We had them within a fortnight. They were slightly adapted to take passengers. By simple tests I found the right men for the job. Men who had never touched a Drag Line Crane before mastered this machine within three days. Men showed me their driver's permit and I sent them to have a go at a tractor. After a short while the American technicians were clamouring to be sent back home because the local men could do the work.

The base was humming. Rommel was in Egypt. Pearl Harbour erupted.[65] I finished the task Sweeney set me ahead of schedule and went back to land acquisition. Teteron Bay and Scotland Bay lay ahead. America was now fully at war and the security of the base was put in the hands of the Marines. A series of deadlines had to be met. The fisherfolk of these districts lived precariously, sometimes dangerously. A German U-boat sneaked into the harbour and torpedoed a British ship loaded with Argentine meat. The limping ship dumped its cargo. A few days later the tide threw the carcasses into Teteron Bay and the people had to take to the hills because of the smell.

Teteron was the most beautiful of the poor man's beaches near Port of Spain. You looked down from the hill and it was inviting. Smooth, cool and blue-green, like an emerald. The road ended at Teteron Bay as if to say, "You can go no further. This is paradise." The beauty of its sunsets complemented my sunrises at Mayaro and many were the evenings I stayed in Teteron to watch the sun go down.

Many Venezuelan revolutionaries set out from the bay with tired eyes glaring, tortured and taunted by the ubiquitous myths and ideals of freedom. Sometimes never to return. Only to catch the big sleep. Others would be caught by Gomez, jailed for three months and given a big banquet then sent back to Trinidad to prepare another revolution. That bastard thrived on opposition. But he would hang you if he caught you stealing. He'd say, "The whole of Venezuela is there. Go plant food."[66]

What other items of history are there at Teteron? Columbus used a stone as a Trig station. This stone is called Woshmakay. Very few people know it. Over there on the left is a stone building. That is Canning's Point.

The Duke and Duchess of Kent, parents of the present Duke, came to Trinidad to spend their honeymoon. They stayed at Government House and in a special suite at the Queen's Park Hotel. It is said that old man Canning wanted to improve the value of Canning's Point, so the Duke and Duchess were invited to spend at least one night of their honeymoon there. On the morning of the day in question about eight truck loads of victuals, stores and other paraphernalia arrived at Canning's Point. These were augmented by a busload of cooks, butlers and chambermaids. The bus was called 'Princess Marina'. They spent the day preparing for the royal guests.

At six o'clock several platoons with European officers arrived to guard the castle and concealed themselves at strategic points. The guests were expected at seven o'clock. When at eight o'clock they had not arrived, the head butler and a chambermaid decided to play "Duke and Duchess". Accordingly all the cooks and butlers drank a toast to the royal guests.

They arrived at nine o'clock. The heat from the stoves and the cooking made the place so hot it was unbearable. They smoked a cigarette or two and left for Port of Spain at nine-thirty.

After notifying the officers that their services would no longer be required, the militia was called in and made to swear secrecy. The chief butler and chambermaid resumed their parts as "Duke and Duchess". They celebrated all night. During the proceedings it was common to see butlers with drumsticks of milkfed chickens in their buttonholes. Several cases of liquor were mopped up. They danced bongo and Shango. Just before daybreak everything was tidied and made neat. They were all at peace with the world. No one dared question how much the Duke and Duchess ate or drank.

I do not think Major Liddelow was pleased to see me at the station. We met to assess the losses of the fisherfolk of the area. They secretly asked me to look after their interests although I was working for the Americans. I made no comment on any point made by Liddelow. He was a top officer in the Trinidad police. I was a constable in the Force. My silence was more eloquent and upsetting than anything I could have said. I was sure Liddelow wanted to get rid of me and would do anything to get his way.

The next morning the *Queen Mary* was in harbour, packed with troops. I knew they were heading for East Africa and were passing this way to dodge the submarine and aircraft attacks. Soon as the meeting started Liddelow asked, "You see the boat in the harbour?"

I said, "Yes."

"You know what boat it is?"

I said, "Yes." I knew with the next question the cat would pounce. The mouse decided to taunt him.

"What is the name of the boat?"

"I know, but I won't tell you."

"You know where it is going?"

"Yes."

"I don't know. Can you tell me?"

"No."

If I had answered those questions as he hoped I would, he would certainly have had me arrested. That's the way with Trinidad and that kind of person.

The fishermen were fairly treated. Liddelow brought Botha Tench to sell them outboard motors to take them to the further fishing grounds. It was progress for the fishermen and a commission for somebody. Strange, I was not even mentioned in Liddelow's report.

Owing to that report, J.P. Tiernan, Roosevelt's special envoy on land acquisition, not having seen a base representative mentioned, came down to Trinidad to see what the devil was going on. He was pleased with what had been done and we became friends immediately. He was rather concerned about the cemetery. He need not have worried. I had thought of that long ago. I appealed to the American sense of the dollar and Tiernan's sense of thrift. It was the only lever for keeping the base open to the local people after it was built.

The scheme accepted was that the graves should be tended by the United States Government. The relatives of the deceased would be allowed to visit and put candles on the graves every year on All Saints' Day and visit at other times when appropriate applications had been made. This was much better than not being able to visit the base for ninety-nine years.

Although attached to land acquisition I had nothing to do with the fixing of prices for the land or the final compensations. These were the problems of the local government and Washington. V.L. Guppy, a top brass of Lands and Surveys for the Local Government, had the delicate task of formulating the prices. The United States Government would have to pay for each coconut or cocoa tree, and for the loss thereof, in future years, to each landowner or peasant contractor.

Let me say here and now, the prices fixed were too low. The United States Government was prepared to pay more. Fixing the price of land is entirely different from fixing the rate for daily labour. Lend-Lease required labour to be priced at the Local Government minimum, plus. To put the valuation of land in the hands of the Local Government was very dangerous indeed. There was no room for bargaining. Land is real property and improves with age. Mr. Churchill, and the British Government, still have a lot to answer for in this department. We were acquired and occupied without consultation.[67]

Tiernan and Guppy got tangled over land prices. But dark sunshades conceal American fears and mask their shrewdness. You get nothing to go by. No pin point pupil. Just deadpan features and the dotted line on which to sign.

The appalling revelation of the agreed land prices sent me straight to Lt. Thompson. He had no control over Tiernan. Tiernan was responsible only to the Secretary for Lend-Lease in Washington. He was in turn responsible to Franklin D. Roosevelt, President of the United States.

Thompson saw the utter hopelessness of the dilemma. He understood what I did not actually say. I faced the possibility of being murdered.

We drove slowly to Teteron Bay in his charabanc, turning the whole thing over in our minds. A man was stealing a pumpkin. Thompson braked the charabanc, got out, and made him put it back, shouting, "It is not yours! It does not belong to you!" This was my only clue to Lt. Thompson's real anger. It was the first time I ever heard him shout at anyone.

We arrived at Teteron, got out and stood in the cool of the Depot. I suppose he found it necessary to stay with me a little while. In turn I was grateful. I needed the shelter of his power.

"What will you do, Edric?"

"I do not know. But please get them to say nothing about the prices, at least for a fortnight."

Thompson went back to his office. I had to work very fast. I tackled the shops and places with foodstuffs. They were the first to go. I was fighting for my life. I waged a veritable blitzkrieg on the remainder of Teteron and Scotland Bay.

You got through to Scotland Bay by a track which followed a steep ridge overlooking the bay. Jimmy Tardieu, who owns Scotland Bay, was a big man. A strong man who did nothing without the instructions and advice of his lawyers. He was out in the sea fishing when I gave him the deadline for the family to move.[68]

"But they haven't given me any advance yet," he said.

"I will see that you get an advance. Would $7,000 do?"

"I have to wait to hear from my solicitor," he replied.

I figured $7,000 would be about one tenth of the value of the estate according to Guppy's figures. It would not be an amount that could jeopardise the final compensation by being too large. The solicitor told him, "Don't move. Hold out." The Base authorities had already signed a cheque for $7,000.

I went to see Jimmy and his family every day for fourteen days, including Sundays. I wanted to be with them in their final troubles. There were ten houses to be demolished carefully. Eight boats and boathouses to be saved, several cast nets and about six seines. I walked through the plantation and advised on what they could reap before going.

Out of five plantations workers, four had already gone — leaving an Indian girl who could not bear to go without the Tardieus. I came upon her quietly sitting under a mango tree. She stood up, eyeing me as only a woman could. We stood there looking at each other. She was beautiful in a rough sort of way. Her eyes were honest and heavenly. She untied her head and her black hair fell, cascading around her shoulders. She moved forward and took me by the hand.

"You come to take me away?" she asked.

"No," I replied. Our eyes were searching each other. She was sweaty and firm of breast.

"Come to my house and see what I have to move." I followed like a little child. It was an old house but her room was very clean. Yards of cretonne hanging from a string parted her bed from the table where she ate. There was one chair that could do with some polish. A goblet with cool water. I waited for her to sit but she showed me the chair. I said, "No."

She put her finger to my lips. The birds sang sweeter and louder. The wind blew. Coconut fronds told us they were there. Butterflies swarmed and grasshoppers leaped as she took me.

After we finished she wiped the sweat from me and said quietly, "You don't have to go, you know. There is nobody here." And she loved me plenty.

The next day I took her to Boissière village where her relatives lived. Near a little church. It boasted a little steeple and a bell that threatened to ring.

Three days before the deadline the United States Navy mined the Bocas. The Tardieus were now hemmed in from the sea. He was still holding out, on his solicitor's instructions. Two days before the deadline Lt. Powers, Legal Officer, handed me a letter to be delivered to Jimmy Tardieu. It was "urgent". It was from his solicitor. While Jimmy read the letter veins in his neck began to bulge and fury boiled within the man. The solicitor told him to accept the $7,000 and get out as quickly as he could. Tardieu was a Frenchman one-eighth removed. The angry eyes darted and his body shook.

"Mr. Connor, if you were a white man I would shoot you, dead, dead, dead, dead, dead!" Then turning to his brothers and sisters, he commanded: "Burn the houses down! Set the plantation alight!"

His brothers were ready and willing to carry out his order. I picked up a hatchet and rushed to the nearest house. Holding the hatchet aloft

I shouted: "Come! We've got time! Two days! We'll make it!", and began to dismantle the building.

The example sparked and the other brothers dismantled their own houses. It was some time before Jimmy caught himself. But he joined us. We packed the boards and the galvanised iron sheets. Then, one by one, we rowed out of Scotland Bay, hugging the coast by the mined area breathlessly. Two days we shifted the boats and the materials. The last boat came in on a storm in the Caribbean and we were nearly drowned in La Vache Bay on the north coast.

When I returned to the office the next day Lt. Thompson said, "Methinks I see a ghost." In cod Shakespeare I replied "Pinchest thou me and see if I holler."

There was a big case in the High Court between the Tardieus and the Government. The solicitors and lawyers were well paid but the Tardieus did not get any more money. I still think it was a terrible carve-up.

A letter was written to the *Trinidad Guardian* by an artist named Simmons.[69] From St. Lucia. It could have been written direct to me. I replied in the *Guardian* so that the general public could get the benefit. It dealt with the cultural history of the island and the West Indies. My letter was published without any cut and occupied one full column. I understand that edition of the *Guardian* sold out completely. That letter reached the BBC in London. They enquired of Radio Trinidad about the songs and history mentioned. Apparently no one else had done the research. My grandfather was proved right.

The letter created so much discussion throughout the island that May Johnstone, Chairman or President of the Trinidad Music Association, asked me to give a lecture on West Indian Folk Music. This was the top stratum of Trinidad society. I called May Johnstone the original hard core.

I took some of the people I evacuated, from Carenage, Teteron and Chaguaramas. Many were the nights I spent with them, learning their songs and dances and folk tales. Now I would spring a surprise on "high society". Now I would show the great talents to be found in the lower strata of this island. I had my friends lolling about at the back of the platform. As the lecture progressed I would lead a song and they would burst forth spontaneously in the background. At a given signal they would leap forward and dance naturally. Limbo, bongo and belair.

The impact was terrific. The lecture lasted past midnight. Everybody stayed to the end. The *Guardian* carried a full page next day and West Indian nationalism was born. This was 22nd July, 1943.[70] In the audience that night was an English producer named Hedly Briggs. He was in the Navy, stationed at HMS *Goshawk* near Piarco Airport.

The base was building apace and won the E-pennant which is a civilian medal for war work. News had been going to the United States about me, taken by Americans with whom I came into contact. Out of the blue I received the offer of a job to teach building construction at Tuskegee Institute in Alabama.[71]

I had gone back to the Royal Victoria Institute for night classes under Robert Pattison. He taught me structural engineering. His wife Olive was my accompanist.

In spite of my diverse activities, I found time to visit my friends of the Police Force, the Fire Brigade, the *Trinidad Guardian* and the City Council. From time to time I would play a game of cricket. I seduced and was seduced.

The offer of the job required three references. Bob Pattison gave me one, the late Dr. McShine another. I am still waiting upon Audrey Jeffers for the third. There were others who knew about the offer of the job before the letter even came to me: Sir Bede Clifford, Governor of Trinidad, and the late Sir Edward Cunard, his private secretary.[72]

Sir Edward complained I would come to him only when in difficulty. "Because I don't want to waste your time," was my reply. The war and its relationship with Trinidad had taken some curious turns. At first it "didn't concern us". Then there were recruiting campaigns. Many of our boys volunteered. The authorities held garden parties at Government House and local coloured people mixed ceremoniously with the white people.

The respite of the war gave Britain ample opportunity to fulfil some of the policies set out in the Moyne Report. The review of police pay. The establishment of social welfare. Better housing conditions for oilfield workers. Better housing conditions for sugar workers. An all round increase in the basic wage.[73] Many invitations came to me to go to parties at Government House. I never went. I hadn't the time.

Some of the new social improvements were proudly rejected by the people they were supposed to help. Many of them thought it was a new dodge to keep them quiet. Edward Cunard complained because I would not bend. The Government had a lot of explaining to do before they were accepted.

Dora Ibberson came to Trinidad to head social welfare, armed with a letter from Irene Nicholson.[74] I presume she also had a copy of the Moyne Report. She never showed it to me. All the new Government officers had one. I was well looked over one Saturday evening at the Queen's Park Hotel. I had the feeling after I left that Dora Ibberson went straight to her diary and wrote a report. A man named Harold Stannard, of *The Times* but representing the British Council, had done the same thing.

I had seen enough and heard enough and learnt enough not to pull my punches. I was not aggressive. I just presented the facts. I think they all respected me for it. At least they ought to know. I was leaving for the United States any minute.

I applied for a passage on an Alcoa boat to take me to the United States. My application was promptly rejected although I showed the offer of the job. I went to see Cunard.

"Why not repeat that lecture at the Princes Building? I will get the Governor to attend and give his patronage."

A Youth Council I was interested in jumped at the idea.[75] We were all playing for time. Then Dora Ibberson put the question, "Why don't you come and work with me? Help me establish this office."

I put the matter to Commander Thompson. He said the only thing he could do was smuggle me out on one of their ships. But taking me out that way would be poor thanks to Trinidad. He felt that he would have difficulty in placing me after the base was complete and I should take the job in welfare until I could get away to Tuskegee, Alabama.

It was a very friendly parting. Old man Sweeney had evaporated long ago. There were Jones, Geiger, Thompson and Powers to see me off. A job that should have taken seven years was completed in half the time. Eighteen square miles of territory had been transformed into a bastion of military might. The American had come to stay. He brought prosperity and stimulated prostitution.

This, my last journey through the base, took in everything: seabees, airmen, sailors, warehousemen, offices, cinemas, clubs, playing fields.[76] All resplendent and spelling success. The Marine barracks jarred my thoughts back to the one who tried to beat one side of my face until it touched the other. The following day he was transferred to the scene of hostilities. We saw the piers where a dozen supply ships were offloading cargo, and the Bullpen, which the Marines built to control the labour force as it came and went. I was once dragged out of a jeep here at the point of a gun. I have often wondered why that Marine did not shoot.

Goodbye base. Goodbye Chaguaramas. Stop on the curve. Just near the point. The harbour now has the garbage and bilge of ocean-going ships and destroyers. Once it was blue, clean water. Three men were shot at and killed here — for fishing in a restricted zone, they say — three good fishermen. Three good farmers. Three husbands. Three fathers. They came from Hart's Cut. And I remember Sister Faith. Yes, Sister Faith. I saw them bring prosperity, and we over-paid with our lives and morality. Yes, Sister Faith. I saw the reason in death and fear. In progress and health. And in the power of the bulldozer. Amen. Amen.

Dora Ibberson was one of the first officers sent out to us by the Colonial Office to set up reforms that were to save the face of Britain. Ibberson was there to organise the Social Welfare Department. She was plenty woman, more than a match for any man. I was now working for her. As if it was lost she sent me to find Trinidad. I teased her: invited her to come with me. "Ibbs" had two hats. One was like those worn by Nellie Wallace, a bloom sticking up the front like a daisy. The other had a whole basket of fruit — pears, plums, peaches as big as a mango cochon. She wore this one when she had a conference where she might come to blows. I worked only ten weeks with her. Once more I covered the whole of Trinidad. Found the remotest villages in the depths of the bush. Found their meagre communications. There were children in all these places. They needed schooling and government care, thanks to Butler, Rienzi and the Royal Commission.

I returned to Port of Spain in time for my lecture. It was attended by Sir Bede Clifford, Sir Edward Cunard, Vincent Brown, the Chief Justice, and other brass. The place was packed with top people.

Owing to the untidy ideas of police officials, the steel band was already among us. Great efforts were being made to have it banned. There were many complaints: "They are too noisy." Some of these came from top Negro people. Some said they induced street fighting and brawling.

I lived among the men and knew their potential. The majority of them had not been to school. In normal conditions, to learn to play an instrument they would have had to kill one of their parents. Or commit some misdemeanour so they could be sent to the Orphanage. Or to the Young Offenders' Detention Institute. Or to Borstal. After having been to these institutions and having learnt to play music, they could not leave with the instrument.

They did not do this. They invented something new and taught themselves to play it. In the Princes Building that night a flood of steel band music was unleashed. It had these socialites gasping. They caught the tails of their jackets, lifted them, then twirled and twisted their behinds sensuously. The music appealed to the beast in them. Inhibitions went to the winds. The 16th December, 1943, must be recorded. Nobody tried to stop the steel bands after that day.[77]

Some remarkable facts came out in the lecture. The legislation against folk dancing. The restrictions against drumming and the Shouters. The way lithographs of orthodox saints infiltrated the unorthodox religions under the names of primitive gods.

A letter from Sir Edward Cunard took me to Government House to discuss my future plans. "I will not allow you to go to Tuskegee Institute, Alabama, to waste all your valuable talents. I cannot be party to such a crime," he said, in very indignant tones. Then, in direct contrast, "Why don't you go to England? You will be better appreciated there. Much better."

I beat about the bush. Then: "People are not being allowed to travel nowadays."

"Oh, we can arrange it," he replied quickly. After a cup of tea he said, "Go home and think it over."

Gervase Casson I knew as British Intelligence. He scraped the fiddle in the Royal Victoria Institute Orchestra. He was waiting in my rooms. My door was always open. "Go to England," he said, "You won't regret it." We talked about music and he gave me the address of his friends in Chelsea.

Next day I had a call from a shipping company. "A passage is booked for you to go to London about the 30th December. Would you please come and collect your ticket? Bring $192 with you." Within an hour I had my ticket and other papers in order. I transferred money to Robert Pattison. He was now Head of the Engineering Department, South East Essex Technical College. This was the only clue about my coming to England.

I went to Mayaro to get my father's blessings and to see my grandfather, probably for the last time. He was ninety-five. I took him his usual bottle of rum. He promptly enquired whether I had started drinking yet. I answered in the negative.

"You too foolish boy. It is the first thing they bathe you with when you come into the world. It is the last thing they massage you with when you going out. It's bound to be good for you in between." It was a promise I had made my mother and I was determined to keep it.

On taking leave of my father he said, "Honesty is the best policy. But son, make money. And always remember a nice man is a damned fool." Perhaps I have been a damned fool. Perhaps I have not made money. But I sleep well at nights.

How different the parting this time. My mother had passed on during my first year as an apprentice at the railways. My three sisters were now married. My father had lost his sight from the strain of shoemaking. With bristles and flax and beeswax and leather welt. In spite of this disability he built me a house with his own hands. "He only fell off the roof three times," my aunt said, when asked how he did it. The Crucifix and the Sacred Heart were still over my bed. My window opened out to sea and sunrise. "New horizons! Here I come! This is it!" I went and said goodbye to my sisters. They were not to make a fuss. They were not to see me off because of security.

My friends knew I was going. My underprivileged children of Gallus Street were now a match for the world. I had done as much as I could in Trinidad. Lennox Pierre was the only person to see me off at Customs.[78]

It was only when I got aboard that I realised the ship was called SS *Settler*. It carried a cargo of sugar and rice and forty-four young officers from the Fleet Air Arm. They were trained at HMS *Goshawk*, Piarco. Also eight intelligence officers and three civilians, two of them civil servants. I settled in quickly and made my way on deck to watch Port of Spain.

The dry season had come early that year and the mountains around the city were ablaze with poui as if to say, "A bouquet of gold for your journey." We passed the Five Islands and the Base.

A thousand drums seemed to beat and the power of my own individuality took possession of this simple frame called my body. I shook visibly. Some people call it personality. This is the thing that makes kings rule from thrones. Sends revolutionaries to ramparts and tyrants to their deaths. The drums beat furiously, the ozone was perfumed and salty. "Lead kindly light. Lead me on. There can be no turning back."

London is the Place for Me

We went straight to New York, and I met Beryl McBurnie. She went there to dance and stand-in for Carmen Miranda. I saw my first snow. We went to see Paul Robeson in *Othello*. Paul received a wonderful ovation. My personal view at the time was that the glorious voice and marvelous physique were not enough for the Moor. There was a tiny actor who played Iago. His wife played Desdemona. He was a West Indian from Puerto Rico and never looked back since that production. His name — José Ferrer.

The skyline of New York is very impressive when you sail up the Hudson River on a bright winter's morning. To a newcomer they revealed the confidence of a nation and the enormous skills of humanity! To me it was the challenge of an horizon which was met by man: therefore an horizon for me to conquer. The Statue of Liberty was the least impressive. It meant work for somebody, and children were fed. The bustle of the tugs and barges of the Hudson foreshadowed the hustle in the streets of Manhattan.

Settler was the hotel from which I made my attack on New York! Greenwich Village, Harlem, the Bronx. I got to know them and was impressed by the stagnation of the slums. I was surprised to see dingy rehearsal rooms in New York and gaping potholes in the streets. Concrete, terracotta, and neon lights. The physical fascination faded. But the people moved. Broadway and Radio City. The plush and the resplendent, the glamour and glitter I read about in the magazines, the Dollar supreme, and Coca Cola calling dames and dimes.

I met Paul Robeson in his Council on African Affairs.[79] A luncheon brought me into contact with some of the influential Negroes in New York City. I asked them for a single scholarship for one of the underprivileged children. Promises were made and my hopes were burnished. A rich contract was used to tempt me to stay in America. When this failed, great pressures were put upon me to leave my research notes and songs in New York. "If only I could have another three days I would know this place."

We lined up to join the convoy in the Hudson River. A crunching, crumbling sound made the *Settler* lurch forward. We were back in harbour for another week. German U-boats reaped a harvest from that convoy, five hundred miles from Brest.

Beryl and I moved around the city and took in the sights. Then she took me into an Automat. I had grown accustomed to meeting the surprise around the next corner but I did not bargain for the Automat. The soup was all right. It was ladled into a bowl. The roll and butter came for another dime. A piece of cake after yet another. A fourth unlocked a compartment with an empty cup and a tap. I pressed the tap and just one cupful of cocoa came out. This spoilt my lunch and ruined my entire stay in New York. I would have liked the tap to have made a mistake and not pour. Or even overflow the cup. I couldn't eat. I kissed Beryl goodbye and went back to the ship. I did not come ashore again. I had had New York. I waited patiently for the ship to sail.

We joined the first of the D-Day convoys — 73 ships — and zigzagged across the Atlantic, dodging submarine lairs. One day we would be up in the Arctic, three days later down in the tropics. We travelled as fast at the slowest boat and engaged in the ways of ships and men in times of war. The only new twist: I danced bongo in the Arctic to keep warm.[80]

The black flag went up when we were five hundred miles off Brest. It came down five hours later. Five hours' tension in the North Atlantic is no joke, let alone being torpedoed.

The passengers cheered vehemently when we sighted Land's End. This gave me a vital clue how an Englishman feels on returning home. We sailed past Avonmouth and the Bristol Channel. We hugged the edge of the Irish Sea past Liverpool, dropping ships of the convoy as we went. We sailed past the Clyde and Glasgow. Ominous grumblings came from the Fleet Air Arm and rumours were wild about the next port of call. I saw the Scottish Highlands and remembered the songs taught me by Olive Pattison and John Cannon. I remembered the nights when John Cannon would pull out his 'cello and describe how a note should sound. Ah yes, I remember John Cannon. I remember Olive. And that white dress with the red buttons.

We passed Aberdeen and Inverness. In the dim sunlight Aberdeen seemed a city just washed by rain to discover it was built of marble slate and granite. The rumblings grew to near explosion when the Fleet Air Arm threatened to mutiny. We had travelled six thousand miles without incident or enemy action. To sail down the East coast to London at this time was inviting disaster. The Captain dropped all passengers at Methyl. At the best of times Methyl is not pleasant to look at. But on that afternoon at 4:30, it was the most beautiful piece of terra firma I had ever stepped upon. I vowed not to eat until I arrived at my destination: South East Essex Technical College, Dagenham, Essex.

My knowledge of English geography was good. I knew the way to Dagenham. I knew I had to change at Waverley Station, Edinburgh. After that it would be easy to get to King's Cross Station, London.

I found myself in a train packed with servicemen. I felt out of place but the blackout concealed me. A single question next morning at King's Cross. A white porter took my bags and said, "Follow me." I began to walk behind him, until I fully absorbed the meaning of the moment. The complete transformation, the reversal of positions. I changed step in military fashion and another horizon vanished. The porter put me on the train to Aldgate East. Told me to change there and get off at Barking. Then take the bus going to Becontree.

I arrived at the college at 11:15 a.m. Bob received me like a long lost brother and we lunched with the Principal and his staff.

I formed the impression that they had never seen a Negro before. They seemed so avidly curious. One man wanted to know what I thought of London. I said I had not seen it yet, I just arrived. He seemed surprised that I spoke English. He pressed me further, wanted to hear more.

"Well, what do you think of what you have seen, so far?"

"It needs a coat of paint," I said flatly.

"Oh, the war, you know," he excused.

"Oh no, I can see peacetime dirt there." That shut him up.

Bob sent me back to London to live at the Colonial Centre, Russell Square, where he arranged a room for me.[81] There was an invitation to return to Barking to have dinner.

I missed the last train and the last bus from Barking. Bob put me on the all night bus at midnight. The conductor dropped me at what I now know as Aldwych at one o'clock. He told me to walk up to the square. "You can't miss it," he said.

I found the hostel but it was closed. My first night in London and coming in at 1:15 in deep blackout. A damned bad beginning. I waited at the door for someone with a legitimate reason for being out. Someone with whom I could slip in. About two o'clock it was bitterly cold. I knew Irene lived at 36 Campden Hill Gardens, Notting Hill, and I set out to find her.

I walked to the corner. A policeman gave me the direction and the distance. I walked a quarter of a mile South and found Holborn to be the apex of my hypotenuse. I turned right and walked five miles. The next person I asked for direction was a taxi driver. "Just up the hill, mate! Jump in, I'll take you."

I rang the bell several times. "Yes, who are you?"

"My name is Edric Connor. I have just traveled 4,500 miles. I am looking for Miss Irene Nicholson, my friend."

"Miss Nicholson doesn't live here any more. But wait, I am coming down." The lady, in her dressing gown, opened the door. I entered quickly from the cold. She was Mrs. Mayor. She put on the kettle and gave me hot tea. Made me a bed and put me to sleep in the living room. I was awakened at eight o'clock to wash and sit down to breakfast. I told my story.

Mrs. Mayor gave me Irene's telephone number, and showed me the way to Russell Square. To my amazement, I discovered that Mr. Franks would have been only too delighted to open the door for me if I had rung the bell. He was the Warden of the hostel.

Irene worked just around the corner, at the British Medical Association. We had dinner that evening at a Chinese restaurant in Greek Street. Here we reminisced. I brought her up to date on news at home. She told me the film was called *Callaloo* and it was in a vault in London. The *Guardian* refused to complete it. She corroborated the information given to me back in Trinidad. We sorted out the letters of introduction I had with me, two from Ibberson, one from Radio Trinidad to the BBC. "Margery Perham is at Oxford.[82] You won't be able to see her just yet. The other lady lives at Gower Street. Just behind the University Senate House." We arranged to meet for lunch next day and to attend the Albert Hall concert on the Saturday afternoon. I had to be introduced to the Albert Hall before plunging into it.

Ivor Cummings introduced himself. He replied to my questions, "Ah, that's what you think. We know more about you than you know about yourself." Ivor is a master diplomat.

"Who are *we*?"

"The Colonial Office." Then with a light pat on the shoulder he said, "Don't worry. You'll be all right." Wherever I went I felt the umbrella of the Colonial Office. From time to time I looked back to see who was following me.

I spent a week knocking about London and Essex before going to the BBC at 200 Oxford Street. I was four minutes late for my appointment. Mollie Croft 'phoned up to John Grenfell Williams. "Mr. Edric Connor, and he says he is four minutes late ... Yes sir, I will sir ... Mr. Williams says you are three months late, but send you up."

John met me in the lift. He took me to his office where Cyril Conner and Una Marson were waiting.[83] "We expected you three months ago. We have been making enquiries every week. For a moment we thought you had gone to Alabama." I laughed heartily. It was only then I realised I was a pawn in a very big game of chess being played on a board as big as the world, and that Britain had won. We arranged to meet at Bedford College, Regents Park, one week later. I left the BBC feeling I was among friends.

Came the day of the big quiz at Bedford College. Some of the top experts of the BBC were there. I didn't know they were experts — they looked like people to me. I told them about our folk music and our people and history but refused to withdraw the criticisms I had made in the press.

Then I played recordings made in Trinidad of the folk from Carenage, singing their songs spontaneously. At the time there was very little, if any, recorded folk music except those songs notated, harmonized and sung by the great singers — Totti dal Monte, Josh White, et cetera. On some of these recordings I took the lead. The audience wanted to know whose voice it was. I raised my hands in surrender. "You may shoot if you wish. It belongs to me." The lecture was over. I received a cable that morning saying that I had passed the City and Guilds of London Institute exams in Structural Engineering with second class honours. This pleased me more than the success of the lecture.

In the bull session that usually follows these things, Cyril Conner asked me if I could lend him the records. "By all means." This was my biggest test. I passed. I was able to trust people. He took the telegram and wrote a receipt. John Grenfell Williams wanted to know if I could do a broadcast to the West Indies the next day. Of course I could.

Fog and February are synonymous in London. I saw English people reacting unpleasantly to the cold. I had been in London only two weeks. It was February 29th, 1944. "Proposals" came; the BBC sent the contract to Russell Square the same afternoon. I spent the whole night studying the fine print and filling up all those papers. The recording was done at the Criterion Theatre, Piccadilly Circus.

Meanwhile Bob Pattison arranged for me to take up a job at a factory in the East End of London on West India Dock Road. With Blundell's and T. Albert Crompton, coppersmiths and makers of ash-hoists for ocean-going ships. They also made munitions. I opened my account the following Monday by machining breech blocks for three-inch guns.

Although I had been away from lathes and milling machines for many years, it took me only five minutes to recapture my touch.

A BBC Press Officer named Frank Cobb came to interview me at the factory. As we could not speak over the noise of the machines he looked on, fascinated, while I set up breech blocks and sent the milling cutter running through the steel. I showed him every phase of the work. Frank was so excited I thought he would give up his job as a P.R.O. We lunched in a pub overlooking the junction of Mile End, Commercial and West India Dock Roads. I shall never forget that lunch.

The BBC provided the opportunities. I did all that was requested of me without compromising my conscience.

Eric Fawcett was producing *Travellers' Tales*. Charles Groves conducted the BBC Revue Orchestra. Leslie Baily wrote the scripts. And I brought what seemed an inexhaustible supply of material. I knew nothing at all about the machinery that ran the BBC and I didn't care to know. I worked hard. Made friends.

I was now living at 39, Capel Gardens, Ilford, Essex. Very near the Technical College. With an aged English couple, Mr. and Mrs. Thomas Bunt. Mr. Bunt was a Master Mariner, retired. Apparently his retirement was hastened after he manned one of the "little ships" during the retreat from Dunkirk. There was an illuminated scroll from his employers to prove it. He suffered terribly from shell shock. He and his wife became my English parents. I could not wish for any better. They helped with constructive criticisms of my programmes.

The month, November. The year, 1944. I made my first West End appearance before a West End audience. The place: the Palace Theatre, Cambridge Circus. The occasion: a Green Room Rag. Margot Fonteyn and Robert Helpmann danced.[84] The first of my two songs was the Negro spiritual, "Weepin' Mary". At the end of the song there was no response from the audience. I thought I had failed, but the lights went up, to reveal a theatre audience dressed in black, with white handkerchiefs pressed against their faces and mouths. I went into the wings. The applause broke out. There was panic in the prompt corner when the stage manager found I wasn't on stage and couldn't be found. Somebody found me eventually and fought like hell to get me on. The superhuman effort won. I was bundled onto the platform unceremoniously. Just imagine listening to thunderous applause immediately after having a kick in the backside. I thought I had failed, that's all. "Ole Man River", which followed, was an anticlimax. The unforgettable point was already made. So many members of the audience had lost brothers, husbands, sons and daughters in the war. "If there's anybody here like Weepin' Mary". All of them answered, "Yes".

Every morning I ran two to three miles around Barking Park. Came the morning of 18th December, 1944. I put on my togs. Wearily. Went downstairs. Lazily. Opened the door. Apprehensively. Went to the gate and coldly turned back into the house. Five minutes later the explosion of a rocket occurred somewhere over Upminster. I began to count slowly. One. Two. Three. And the most awful explosion roared on Longbridge Road, at the foot of Capel Gardens. The house swayed. The blast ripped the glass from all the windows. All the pictures left the walls. My bed was in another corner of the room. The rocket dug a thirty-foot crater just at the point where I would have been had I gone for my exercise. Thirteen people were killed in the houses nearby. Five of them could not be identified. I would have disappeared without trace. Mrs. Bunt to this day talks about the incident.[85]

Godfrey James, Head of BBC Talks Department, took me under his wing. I did three talks at a peak listening time: 9:15 p.m. on Sundays, after the 9 o'clock news. The talks were based on West Indian history and its effect upon the culture. We had musical illustrations and Alec Robertson held our hands. He saw that we had a safe passage. Studio 3A Broadcasting House rang with the birth pangs of a new nation. This was before the Reith Lectures. The 9:15 p.m. programmes were important and the whole nation respected them. Here was West Indian history and culture presented so that the scholastic deficiencies of the listeners went unnoticed. Trinidad was almost unknown. Jamaica and Barbados were known simply for Henry Morgan and rum. At that time it was almost theatrical suicide to say an artiste hailed from the West Indies. I was determined to let people know I came from Trinidad.

On this programme I sang the West Indian version of The Lord's Prayer, then told the story of the way it was collected. Almost immediately laws against the Shouters were repealed in Trinidad. I sang "Pain Oer Ka Mange" and described its association with insurrection during the first decade of the nineteenth century.[86] I sang "A Little More Oil in your Lamp", the song that fanned the flames of the oilfields riots in 1937. Work songs, lullabies, folk tales and the customs of my people were presented to Britain. The list seemed endless.

However among my mail was a letter from a very prominent Negro citizen of Trinidad, pleading with me to refrain from broadcasting West Indian songs and customs. In another programme I sang a bold modern composition by a West Indian whom I called "Charleski". This song met with the approval of my prominent countryman.

In all this, the only thing I prayed for was health to do the work. My childhood was ever present. The people in the country districts of

Trinidad, including those without even a radio, supported my every effort. I was now well known at the BBC, around London, and, as a voice, throughout the world. Letters and requests came to me from men at the Front. Among them film stars, American and British.

Sunday night was gala night at the Stage Door Canteen. The world famous husband-and-wife team, Alfred Lunt and Lynn Fontaine, would be there, washing dishes and serving tea.[87]

The day the war in Europe ended (May 8, 1945), Eric Fawcett, Evelyn Dove and I were to broadcast the first instalment of a new series of programmes called *Serenade in Sepia*. Our work was postponed so that the BBC could do justice to the occasion. Nevertheless we recorded the programme. Most public transport stopped running. Housewives left kitchens. Shops and schools were closed. All commercial and industrial activities ceased. The only way I could get to London that day was in a hearse. As I sat near the coffin I contemplated the dead body it contained. What a day to go. Then I thought of the millions of people killed in the War and wept quietly. Somebody had to cry for the steel that is bent and the body broken against its will. Somebody has to cry for the children unborn and those born but hungry. Somebody had to cry for humanity. They put me down at Oxford Circus.

We recorded the first edition of *Serenade in Sepia* at the Mission House on Marylebone Road. Of course we were disappointed at the delay but it gave us a week's respite to study the programme and find its flaws. The same evening I had dinner with Liz Foster at Verrey's. Afterwards we left for the Mall to join the revels. The War had torn a big hole in British society. Flags were lowered at all levels. Liz and I walked down Regent Street a few paces behind an American who was wrapped closely to a blonde, so closely the wind could not pass between them. We could not hear what they were saying until suddenly, with a cry of anguish, the girl shouted, "Awoo, Nawoo! Not Claridge's agaeen!" The hole gaped wider.

We made a lot of noise. Marched up and down the Mall in bands. Made yet more noise, until we were hoarse. Everyone celebrated victory in his own way. It went on for several days. The abandonment was contagious and I enjoyed myself. Army, Navy, Air Force, factory, office, hospital. Even the clergy went wild. "Lift up your cassock! There's a hot time in the old town tonight!" And they did.

Serenade in Sepia was an immediate success. After the second week the option was taken up for a further eight programmes. The pall and dust of war hung grimly over London. All eyes were turned to Burma and the Far East. Chipped and cracked cups were used in the best restaurants. At the BBC and elsewhere we stirred tea with the handle of a fork, a makeshift that becomes a habit. A universal habit.

The orchestra we had in *Serenade in Sepia* was constructed to give a thick sound. There were ten pieces: Eugene Pini, violin; his brother Anthony, 'cello; Monia Liter, and sometimes Sidney Jerome, piano; Michael Krien, clarinet; Henry Krien, accordion; Peter Akister, bass; Freddie Phillips, guitar, and Arthur Cleghorn, flute. Sometimes Reg Leopold, second fiddle. Max Saunders and Hal Evans did the arrangements. Jack Byfield stepped in when the other two were not available at the piano. They were the best musicians in the world and all had their own orchestras. But we looked forward to working together once a week. We certainly had a lot of fun. We knew we were doing something good.

The fan mail was enormous. We ran for forty-five weeks with one repeat at home and five repeats overseas and throughout the world. Apart from London transmissions, the ensuing work from this popularity gave me a chance to see Britain in more detail. Britain was on her behind. She had to be put on her feet again. A new government was in power. The blasted windows and doors of all homes and houses were sealed from draughts with paper. A girl with nylon stockings no longer carried her own name but "the girl with the nylon stockings". At home I had Brussels sprouts and potatoes or as a change, potatoes and Brussels sprouts.[88]

I worked hard. I was famous. My programme was a success. One of the penalties of success is the rattlings of the green-eyed monster. I dismissed it at first. Then I looked around and saw the vast number of unemployed singers who had spent years training. I remembered the number of times the so-called intellectuals in Trinidad had said I had no voice training. What is training? I became famous with nothing but a God-given capacity to make people pay attention to music sung with deep sincerity. I became nervous before the microphone. It was easily noticed. This affected my breathing and control, so Eric Fawcett took me to a teacher who wasted a whole year trying to get me conceited. He discovered that when I sang a song I didn't give a damn about, like "Land of Hope and Glory", it was always well sung. But on singing "Let My People Go" or "Go Down Moses", I would become emotional and tremble. I suppose that is what is called vibrato.

Eric then thought I should go to drama school. I was on the point of becoming an ordinary student at the Royal Academy of Dramatic Art (RADA), when difficulties appeared. I was a Negro. The principal would prefer me to take private lessons from one of his teachers.

I had eight lessons at the Dineley Studios from Mr. Frederick Ranalow. We worked mainly on *Othello*. They were very good lessons, and Mr. Ranalow a very great teacher, but as I couldn't go to the Academy I felt I was getting second-best and merely being tolerated. Mr. Ranalow and I came to an understanding. He gave me a fatherly pat on the back, then said, "I understand. I understand completely. But go on, boy. Go on. You have it in you to be great. I listen to your programmes. I have thoroughly enjoyed the couple of weeks we have worked together." It would have been unfair for me to continue working with him, considering the way I felt about the whole business. Conscience prevailed.

Gossip and rumour are diseases as prevalent and contagious in the metropolis as in a country village. Somehow the RADA affair leaked out. Teaching circles were humming with it. Mara Watson, wife of a welfare officer at the Colonial Office, invited me to dinner at the home of a very close friend of hers. This was the way in which my circle of friends expanded. Although I was very popular and famous, very few people knew me personally. The friend turned out to be Rose Bruford, Head of Drama at the Royal Academy of Music. After the usual soundings, table discussions and a good meal, she handed me the play *Green Pastures* by Marc Connolly. To read "De Lawd".

I read the whole play, voicing all the characters. I enjoyed every minute of it, almost recapturing my savannah at Mayaro. I struck up an instant friendship with Rose and Juno, her companion. Three days later I received a letter from Sir Stanley Marchant asking me to play De Lawd in *Green Pastures* at the Royal Academy of Music with the drama students. They were all women.

I replied to Sir Stanley accepting the invitation. We arranged my first visit to the Academy. It was a very generous welcome. "You come here and play with my fifty women," he said.

We rehearsed twice a week. These rehearsals took place during one of the bitterest winters in the history of Britain. Most houses were draughty. Almost everybody in London was ill. More people died in London from fog and cold than were killed in the blitz.

Green Pastures had never been performed in Britain on a stage before. The Lord Chamberlain said you could not personify God on the British stage. However, the film had been shown before the War, with Rex Ingram playing De Lawd. The theatre at the Academy of Music holds four hundred people. We gave fourteen dress rehearsals in front of audiences before the official performances.

It is not easy to play God. His greatness transcends humility and nothingness. To understand this I had to carry out painful experiments on myself. "Gangway! Gangway for the Lord God Jehovah!" This is the greatest entrance ever written for an actor. The only way it can be made is with the utmost humility. "You walk like a cat. Behave like a tiger. If there is to be any other movement — dance."

Apart from its being a British premiere, *Green Pastures* was a great success for all concerned. Including the Academy of Music. All the girls blacked up to look like Negroes. I was the only white man. Some stirring performances were achieved. It attracted the Press, film, and theatre moguls. Sir Stanley Marchant was very pleased. He told me to choose any gift I wanted. I chose a Bible. The one my mother had given me as a boy was now battered.

I made very good friends at the Academy. Including the fifty women of the drama class.

The BBC resumed television. Eric Fawcett was transferred to Alexandra Palace and took *Serenade in Sepia* with him. Now I didn't only have to sound good. I also had to look good.

Julius Guttmann called and threatened me about my breathing. "If you don't do something about that voice you'll lose it in five years." He straightened out the problem in an hour. Then he said, "Let nobody interfere with your voice. Now let us work on repertoire. Yours is a natural gift. It doesn't need blessing. It's there." Guttmann was chief bass at the Prague Opera House in his day, and in Berlin. Because of the Hitlerite pogroms against the Jewish people he fled to England.

With the lifting of travel controls many people went to France to get a good meal and do business on the black market. They all complained about the high cost of food in Paris. Then came the first national strike of the French railways. Many people were stranded. I booked a return ticket to Calais intending to hitchhike my way to Paris. Sleeping in haystacks if necessary. I set out for Paris from Calais on the Abbeville road. Fifteen kilometers out I came on a military cemetery. It housed many Canadians. There must have been a lot of mourning in Canada after that encounter. Some of the dead were 19, 20, 21, 22, 23 years old. There were many thousands of little crosses. God of the brokenhearted, do you see?

I had helped to build a Base. Broadcast British propaganda. Entertained troops and civilians alike. Made breech blocks and ash-hoists and condensers for breweries. Part of me also died. For them it will be no more the call of the postman or the Angelus ringing. No sunrise, no sunset, no horizons.

Nine hours later I arrived in Paris. I was picked up by a coach. On the journey we followed a trail of destruction. The cathedral at Abbeville stood busted, half naked. Like a skull that has shed its skin and flesh. But it defiantly remained to be seen. To frighten naughty children. I heard the battle for Abbeville described on the radio. It was gruesome. What a monument they left. Just for the hell of it. I thought a soldier was just around the corner, writing "Clochemerle".

The Place de la Concorde was quiet. There was no fighting at the Quai d'Orsay. But they were arguing the strike. Another government was on the verge of collapse.

I went to Maxim's and asked for a job in the kitchen, washing dishes, to be near the food. They told me to come back next day. I spent a week in Paris, went to all the places that needed to be seen, and marvelled at the pissoirs. At first I thought they were relics of war put up as a warning, only to find that many French Governments fell because they tried to have these pissoirs removed.[89] I found Paris fascinating in many ways. The Opera House, like a fruit cake with icing. At the markets, like a chicken-farm at feeding time — in sound, at any rate.

I returned to Calais on a cattle truck. There I spent my last fifty francs on a slice of bread and butter. I slept on the ferry boat that night. The strike was still on. Twenty-one miles of sea divide two different worlds. Twenty-one miles of sea have been a barrier to revolutions. Twenty-one miles of sea mark the difference between political calm and hysteria.

Dover – London – Barking. I was welcomed with great relief by Mr. and Mrs. Bunt and the dog, Tracey. After France my appetite was whetted for other countries on the Continent. Especially while the destruction was still apparent. There was a so-called World Youth Congress in Prague and the Trinidad Youth Council asked me to represent them.[90] I had never been acquainted with any of the isms — Fascism, Conservatism, Communism. Judging from the rumours coming my way it was time I got acquainted. A party of eager young people set off from Victoria Station for Folkestone, Boulogne and Paris. We changed from the Gare du Nord to the Gare de l'Est.

The destruction along our route was sickening to see. At Nuremburg one wondered where the people lived. They seemed to come out of holes. The children were thin and hungry. They looked at you accusingly. I had taken along a huge supply of chocolate to eat on the journey and to give to friends in Prague. But the children of Nuremburg needed it more than any of us. I gave them the whole lot. It was difficult to keep calm after that.

We arrived in Prague after forty-eight hours. Despite Nuremburg and the horrible carnage and destruction through which we travelled, the trip was enjoyable from an educational point of view. I renewed my acquaintance with my old friend, Masaryk. He was now Foreign Minister in the Government. He had worked in a factory in London, and we had met several times at Czech and Austrian parties.[91] Churchill had already made his Iron Curtain speech and the trip was full of it. I asked Masaryk to show me the Iron Curtain. He replied, "Go to any part of Czechoslovakia. If you find the Iron Curtain, come quickly and tell me, because I would like to see it."

The British group were to stay at a hostel in New Prague. The water was too cold. I did not wish to catch pneumonia, so I installed myself in a hotel in Old Prague. While in Trinidad I always thought the words "Englishman" and "capitalist" were synonymous. Because of my hotel some English people at the conference called me "capitalist". But I co-operated with the food rationing and enjoyed the Czech dumplings.

After the first snows of the next winter — (1947–1948) — I began to pine for the warmth of the West Indies. British South American Airways had just started its flights to that area. All seats were booked when I went to make my reservation and I had to go on the waiting list.

I returned to my friend's place at Dorset Square, where I was now living because of pressure of work. Shortly after there was news of a plane crash. The expected call came and next day I was chasing the night before. In a converted Lancaster bomber it took us nine hours to reach the Azores. We stayed overnight at the Santa Maria Hotel. The weather report over the Atlantic was very bad. We took off next morning with instructions to fly south to Dakar. After being airborne for two hours we were told to fly diagonally to Natal in Brazil. The flight lasted fourteen long hours. We landed in Natal with a few gallons of fuel to spare. At the airport the heat was stifling.

Then we took off for Trinidad. We flew over barren wastes of grassland with here and there a coffee plantation dotting the scene. Over the mouth of the Amazon River, a hundred and fifty miles of it. Over Devil's Island off French Guiana and Georgetown, in British Guiana. Then to the Serpent's Mouth, where the red clay and shale of the Orinoco River coloured the sea. Over Guayaguayare and Mayaro, where I had a bird's-eye view of the scenes of my childhood, the school, the police station, the doctor's quarters, the warden's office, the savannah. And Peter Hill, my family home. Then on to Piarco.

I desperately needed to renew my cultural ties. That was why I came. I could not have stayed a day longer in Britain, I just had to go home. Some people commit crimes to do this. Some walk. Others ride. Some even swim. I didn't care if I got killed in the attempt, I just had to go home.

It was my first visit since I had been away. Nobody knew I was coming. How would I fit in? Would my friends remember me? I became very nervous over the last five minutes of the journey. We were down safely after eight hours. I was the last passenger to leave the plane. I looked up at the hills of the Northern Range. Their distant mauve-blue tint told me I was home. And there's Mount St. Benedict on the left. I look down, and "Eh, eh! What you doing here? I say I'm going to listen to you on the radio tonight and here you come out of the plane right in front of me eyes."

It was a policeman greeting me. Thomas. We were in the Force together. Then I knew I was truly home.

This was news and the *Trinidad Guardian* made the most of it. The Governor, Sir John Shaw, took me to open a railwayman's club at San Fernando.[92] "You're an ex-railwayman. You're the best person to open it." We travelled up to San Fernando in his coach, a coach in which I slept many times as an apprentice, when I was too weak and hungry to continue working. The coach in which Robert Dick caught me sleeping. "If ye wrong, face me. If ye right, face me. If ye run, ye show guilt." I couldn't run. I was too weak. "Ah, Connor, if ye don't pull yourself together, ye'll be buried and covered up soon." Those words of Robert Dick made me pull myself together. And now I was riding in the coach.

John Shaw had gone to Trinidad from Israel with a price on his head. I am sure the Israelites have forgotten that now. He was not a bad man. He investigated everything personally. That year the people sang a calypso about him:

> De Governor tall, tall, tall.
> De Governor peepin' over the wall.
> De Governor tall, tall, tall,
> But he is the best Governor of all.

This says a lot. Our calypsonians seldom hand out bouquets.

I went to the railway workshops to see Mr. Niles, Eugene St. Aude, Laurie Cooper, de Freitas, and Birdie, who doled out my glass of mauby without my asking for it. "You remember what I did tell you? You see it come to pass?" "Many, many thanks, Birdie."

I crossed the Dry River to the East End Foundry to say hello and thanks to Mr. Carmichael. He had retired as Railway Superintendent and bought himself deep into the East End Foundry. Still impeccably dressed. With that very conservative necktie. He showed me around, all over the shops. I went home to Mayaro and saw my sisters. Visited the calypso tents. These had become more commercial but as bawdily philosophical as ever. Then came Carnival days (1948). How I danced in the streets! After five whole years and no Carnival there was a lot of catching up to do. The Stokers' Dance and the Toeboe Foot Dance were the ones that caught the imagination.[93] Those two dances were combined later to form the basis of rock 'n roll. That is the reason rock 'n roll never caught on in Trinidad. It originated there.

The mass cultural intoxication of the people of Trinidad, the spirit of Carnival, is one of the most remarkable phenomena of this modern age. For the two days before Ash Wednesday the whole island goes crazy with ribaldry and song, with dance and the splendours of costume and mimicry, healthy competition and uninhibited participation. Two days out of three hundred and sixty-five. In Germany you call it "Fasching", but that's tame. The carnivals of Rio, Nice and Cannes and the Mardi Gras of New Orleans are kiddies' tea-parties next to the Trinidad Carnival. It is twenty-five per cent organised and seventy-five per cent spontaneous. Although it is now a Roman carnival it came out of the Camboulay of the slave days.

I had taken a cine-camera with me and some film. The revellers! The people! Sailors, robbers, Red Indians, bats, Breton fisherfolk and dozens of other disguises. According to the calypsos, "Jump in the line and shake your body in time!" "Off and on I hug anybody and join in the steel band melody."

The phrase "hug up anybody" is operative here. That is exactly what it means. Regardless of race, colour or creed, everybody joins in the fun. It is even unnecessary to wear a mask. If you exchange names with a girl you know it's for keeps.

The steel bands had improved considerably. It was worth travelling all the way from London to hear the pan beat properly. Oh, that music! It permeated my bones and I was refreshed. Ting tang boom, bi doum bi doum boum. "Pan boy! Oh God, hold me! If you don't hold me, I'm going to fight them! Fight them! Ah! Beat me with the music!"

We followed the band, dancing. For miles, with our eyes closed. Midnight comes on Tuesday night and we walk home, tired, but refreshed. Rejuvenated. Intoxicated. It is then we formulate our plans for next year's Carnival. What mask? What costume? What band? To sleep, perchance to dream. It was then I discovered that the whole of Trinidad is one vast theatre.

I returned to England via America. All British South American Airways planes were grounded. I travelled via Aruba, Caracas, Curacao and Jamaica by British West Indian Airways. Stayed over in Jamaica for a couple of days with Crab Nethersole and Theodore Sealy. They took me into the "Presence". Otherwise known as Alexander Bustamante. He seemed uncomfortable. He kept rolling up his sleeves every few seconds although they were already rolled up. That head! With that grey mop of hair. Picked up in the crossbeams of pinpoint spotlight it has sent many a man on the road to defiance, culminating in the independence of Jamaica.[94]

A girl stepped on my toe while dancing at the Sugar Hill Club. It became septic. I limped out of Jamaica on a Constellation.

At La Guardia Airport, New York, Pan American Airways did not bring out the brass band for me. The photographers came and snapped. My sick toe was prominent. So was the doctor's needle. In the sick bay they suggested I should stay in New York a couple of days. But no. "When's your next plane to London?" "In two hours, sir." "Good. Put me on that."

This brand new Constellation had only ten passengers. Three hundred miles off New York we ran into a terrible storm. The big bird of steel was buffeted all over the wind. I had experienced storms at sea. I had experienced a hurricane as a boy. But nothing like this. There were times the plane seemed to stand on its tail. Level out. Then stand on its ruddy nose. Bowels seemed to touch throat. Its fury struck me down and I went to sleep. They woke me at 11 o'clock next day over London. The storm lasted a thousand miles. I slept through it all. London never seemed a nicer place. The early green of spring was good for the eyes.

The War and the general reorganisation of Britain showed up in Britain's overseas policy. India was given her independence (1947). You couldn't hold Burma with a free India next door. Indonesia was already ablaze. The Dutch were out. British colonies all over the world were clamouring for independence. In fact the British colonial empire was ablaze. All wanted a little bit of what was given to India.

While building the base in Trinidad I had seen the reaction of the local people to the coming of the Americans. Singapore was overrun easily because many of the local inhabitants went over to the Japanese. The same thing would have happened in Trinidad, regardless of who was the enemy.

Owing to the clamouring, the arson, and the violence, the Fabian Society called a weekend conference of responsible colonial people in London.[95] The conference took place at Webb House in Dorking. On the Friday evening the first session took the line: "Please tell us what to do." The next session, on Saturday morning, we colonials replied honestly. By Saturday afternoon, Webb House and the grounds were swarming with MI5, Special Branch men, FBI and what-have-you. Their questions were very penetrating. All of us colonials remained very honest.

When the last session came up on Sunday afternoon a spokesman made a speech summing up the Fabian view. We were not allowed to reply. It said that we must behave ourselves, we people of the colonies. If we didn't know how to behave, we would be taught.

We had a lot of fun at that conference. We were able to laugh at some of the antics, having been at the receiving end of colonialism. It was then I predicted the possibility of world war in Africa. Starting in Lobenguela's lands, on the border between Northern and Southern Rhodesia.[96]

West Indian students had nowhere to meet, so I opened my house to them. For this all sorts of political epithets and invectives were hurled at me by the Colonial Office. The first shipload of immigrants from Jamaica came into London. They reflected a pitiful sight. Some wore face towels as scarves and woollen socks to keep their fingers warm against the cold. Some lived in temporary deep shelters at Tooting, some in hovels. Some of them were the sons and daughters of highly respected people and came from good homes in the West Indies. Some of them died in the emergency shelters.[97] Ah, those horizons ... ubiquitous and fleeting. Horizons tempting, bewitching, beguiling, with the cackling laugh of Mephistopheles echoing in the wind.

These immigrants preferred not to burn down the Empire. Their ancestors worked as slaves on some of the largest plantations in Jamaica. The Barclays and the Barings owned hundreds of slaves in the West Indies. British families in Bristol and Liverpool, Southampton, Plymouth and Cardiff had taken part handsomely in the slave trade. The vast profits made out of slavery they invested in the Industrial Revolution. This has resulted in today's Welfare State in England. The immigrants have only come to collect what their ancestors invested for them.[98]

Some English people accepted them with sympathy, some with pity. But the exchange was unequal. Every week, every day, there are dozens of Europeans going to the West Indies by plane, by boat. Nobody talked about them or made television and radio programmes about them. One of them even broke out of Newcastle Gaol. Within a couple of weeks he was installed in a big job in Port of Spain.

The colonies were still being used as a dumping-ground. Immigration is not a disease but a symptom of very serious human problems. The anthropologists, sociologists and psychologists do not seem to have any part here. They give the impression of only studying and not practising. Everything seems to be left to the economists and the law. And to hell with the human being.

Paul Robeson came to England to do a concert tour. I met him at Waterloo railway station. He stayed at a hotel off St. James's Street. I visited him there on three occasions. He asked me not to see him there any more because he thought I would get hurt. Not physically but politically. "All right. Then you come to my place." He welcomed the idea. He needed some rest. He always had to be looking over his shoulder when he walked the streets.

This invitation did me irreparable harm. Later that year it prevented me from getting a visa to go to the United States. True, I had taken some risks in the past. I had gone to Czechoslovakia without a visa, to see how Masaryk died. And to Budapest to see whether the Danube was blue. Instead I found they were heading for a Red regime. Notwithstanding these risks, which were taken because of my deep concern for my fellow human beings and a burning desire to learn, I had done no wrong.

I wanted to go to the States to get some new songs. *New material.* American theatre was the vogue. "No. We cannot give you a visa." No reason was given. The press told me it was because I had spoken to Robeson. I thought of the base I helped to build, the people whose lands I acquired for America, the people I evacuated from those lands.[99]

Paul went back to the States, and his passport was taken away from him. He was incarcerated for nine years.

In order to occupy myself, I went to the British Museum and the libraries. I carried out research on Ira Aldridge and slavery.[100] I received a great amount of help from the Anti-Slavery League. Then I met a man named Harold Sharpe. I cannot remember the circumstances surrounding this meeting. We discussed cults and I mentioned my researches among the Shouters and the Shangos. I thought it would be interesting to follow up a British cult to see how they compared. Harold sent me back to Russell Square, this time to the Marylebone Spiritualist Association. There I met Ralph Rossiter, who in turn sent me to a lady named Mrs. Hardwicke.

Mrs. Hardwicke sat me down. After a few explanations she went off into a trance. She became completely possessed by an entirely different personality. She told me I would be going to South Africa. I said I didn't care to go there. I had nothing there. Then she said, "If I tell you why you will be going, you will want to go." "Then tell me." "You will be going to make a film. Has nobody talked to you about it yet?" "No. No one has approached me. No one has talked to me about it in any way."

"All right. Remember what I have said." After some remarkable revelations I left Russell Square. I had taken a step beyond Sister Faith. When we research we search for truth, and caution is a very important ingredient in the examination of the facts we gather. In my walk back to Lancaster Gate I met Orlando Martins in front of the bookshop called Bumpus. He made me a present of Alan Paton's *Cry, the Beloved Country*. It was all about South Africa.

The next day a call came from Zoltan Korda.[101] Would I go to his office? He would like to talk to me. After five minutes with Korda he asked, "Would you like to take a test for my film?" He was making *Cry, the Beloved Country*.

Several weeks passed. I heard nothing more from Korda. In the meantime I did whatever work was going, including the buffetings of cabaret and my dear, beloved, Players Theatre, always a haven of rest and nice people.

A test piece was sent for me. I had to be at the studio the next day. I did not want to lose this job and could not afford to lose it. Leonard Sachs coached me that night.

Korda was in a very sour mood at the studio. "I am only testing you to prove to someone that there are no Negro actors in England," he said truculently. Then, when I stood before the cameras, in front of the entire unit, Zoltan Korda asked, "Are you a Communist?" "No," I replied. "They tell me you are a very big officer, high up in the Communist Party."

I was shocked. With equal truculence I replied, "I do not belong to any political party. And that is the absolute truth." Then, out of the prevailing silence, "All right. We'll start the test."

He printed five takes of different angles of the scene. Then he came in front of the camera. Took off his hat and stretched out his hand. "I never thought it possible," he said. "No waste of time or material. Thank you very much sir, thank you. Perhaps you'd like to see the test? I'll call you tomorrow, yes?" "Yes, please," I replied.

It was Saturday morning. Zollie kept me waiting at 146 Piccadilly until long after the banks and shops closed. He wanted his brother, Sir Alexander Korda, and his wife Joan, to see the test also. It was good. Then he asked me to be tested for two other parts on Monday.

I got in at one-thirty on Tuesday night from work to find a note asking me to call Mr. Korda any time I returned. He was waiting up for me. "Edric, don't tell your agent I said this. You are a great actor. Take five hours, five days, five weeks — five months if you like. Choose whatever part you want in the film. You are a great actor."

It was very difficult to sleep after that. The 'phone rang at 7.30 a.m. Zollie wanted me. "Edric, I know you see yourself as Msimangu — but play John Kumalo for me. I have tested a lot of people, and I cannot get a John Kumalo. I know I haven't tested you for this but I am sure you will be able to play it well. Because you are a great actor. Don't tell your agent I said this. But play John Kumalo for me and I'll make it up to you."

"You are the boss," I said. "You tell me what to do." I said my thanks. Then came the usual battles between agents. The blackmail and the threats. When an artiste is going into a film many agents claim ownership of him. I just sat and waited to be called to go to South Africa, regardless of anything that might happen. Korda wanted no one else to play John Kumalo. I fattened myself up to play the role. From 13 st. 11 lb. I became 15st. 8lb., and at times felt very uncomfortable.

A new form of schooling had begun. A new field was opened. I learned the meaning of fear, once, on a street in Johannesburg. Fear can only be created from the things seen. I had greater trust in those things I couldn't see. Like the horizons, I was no longer afraid of anything.

Two men in the film made great impressions on me. Sydney Poitier and the late Canada Lee. Both American. Canada Lee was born Canagata in the island of Montserrat in the West Indies. He went to Canada with his parents. Fighting for existence, he became a jockey and when his weight got out of control, a boxer. He fought five times for the world's welterweight title. He gave up after losing an eye. He was a vaudeville star and band leader and left this to become a great actor. Sydney Poitier, on the other hand, was born in the Bahamas. He went to America at eleven. Born in a different generation, he did not suffer the misfortunes of Canada, though he had his troubles as a Negro.

My baby daughter, Geraldine, was only about a month old when the premiere of *Cry, the Beloved Country* took place at the Carlton Cinema, Haymarket (London), in 1952.[102]

Mine was the only unpleasant character in the film. The politician, John Kumalo. I had four short scenes in which to give him dignity and then take it away from him. If he had not been properly played, the whole film would have collapsed. In the proverbial theatrical cliché, "I never looked back".

I was then appearing in cabaret at the Celebrité Restaurant. Though I looked £500, I was paid only £25 a week. The salaries paid to artistes in West End cabaret are guarded like military secrets. I made very good friends among the hostesses. They would applaud like mad every night. It is still one of the toughest cabaret spots in London. For several years I played there as a test. To prove that I was not slipping I would go to the Celebrité for two weeks. I test my success in cabaret by the amount of quiet I am able to maintain. The applause which will erupt when the song is finished. To make the drunks keep still and the food go cold are the hallmarks of a good cabaret artiste. Sometimes I would throw an operatic aria among the popular songs. It went down well. Nobody can tell me people do not appreciate the better things in cabaret or night club life.

The Prime Minister, Mr. Attlee, and his wife, came to see us do *Serenade in Sepia* at Alexandra Palace. Mrs. Attlee confided to me that they hadn't a television set at No. 10 Downing Street. Admiral of the Fleet, Lord Cunningham, who incidentally was born in British Guiana, also paid us a visit. Photographs were taken on these occasions. Government machinery goes into operation on a worldwide scale.

One of the most dynamic items in the Festival of Britain of 1951 was an item that was not exactly British. It came from Trinidad. A steel band. The people of the islands of Trinidad and Tobago subscribed just over $13,000 to send the band to England to participate in the Festival.[103] Through my friend Mariann Lomas of the Council of Industrial Design, and other friends at the Colonial Office, I got them accepted, passed through the customs and presented at the South Bank. Vic Barton of the West India Committee got businessmen with interests in the West Indies to contribute accommodation, transport and other comforts. I produced a concert starring the band at St. Pancras Town Hall. Artistes were Lord Kitchener, calypsonian, Boscoe Holder and his dancers, myself and others.[104] London shook with the pace and excitement of West Indian art. Carroll Gibbons immediately signed up the band for a fortnight at the Savoy Hotel. After this Mecca Dancing took them on a thirteen-week tour of dance-halls all over Britain. They were due to fly to New York for the Hearst newspapers to do a six-week tour of America but the conductor had other ideas. He took them to Paris to appear in the Modrano Circus.

Top bandleaders left Europe for Trinidad in the hope of getting steel bandsmen to come to England. They found them well-organised and not open to exploitation. Steel bandsmen have since travelled abroad on their own terms: the terms of employment agreed by ordinary orchestra players in whatever country they go to. There are steel bandsmen throughout the world today. They have even been to Africa to teach the people there how to make and play the instruments, Africa — home of the instruments. Where they originated as the drum. They began as dustbin lids in the new environment. But the young men of Trinidad cut oildrums to different lengths according to the depth of tone required. The bottom is then heated and stretched. This becomes the face of the pan. Then the notes are marked off in segments with a caulking tool and tuned according to the pitch required. Some instruments have 23 notes. The range of the orchestra is graduated down to four notes, in some cases three notes on a full-length oildrum. The instruments have names like Pingpong, Tenor Kettle, Alto Pan, Bass Boom, Guitar Pan, etc. A new language has grown up around the playing of the steel band. For example — 'Constacklement' — meaning 'artistic confused dilemma'. And the word 'Chook', meaning 'to prick' or 'to push'. The markings of the face of the pan remind us of the sketches of Picasso and Henry Moore. The poor young men who invented these instruments could have easily committed crimes. Instead they made instruments and taught themselves to read music and play. It is remarkable what the human spirit can do under stress. The singing of Negro spirituals in the face of cruelty and humiliation during the days of slavery is a fair comparison.

Owing to the worldwide acclaim and publicity given to steel bands, and West Indian music, the Central Office of Information (COI) asked me to write an article on the calypso. They said it was at the request of a Russian newspaper. This done, the COI called me in to argue and discuss the contents of the article. The odds in the office were six to one.

They resented the fact that I didn't recognise any great virtue in the abolitionists and the liberal movement on behalf of the slaves. I argued that it was nothing but a trick to get cheap labour. During slavery a master had to house, feed and clothe his slaves, tend and care for them like animals, in order to get the best out of them. To produce profits. After slavery was abolished, during the period of Apprenticeship, the ex-slaves worked for four years for nothing. Afterwards they received sixpence per day to feed, house and clothe themselves and their families. The master was in no way responsible for their welfare. For a hundred years, from 1838 to 1938, the wages were still sixpence a day in many West Indian colonies.

In 1806 the British Parliament set aside Trinidad as a station in which to carry out the "experiment in freedom". But the experiment was painfully slow. This story formed the basis for my article. I am not aware that it was ever published.

The Rev. Elsie Chamberlain, of BBC Religious Broadcasting, asked me to do one week of *Lift Up Your Hearts*. This is a daily five-minute radio programme done by churchmen. I pointed out to the reverend lady that I was not a man of the church but the biggest sinner in the world. She floored me with her reply: "That is a very good beginning.

Now you go home and write me six articles, lasting about three minutes each, and allow for a short song."

I have carried many a cross in my time. But the writing of those six articles was the heaviest load I had to bear in the whole of my career. I took them in to the Reverend Elsie. She liked them. I didn't. Came Monday morning, and the first broadcast. I arrived at the studio at 7:30. I read the script at rehearsal. I thought it an abomination. "Is there a Bible in the house?" I asked. After five minutes' search the Reverend Chamberlain produced one. "Bravo! A Bible in Broadcasting House at 7:45 a.m.!"

The Reverend Chamberlain and I decided upon St. John 13, which deals with Christ washing the feet of His disciples. At ten minutes to eight we were "on the air". I dramatised each character as I read to the 13th verse and ended the programme with the spiritual "Wash me, O Lord."

My wife was away in Italy at the time.[105] By the time I returned home all the national press were on the telephone. It was frightening. I telephoned Frank Cobb. "Say nothing. Get back to Broadcasting House immediately." "I'll be there in half an hour."

It is a wonderful sight to watch an expert at work. Frank was just that. The Reverend Chamberlain was delighted. We had broken through. The fanmail was fantastic. Next morning I had to go on the air and give a short history of myself. Many of the listeners seemed to think I was Jesus Christ. We continued the theme of personal responsibility. It was brought to our notice that many factories called on the management to allow the employees to listen in to those five minutes during that week. I understand it achieved the highest listening figures BBC Sound ever had for the programme. From the inspiration of that programme the late Gilbert Harding started his weekly column in *The People*. It was a hellraising column. His personal responsibility. The black sheep of many a family sought guidance. Many young people who had run away from home asked to be taken back.

In the nightclubs where I worked the hostesses, cigarette girls and other staff achieved some highly interesting standards of discussion on their personal responsibility. Yes. It is amazing what five minutes on the air can do. Some people expected me to set up a new church and exploit this popularity. My reply was very simple. "There are enough churches and religions in the world already. Why not go and make your body a new church? So that God and His other spirits can come in and worship with you?"

It was around this period that I saw Sir Alexander Korda. I asked him to give Negroes parts in films as human beings, people. Without having to wait for Negro parts to come up. He picked up the 'phone. Orlando Martins got the part of a priest in the film *The Heart of the Matter*. A few weeks later I was asked to do the music for the film. Trevor Howard and Maria Schell played the leads. Story by Graham Greene, directed by George Moore O'Ferrall.

When I saw the rough cut I found I had a film about African life without African atmosphere. It was the life of Europeans in Africa. Apart from the priest, played by Orlando, all the Africans performed menial tasks. There was only one thing to do: give it African atmosphere with African music.

There was a scene of a brawl on the wharf. I made that my key. Added ritual drumming. The music of Shango. The fiercer the fight became, the fiercer the drumming. The result was glorious cinematic excitement. I am proud of that. When the real films of Africa and the West Indies are made, the drum will play a very important part.

I played Joe Major in *The Shrike* for Sam Wanamaker.[106] He paid me £22.10s. a week. It was all he could afford. One week after the play came off I was at home alone with Geraldine, my daughter. She had recently celebrated her first birthday. She could not walk or speak. A dull tingle of pain began to creep from my solar plexus to my right shoulder. I tried everything possible but it did not go away.

I called the doctor. He was a long while coming. The pain was blazing across my chest. I began to sweat and felt unable to hold on to anything, even life itself. I lifted Geraldine into my room and placed her on the bed. Then knelt down to say my last prayer. "O dear God, my baby Geraldine — just one year old!" I looked at her. She looked at me accusingly in return. As if to say, "How dare you go and leave me now?" I took her little hand in mine while she just sat there. I was on my knees, my head resting on the bed. We were there for two and a half hours before the doctor came. And that child had never moved.

I had taken the precaution of leaving the door open so that the doctor was able to enter the house. He took emergency action, then called a specialist. They took me round to St. Mary's Hospital in an ambulance. I was well known at St. Mary's. From 1947, every Christmas Day in the afternoon I went through the wards, singing to the patients. I knew Sir Alexander Fleming, Derek Sylvester and Harry Cockburn. They looked after me well. I was discharged the day before the Coronation of Queen Elizabeth II.[107]

One month later I was on a Union Castle boat bound for Mombasa (Kenya). We sailed from George V Docks, passing teeming cranes and noisy dockers. Industry and exports can make a town look ugly, but the returns are good. The Thames and all its history gradually receded as we floated on the first leg of our journey to Africa. Many of my fellow-passengers were Europeans who had come home for the Coronation. They were returning to work in Kenya, Uganda, Tanganyika, Southern Rhodesia, Northern Rhodesia, Zanzibar and South Africa. Everyone was jolly and friendly. Very friendly.

We sailed down the Channel and passed the Bay of Biscay without incident. We rounded the face of Portugal and made our first stop at Gibraltar. It was good to see the Rock at close quarters. It is a town just large enough to be explored by passing ships and their passengers. Paradise Lane led from the docks, so I set out to prove a point. In the towns of most British colonies there is a Paradise Lane or Street. You invariably find a gaol, a church, a police station or a lunatic asylum on this street. Let us see Gibraltar.

I found the police station. Two hundred yards further on, an alleyway leading to the back of the church. I began to climb the steps. Owing to my recent illness I could not hurry. This gave me time to admire the way people lived. Looked down on, the houses shortened, as I climbed. Revealing the Bay and Alicante in the distance. The caggle and the babble of the town came up with its mad, bustling cacophony. Washing hung across the streets from house to house like bunting. I pressed on to the Moorish castle. The sign said "No Entry". As the gate was open, I entered. Leisurely steps took me through a large hallway built of stone. I saw no one, and continued to the other side, through the yard. Then, bang up against a door with a brass plate: H.M. PRISON. I rang the bell. A warden came. He seemed to have come from quite a distance. He was very polite and kind. He invited me in. I asked how many prisoners there were. Only one.

"May I see him?"

"I'm afraid you can't. It would be against regulations. You see, he's under sentence of death." Only recently I had my death sentence commuted. I would have liked very much to share a few minutes of his agony. "It must be lonely in there," I said. The warden nodded in agreement. I had walked right into prison – at the end of Paradise Lane.

The Bay was peaceful. Reclamation to enlarge the harbour was going on. An airplane had just landed. With a message, I hope. Sparing the life of the prisoner, and the feelings of the warden. The journey down the Rock was easier. I followed a fish vendor. No different from fish vendors in Port of Spain. "Poissons frais! Tazar frais! Nice King fish!" Only this time it was in Spanish.

We went on to Marseilles, in the south of France, to be greeted by heavy chalk-marks on every wall: YANKEE GO HOME. It was so monotonous in its malice it was boring. We spent two days there. I visited the le Corbusier architectural experiments. I marvelled and shuddered. The possibility of being born in a building and growing up to be octogenarians without putting a foot upon Mother Earth. I rode the funicular up to the seamen's church on the hill. I saw the island which inspired Alexandre Dumas to write *The Count of Monte Cristo*, the Ile de Ste. Marguerite. But turn into this church. You see dozens of models of sailing ships: steamers, trawlers, yachts, and yawls, even lifeboats. Their many miniature tears telling grim tales of disasters and rescues. The rescued give penance by this building. By doing time, building a model of what might have been their coffin and offering it up to the saints in thanksgiving. What is man? What is life? He prays for it. Clings to it. Then it goes. It is time to leave Marseilles and go to Genoa.

This is where Christopher Columbus was born. The Italians make sure you are informed of this. On almost every street. In every park the evidence is there in a statue, or a bust, or a name. I went to the yard where he recruited men to sail his ships across the Atlantic. Those ships, the *Santa Maria*, the *Pinta* and the *Nina,* are designed on the side of a hill in live and growing flowers. A great deal of love is put into each blade of grass. These symbols scream: "Don't you ever forget it!"

Next to the yard where he found his crew they are still making broad pizza on a broad platter. Perhaps he got a piece of pizza here.

I went to Portofino and Rapallo. In Portofino the old ladies show wrinkles on their faces matching the age and grace with which they knit fine lace. Rapallo bothered me. Here they signed the Rapallo pact.[108] It is a dull place and they signed a dull pact. I am sure they could sign better treaties in Guayaguayare. At the bottom of the backbone of Trinidad. Rapallo is not very far from Camogli. They are very stingy there. My guide was a man who looked like a cross between Fernandel and Raimu, the famous French film actors. But he was better than both of them together. He was a man of the universe, for the universe. He saw the funny side of everything. The Italian flair for facilities and frowziness. The great homage paid to the dead who might have been hungry when alive. The vast wealth of the Vatican. The abject poverty

... Here were the Italians. He liked being a guide. It gave him a sense of being in contact with the outside world. He couldn't be wealthy. He gave me back half the fee I paid him. "I enjoyed it too, Signor. That is why I must pay you your half!" And the world was a brighter place for sunshine.

After we passed the Messina Straits, heading for Port Said in Egypt, I observed the gay laughter and abandonment of my fellow-passengers receding. Many who had been very friendly and cordial to me became cold and unapproachable. A map of the world showed me that Egypt was in Africa. The status of Bwana had to be established between Negro and White. I kept to my cabin. When they wanted me to sing in church I refused.

Port Said is the seamiest dump I have ever visited. The watermelons were big, red and luscious but the flies were swarming all over. A little boy tried to sell me a little girl. When I did not accept he offered me Spanish fly. A British warship was in the harbour, at the mouth of the Canal. The Europeans cheered when they saw it. The Suez Canal, with its solitary dhows lazing in the languid waters. Sand on the left. And blackhead goats munching. The camel perpetually firing on all cylinders. Into the Red Sea. Israel on the left. I found Mt. Sinai could be only ten miles away. We come to Port Sudan and the Fuzzywuzzies. These men are fighters. Their hair is combed to stand on end. It was their fathers who beat the British under Gordon of Khartoum in the Sudan.[109] To prove it they wore the Sam Brownes captured in that campaign. These dockers worked hard. When the break came they went ashore, lay on the ground, formed a human heap, and slept.

There was hate in Port Sudan. So much you could feel it. In Fuzzywuzzy Town I was shown where people lived. It was disgraceful for human beings to exist here. But I also saw a new housing project in progress. You come into Aden through a series of narrow channels. You pass Kuwait and several small islands which must make navigation a nightmare.

We did not stay long in any of the ports where Britain was expecting trouble, so I limited my sightseeing to bare essentials. I visited the shipyard where Arab dhows were built. The Wells of Solomon — a fine piece of engineering. I looked up and saw the place where the Queen of Sheba took him. Where could he go? He was trapped. From the edge of the cliff where the Palace stood is a 1,000-foot drop into one of the Wells. I took a taxi and drove about 25 miles out of Aden into the Yemen. I passed salt troughs with their windmills turning and towns of the lesser Arab potentates. I returned just in time to catch the last tender to the ship. But the taxi-driver robbed me. Oh, the number of times I heard the word "Baksheesh!" spoken by children from Port Said to Aden. Is no one conscious of this? Is there nothing to be done about it?

As we rounded the horn of Africa I contemplated the things I had seen and the feelings I had about Port Said, the Suez Canal, the Red Sea, Port Sudan and Aden. I came to the conclusion that there would be serious trouble in the whole area. It would be only a matter of time. Would anyone pay attention if an actor, a singer, warned? Or spoke his mind on this? Would anyone hear the cry of another human being? Even in the little world in which we were travelling, camps were set up. Sides were taken with a militancy that was amazing. What else could one do but look over the ship's side, vomit, and watch the dolphins cavort and play.[110]

Shortly after leaving the shelter of the Horn we ran into the teeth of the monsoon. Huge waves were breaking over the bows of the ship and the decks were awash with spray. The ship plunged and lurched in a drunken dance down the eastern waters of Africa. The decks were cleared of those sullen, sulky faces. Many had overeaten on the journey and were fat with the leisure of the trip. No longer the proud promenades, but the cry of "Doctor! Doctor! Aspirin! Aspirin!" They stayed in bed for four days with their 'A-a-aspirin'. When the storm ceased and they crawled back on deck, they looked like purged chickens.

At last we arrived outside Mombasa. The engines were just turning over, but this giant of a ship was travelling very fast, on the tide. Then the engines were put full astern and we braked visibly alongside the pier. Well done, sir! "John Miller." "Delighted to meet you."

The first thing that arrested my attention in Mombasa was the fact that the so-called "Native" inhabitant would go to work in shoes, plimsolls or sandals. He was made to take them off while at work. This happened mainly in homes, restaurants and some shops. I believe the wearing of shoes forms the beginning of a man's real education. It can take him to places where he could not go barefooted — among thorns and harsh scrubland. Boots could take him through swamps. The average life of a jute worker is 29 years. He would be able to live much longer if he were given rubber boots to patrol the swamps while doing his work. The economics of the exercise could be of tremendous help to the revenue. Without considering the preservation of game in Africa, skins for leather could be a thriving industry. China has a population of 600 million at least. If we were to sell one pair of shoes at 6d a pair each year to every member of the population it would reduce the National Debt considerably. Yes, Kenya has its inconsistencies. A beautiful country. Mount Kenya impressed me greatly.

Mount Kenya in its glory. I remember the day. The two snow-capped peaks shining in the distance. At eight o'clock in the morning. They caught the sunlight. This created a beauty that could not be described. Mount Kenya was a hundred and twenty miles from where I was standing. There was a halo of white clouds around the middle. It shot out of the ground like a citadel reaching to Heaven. Oh, what beauty! This, one day, I shall tell my children. This halo of white clouds — it cannot be less than fifty miles across. Mount Kenya does not deign to show itself every day. What did the driver say? "Is it worth fighting for?" Yes, it is worth fighting for. I have nothing against anybody who worships this as a god. So there! As if I have loved deeply, I feel small. There was a war going on out there. The Mau Mau against the British. We were standing in the heart of Mau Mau territory.[111]

I remember, accidentally almost, wandering into Africa. Particularly Cairo. I was on my way to make a film in Johannesburg. On leaving Tripoli we were flying in the direction of Khartoum. Suddenly the captain of the aircraft said: "I think we will go to Cairo. The coffee is better." There, at the airport, in the waiting room, I was being served with coffee. A man of aquiline features. About fifty or fifty-one. A beautiful man. Well built. He did not give his name, but we shook hands. He said:

"Welcome! Welcome! You are walking upon old streets with new feet."

"I beg your pardon?" I replied, as if I did not hear correctly.

"You are walking upon old streets with new feet."

"Who are you pray?"

"Don't worry. We have been expecting you. Welcome! Let us leave it at that." And he walked out into the night.

I have thought on this most of my days. "You are walking upon old streets with new feet."

Once in my life I have found myself afraid. Very much afraid. This was at high noon in Johannesburg. In one of its main streets. No taxi would take me up. No restaurant would give me food. I began to run – run – run. Until I found the garage from which the film company had its cars.

I am not going to dwell on South Africa. Africa has too much in its favour to dally upon this part in the south. There are so many geological freaks. High veldt, rain forest, millions of square miles of desert, shining desert. Beneath which is oil and gas for mankind. The foodstuffs! You only look at the ground and it begins to produce food. Boulders, precariously perched on the edge of a mountain. Any little boy with a lever and fulcrum can move them. Boulders as big as a house.

Wild life. Roaming, rampant. Flying, weaving, herding. Here is a safari with guns. The birds have spotted them. By some form of telegraphy they have conveyed a warning to the giraffes, the water hogs, the dik-diks and the deer. They scamper out of the way. The elephants too, have been told. Their trunks cleave the air. They trumpet a call and dash to safety. The lion and his mate perch upon a rock with whiskers touching. They have seen the safari. "Let them come. We are ready …"

Acting and Travelling

*M*y film career was about to take off. I met a legend in Bob Lennard's office. It seems I was in demand. Bob invited me to his office to meet John Huston. "They are making *Moby Dick*", he said. "And Mr. Huston would like to meet you."[112]

Huston was half an hour late but he phoned his apologies. Bob kept me company in the office next door. It reminded me of the office I had on the base in Trinidad, when I had gone to reorganise the employment and transport office. My seat was high, that of the person being interviewed was quite low, so I would have the advantage of beaming down on him. Bob Lennard and I joked and played around and changed places as we went. Huston arrived and Bob went over to his office to meet him.

Then he took me to the legend. It looked as if it had just come from round the corner selling papers. All whipcord and man. I couldn't say, "Good afternoon" – it would have been out of place as a greeting. But we pumped hands: "So you're the man!" And John replied, "You're Dagoo." "Well, I'll be blowed!"

"Me too," he replied. "I don't want to see any photographs, newspaper cuttings, or anything you've brought. You're Dagoo." There was nothing more to say. I left for my agent's office in Jermyn Street. It took about five minutes to get there – to find contract terms and arrangements had been agreed over the 'phone during my short walk from Lower James Street to Jermyn Street.

It was a Saturday afternoon, the 10th of July, 1954. We were gathered on the railway platform at Paddington. My wife and my baby daughter came to see me off. Father George Long had come to give us his blessing. Kevin McClory, John Huston's second assistant director, was taking us three harpooners to Youghal in Ireland. The others were Clegg, who played Tashtego, and Count Friedrich Liederbur, an Austrian who played

Queequeg. It was our first meeting, we three harpooners. We were to live together for the next six months. I had met Kevin McClory before. He was boom operator on *Cry, the Beloved Country*. We have always had wonderful times together.

We arrived in Fishguard in Wales at about 10:00 p.m. and changed to the ship for Ireland. We hit Cork at eight o'clock next morning and drove to Youghal. My hotel was a lovely place. It looked out across the bay to the golden cornfields on the hill above the harbour. Being Sunday, and Southern Ireland still Catholic, you could tell the time every hour the church bell rang. It was beautiful over there. I kept promising myself I should visit that place.

The proprietor and manager of the hotel was a woman. She rejoiced in the name of Savage. Actors, technicians and other staff joined us at the hotel. Next to my room was Charlie Parker, chief make-up artist. To my left was Bernard Miles. Along the passage was Friedrich Liedebur. Our rooms were located so that our windows opened above the not unpleasant roof of the hotel to that lovely view of those fields of golden corn.

About six o'clock that evening John came and saw that we were comfortable. Our ship had not yet come into port. We had time to check on costumes, props and people. Gregory Peck, the film star who played Ahab, lived at a hotel in Cork. Leo Genn played Starbuck, and Harry Andrews, Mr. Stubbs. Seamus Kelly, the journalist from Dublin, played Mr. Flask, the third mate. Richard Basehart played Ishmael. A brilliant actor named Royal Dano played The Ragged Man. I had seen him once before in another Huston film, *The Red Badge of Courage*. He spent only a week with us. His work finished.

Mr. Clarke, the Cambridge don, was there to teach us all about open-boat whaling. An indefinable something about Youghal impressed itself upon me. A whole week passed yet the ship had not come in. She limped into Plymouth for repairs. But the appointment was made, we had to go ahead. Not one foot of film was shot, but film reporters and critics and newspaper men from all over the world descended upon Youghal to have lunch with us. This was the brainchild of John Huston and Ernie Anderson, director of publicity. Guests of honour were Taft, American Ambassador to Ireland; Lord Moyne, one of the children of the Lord Moyne of the West Indies Royal Commission; and the Mayor of Youghal. The actors all attended in costume. After having been well fed, our first real test began. John Huston has a way of testing his men all the time. Every day. Technicians and artistes. I got the impression he was working out his own personal process of elimination.

After the Mayor welcomed us, Lord Moyne spoke a few words. The American Ambassador made a very bad speech. Then John Huston spoke. Just a little. He left us to do the talking. Each head of department had to get up and say a few words. If possible say something that had not been said before.

Then came the actors' turn. Not in order of importance in the film, but according to our positions at the table. This was more than a revelation as to who I should respect during the whole of the six months we were together. I suppose that is exactly what John was trying to find. I lost respect for a lot of famous names that day. It was in the middle of my speech that I discovered why I had never been invited to Ireland before. I found there were more Irishmen abroad than at home. It was quite possible, with my name being Connor, that I might have been mistaken for an Irishman who had gone to propagate the race abroad. I found myself in the unique position of speaking on behalf of many of my colleagues who could only say "How" and "Tut" and "Er – er". I thanked the Mayor for having us in his lovely town. It must have been a good speech. Four years later I ran into Taft's aide in Trinidad. He had made a mental note of it and was able to repeat its salient features. John Huston took me under his wing from that moment. He taught me a lot about films and filming. After lunch we paraded on some of the old hulks in Youghal harbour. They seemed to have been there since 1870 when the town went to sleep because of the advance of steamships and the decline of sail. We were photographed for every important newspaper and television station in the world.

The next day the whole world knew we were making *Moby Dick*. Once more Youghal had its place in the sun. They came from far and near. The women. From the lochs and fens of Scotland. From the Broads and Downs of England. From the Kerries and dales of Ireland.

The following Monday the *Pequod* sailed into harbour. She was a lovely sight in full sail. One of the first scenes shot was John Kilbracken — even then Lord Kilbracken — carrying a squealing, kicking pig aboard the *Pequod*. I learned to tie my harpoon to its shaft. To splice rope. And to coil the payropes. I learned to live in the bow of the boat and to run the gunwales when stationary. This is extremely difficult at sea. I wanted to be a good representative of all the harpooners of all ages. I was dedicated to the task. As usually happens in such cases, I offended quite a number of my colleagues. I was showing too much interest.

The harbour at Youghal had been transformed to look like Nantucket. Thousands of people came every day to see us at work. The town bristled with business. The coffinmaker didn't get good trade and turned to making breadboards. There were some old salts who used to sit in front of Lenehan's bar. They seemed to have been sitting there since 1870 when sail folded up.[113] They found the town was becoming too noisy. They changed their positions and went a hundred yards up the road to Mary O'Connor's bar. These men were used, in their normal clothes, sitting on barrels in a shot that had Mary O'Connor's bar as background. And how the beer flowed that night at Mary O'Connor's!

We sailed from Cork to Fishguard on my birthday. That evening Jack Martin, first assistant director, Cecil Ford, production manager, and all members of the cast, with the passengers and crew of the ship, celebrated my birthday. It is a wonderful thing to have a birthday at sea.

In Fishguard we took over a hotel which was once owned by the railways. Fishguard is a terminus where ships and trains meet. But the town of Fishguard itself is nearly two miles from the terminus. The hotel proved unprofitable. I suppose most passengers preferred to sleep either on the ship or in the train. Some of the best cooks were brought from London and the hotel became a hive of activity and entertainment. In the town I found some very lovely paintings of London theatres. Many guests savoured the peace and quiet of my room. Gregory Peck and John Huston dropped in from time to time. Greg was curious to know why the crowd outside the hotel called for me just as much as they did for him. Greg had been told by Zoltan Korda in Hollywood he should look me up. I think we learned a lot from each other. Greg is a remarkable man. I think he could have become President of the United States if he had wished. Or a great banker, with the knowledge of international finance at his fingertips. Instead he chose to be a film actor. I respect him for this.

Now we were at sea I began to practise standing on the bow of the boat and using the harpoon. With the buffeting of the waves and the dipping of the boat I wasn't long in realising it was ballet. The combined balancing and the sensitivity of the harpooner's eye could electrify a scene. Queequeg was first to go out to do his harpooning scene. I asked John to allow me to attend. There was nothing particular about the day so I stood inconspicuously at a vantage point high in the camera boat. Unfortunately I was not impressed. Friedrich was one of the best horsemen in the world in his day. For many years he was a white hunter in Africa. But the poor fellow could hardly sit in a boat. So you see, I was not wrong in practising.

Next day I was in the hold of the *Pequod* writing a letter to my baby Geraldine. She was then two. Giving a running commentary of the daily activities on the *Pequod*. Huston came up and asked, "How did you like yesterday, kid?" I honestly replied, "I wasn't impressed, John." He was visibly surprised by this. I suppose because he is accustomed to hearing people agree with him. "How come, kid?"

"John, when my turn comes to do the harpooning, will you please get me rough seas?"

"But it has never been done before, kid."

"Then shall we make the first try?" He settled on his heels for a moment, then said calmly, "All right, kid. You'll get your rough seas."

Three days later one of the worst storms to hit Wales ripped through the harbour at Fishguard. The harbourmaster warned us not to go beyond the breakwater and lighthouse. No. 3 boat took to sea, followed by a rescue launch; we got beyond the windbreak and the lighthouse. The waves were about forty feet high. My shipmates were screaming, some of them cursing. "Who the hell's idea is this? Coming out in this kind of weather?" I didn't dare say that I had asked for rough seas — they would have killed me. Ossie Morris, the cameraman, set up and we began to shoot. Halfway through the first shot a wave swamped the boat, camera, lenses, everything. The rescue launch came alongside and took us aboard. Three times the boat broke its tow. The last time was too dangerous for it to be retrieved. We let it go. We had already taken the camera aboard with us. We went back to the hotel, had a hot bath and hot soup, and prepared to settle down for a day of rest. Because the next day was horrible too.

"No. 3 boat and crew on call! Must be before camera in half an hour!" As harpooner, I was responsible for the ropes and most of the fittings in the boat. But personally, as an engineer, and in my own private capacity, I always gave the boat a thorough inspection before we put to sea in it. We had lost our boat a few hours before and were getting a new one. My inspection would be even more thorough. I warned my mates not to go in it. It was the breakaway boat we had been given. It was completely wrongly fitted out. Our protest was so strong, closer inspection was necessary. It would have collapsed as soon as we touched fifteen knots through the water. With the seas as they were just one good wave would have done it. We transferred the fittings to a new boat and went to sea, my colleagues swearing blue murder. At the lighthouse an Royal Air Force motor tugboat took us in tow and away we went with death riding on our shoulder.

We had twelve runs of the sleighride, each one more dangerous than the last. The sleighride shows what happens to a boat when the whale is running, stabbed mortally by a harpoon. Running for its life with a boat in tow. It sometimes gets up a speed of 40 m.p.h. On one occasion our boat was idly bouncing like a piece of cork in this great rough tub of an ocean when through the loud hailer came the command "Don't look back!"

Men at sea under those conditions are very suspicious. And to ask them not to look back is as good as asking them to do so. With a tug we were away. And there, following us for almost 150 yards, was a wave about sixty feet high. Then we went to the crest, the tug below. We disappeared over the crest, the towline cutting through the water. After a few seconds the tug appeared on the crest of the wave high above us. This was filming at its most exciting. The only way to get good results is to be lost in it.

The order came: "Change places!" Mr. Flask had to take over the tow, with his lance. I had to get the stern and the tiller. I ran along the starboard gunwale, waving, while Flask, hugging the men, crossed on the port side. The seagulls were wild in their praise. Then faint applause broke through on the wind. It had come from the tug and it was John Huston's way of saying 'Bravo!' Over the loud hailer he said, "Well done! We go home now."

Do you know, most of those scenes have been left on the cutting-room floor? We returned to base, my colleagues and I, and we were better men. We had seen death, and had conversed with him. That gave us something to tell our children. We didn't even talk about it at the bar. All the talking was done by John.

A scene was being shot on the *Pequod* while eight boats with forty men lined the horizon. The distant horizon. There were two tow launches. We did not have to do anything in particular, just sit in the boat. We left the ship at 8 o'clock that morning and formed the leading group — four boats on a short tow. It was also a short sea and the bumping and bobbing about was disconcerting. Being on short tow, we had a launch that was doing about 18 to 20 knots. It was unpleasant in the extreme, and many times the bow of our whaleboat went under water. Tom Clegg vomited what he hadn't eaten that morning, and I remembered the words of a famous song: "If there's anything inside a man, the sea will bring it out."

Lunchtime came. There was no call from the ship. It went. Still no call. Teatime, and not a thing to eat. It was summer and the days were long. At six o'clock the *Pequod* set sail for home. We were about three miles away but we had to wait for instructions. They never came. We were all famishing and would have eaten raw fish if one had made the mistake of jumping into our boat. Tom was now a very sick man. Darkness began to fall. We had been forgotten. Forty very angry men got back to base at 11:30 that night. I was all right — I was a "natural". But poor Queequeg had to be up at 4:30 next morning to put on his make-up. That's film-making.

We made a whale costing £20,000. It was built on a raft of oil-drums with a skeleton of structural steel covered with one-eighth inch expanded metal. The final thickness of the metal was about 1/64th of an inch. This was covered by a paste of lactic and mica, then felt and more expanded metal, lactic and mica. Then it was painted to the appropriate colour of white, cream, off-white. It disintegrated completely the first day it was put into the water.

A new captain of the *Pequod* took over. The first one had run her against the harbour and broken the mainmast during an important tracking shot. Captain Alan Villiers, devoted seaman, took control. He was the man who took *Mayflower II* to Virginia. We built another whale. This one was more durable and faced the tide as Moby Dick would.

Newport isn't a big place. We could see it from the sea as *Pequod* sailed up and down the Welsh coast while we shot the film. In the distance it looked quaint. I told myself to go and see this place. On location we worked seven days a week. When we began clawing each other to death, the film company would give us a rest day. We worked in Fishguard for three and a half weeks before we had this great luxury. Some of the crew went home to their wives in London. Most of us were too tired to move. We just stayed in bed. I promised to see Newport, and as Greg was going there to golf with Veronique they gave me a lift.

The mountain over the village was much higher than appeared from the sea. I climbed it and saw Cardigan, St. David and Fishguard in the distance. There wasn't much else to do up there, so I came down slowly and made friends with the children I met on the way. By the time we came to Newport town I had over fifty children with me. We were singing nursery rhymes and dancing all the way. We stopped at the prearranged point for Greg. The grownups of Newport came out to join us. In true Welsh tradition I sang at them and they sang at me. Greg and Veronique eventually arrived. They too got caught up in the spirit of the occasion. But we had to leave Newport. The car travelled slowly – the children running behind. Through a rear view mirror I saw Greg looking hard at me. Then he said, "Remarkable! Remarkable! Did you see this ever? You could have taken them wherever you wished."

"Yes," I replied. Then I turned in my seat to look at Greg and Veronique. "Has anyone ever tried marching children onto a battlefield?"

"I don't know, Edric," said Greg. "I don't know," said Veronique. It was a lovely day.

We finished the location work and left Kevin McClory to direct the second units, taking Moby Dick in doubles and long shots. We went to the Associated British studios, Boreham Wood, where various sections of Moby Dick had been constructed. A full ship, like the *Pequod*, built on rockers. While we were at sea I believe we ate enough seasick pills to equal the quantity of fertilizer for five acres of ground for five years. During our eight weeks in the studios on that rocker of a *Pequod* we ate twice as much.

We were set up for the storm scenes. There were two Rolls-Royce engines fitted with propellers. These were taken from Spitfire aeroplanes used during the war. They were to create the storm and drive spray from hoses. Six large hoppers, each carrying two tons of water when full, ranged high on a gallery above us. On command they were released individually over the storm side of the ship delivering their load of water down a chute about three feet wide. This went below the level of the ship, rose, and broke on the deck as a wave. The full impact by the time it hit the deck would be about three and a half tons.

During the shooting many of us found ourselves hauled, mauled and buffeted with great indignity. We had serious colds, sprains and strains. But we went through manfully without any fatality. The rushes were magnificent. People came from all parts of the world to see us. Gina Lollobrigida, Sophia Loren and many other film stars from Italy were photographed with John and Greg.

We next went to Las Palmas in the Canary Islands to do our final location work. However, shortly before we left London, Moby Dick broke away and became a danger to shipping. Even the staid *Daily Telegraph* carried a front-page picture of this fake monster. Warnings were put out to shipping on the radio and on television. I understood later it fetched up in Ostend.

Most days we worked ten miles from shore at Las Palmas in order to match the waters we had at Fishguard in Wales. After a couple of weeks Greg told me there were two locations in view: Cape Town in South Africa, and Las Palmas. He supposed they chose Las Palmas because we might have run into political difficulties in South Africa. He didn't wish to go there anyway. I became very disrespectful. "We want men like Gregory Peck and John Huston and others to go to places like South Africa and Kenya, Southern Rhodesia and the Congo. To show that they treat Negroes like human beings. We want them to set examples. They should not take the easy way out and film in blooming Las Palmas to spare them the trouble of taking a side."

We continued filming. In one scene we were supposed to swim while Moby Dick descended upon us after destroying our boat. The distance: about a hundred yards. My loincloth became unloosed and tangled both legs, preventing their use. I kept afloat for seventy-five yards using just my arms. I was trying not to spoil the shot. But the current was strong and I could go not further. I called for a lifebelt. They dragged me in, wrapped like a mummy from the waist down. That was close.

We spent Christmas in Las Palmas and enjoyed the Spanish festivities. There was a charity boxing contest. John thought some members of the cast should participate. Tom Clegg, who once fought Max Schmeling, was to give an exhibition.[114] I was to enter the ring as a boxer, shed my dressing gown, and sing "The Kid's Last Fight". The other members of the cast were supposed to sing the chorus. I was dressed all in white. A white dressing gown with "Moby Dick" inscribed across the back and "Moby Dick" on the leg of the white shorts. I entered the ring and shed the robe seductively. The women shouted "Olé!" and the men whistled.

I started the song. The chorus came. I got no response from the cast, who were supposed to be singing in the background while I was shadow-boxing. Mind you, there was no musical accompaniment. The Spaniards just gazed. I jabbed. "Come on, Kid! Come on, Kid!" I countered, and hit him "with a left and a right." "Come on, kid! come on, kid!" An uppercut. "And how were they to know it was the Kid's Last Fight?" The second verse. I looked for my colleagues. They were convulsed with laughter. Came the second chorus. Not a note from them. I started shadow-boxing. The Spaniards continued to gaze. It was a hell of a night. I got a lovely bathrobe and a pair of shorts out of it.

The day we finished shooting in Las Palmas, John threw a party to say "Goodbye and Thanks". I helped him a lot behind the scenes with some of the music. We were all very tired — very, very tired. John threw his arms around me and said, "Thank you very much, kid, for all you have done." I replied: "Thank you, John, for all you have done for me. But there were times when I felt I could kill you!" But how could you kill a man when you like him?

He called the press. He said, "Listen to what Edric has to say." I repeated my remarks. Then, "Why did you want to kill me?" I said, "John, out there. Out there in the sea. Some of those men — I saw death in their eyes. So many takes, John." "Aw, heck," he replied. "I knew what I wanted. I didn't hire bloody stars. I hired men. I wanted them to act like men. And what the hell? They were well paid."

He put his arms around me again and said, "You're not among them, kid." And it's true, I was not among them. A few years later he hired me to work on another film with him. And I am today one of the very few artistes who have worked with John Huston more than once in his films.

Friedrich, Tom and I had become brothers. We were harpooners. No one must invade this clan. Tom was quite good as Tashtego. Queequeg was excellent. I was there too, as Dagoo.

We slipped out of Las Palmas early one morning by seaplane. It was just as well we did not keep the senoritas weeping. Perhaps we will return one day to do "Son of Moby Dick". I learned a lot about my fellow actors on this film. We are all terrified of old age.

Bad weather in London kept us in Lisbon for five days. I must hand a special bouquet to Hilda Fox, the hairdresser, and Angela, continuity girl, who stood up to the rigours of the weather and the ships and the sea over the entire six months. It was said we wasted money on this film. One of the backers even came all the way from Hollywood to see how we were spending his money. He was given a good breakfast and a fast launch out to the *Pequod*. We sang him aboard when he arrived, with "Heave away, my Johnny". He looked green, but flattered and pleased. Then he was offered a well-done, fat steak from the galley. He took one look at it and called for the launch to take him back to shore. No, we did not waste your money, sir. A lot of little children were fed — in Youghal, in Wales, in London and in Las Palmas in the Canary Islands, in Madeira, and in Lisbon. On behalf of those children I wish to offer my thanks to you.

Before the film was completed I said, "If *Moby Dick* doesn't turn out to be the greatest film made, I'll be surprised." The public did not see the film we shot. They saw the film they were made to see, not the one we made.

The day after I returned to London my son was born. We named him Peter, after the great Fisherman. It was not difficult to pick up the threads after being away for six months. The BBC knew I was back. They offered me four weeks, extended to a fifth week, on a programme called *Down Melody Lane*. Produced by Frank Hooper. Paul Fenoulhet conducted. Frank and I had very good times on this programme. I remember appealing to him to be allowed to sing "That Old Black Magic" with a sexy beat. Frank retorted: "You can't sing that sort of thing to the staid British public on a Sunday night." My reply was equally forthright. "My dear sir, I'd have you know that everyone who was born in this country was conceived on a Sunday night." We roared with laughter, and I sang the song.

Fire Down Below, for Warwick Films, took me back to the Port of Spain wharves I knew so well. Where I had repaired the government steamships *Trinidad, Tobago* and *St. Patrick.* And in a character and costume in which I was "a natural". A fair-play West Indian seaman, uneducated but intelligent. With a sense of humour in everything he did. Even to the point where Rita Hayworth asks him: "You hate me, Jimmy Jean, don't you?" And he answers honestly, "Yes, Ma'am, I do." Scenes for this film also took us to Tobago. To the beautiful Buccoo Reef. And to Plymouth. It is extremely difficult to sum up one's feelings on returning home on such a project. Civic receptions were given for me in Port of Spain and San Fernando by the City Fathers. My famous American film star colleagues were rather concerned at the fact they were left out. Being more famous than I was they had a greater right to the freedom of Port of Spain and San Fernando. But the City Fathers honoured me for the political and social work I had done for the island while in Europe.

Yes, I had done the State some service, and received the freedom of Port of Spain in my costume. Dressed as a wharfie. The film company did not release me in time to get properly dressed, although they arranged with the City Council that I should be released to accept this honour. My wife and my two little children were present.

Trinidad was thriving. The place had changed considerably. It was vibrant. We had received a form of self-government.[115] I was particularly pleased to see one of my under-privileged children a member of the City Council of Port of Spain. I had nothing to do with it. But I may — I say, I may – have sown the seed. At least he will remember we swept Gallus Street together. And thought, "We might as well clean up Port of Spain." The police were getting much better pay. The Deputy Commissioner was one of my batch. Fourteen more who remained in the Force went on to hold very high positions. The oilfields were throbbing. There was better understanding there. The whole island was organised. With trade unions and a certain amount of welfare. Ocean-going liners were coming alongside the pier and to the wharves. There was a special harbour for sailing ships and a handy dry dock. And the mule-carts were replaced by trucks. Many of the old offices had been replaced by modern buildings. The University of Woodford Square was thriving, giving mass education in world politics and other international affairs. The main tutor, or don, was poised for the formation of a new political party.

The people lived politics. There were others who were prepared to capitalise on it, even to the point of making "bobol".[116] This had always been a great drawback to Trinidad politics. A party is formed. After six months someone runs away with the funds. Sometimes to another island, or Down the Main. The place was on the move. All points read "Go". But where? Who will lead them? Within a few weeks of my departure for England the People's National Movement (PNM) Party was formed. The don was head of the party. Four months later it swept into power. Completely. Absolutely. Relentlessly.[117] The Catholic Church was against it and threatened to excommunicate anyone who voted for PNM. The Archbishop had to lift the ban three days after the elections. The old regime was utterly defeated. It is said that a priest was found coercing people and threatening them if they voted PNM. He was roughly handled. Why does the Church always interfere in these things? Why is the Church so slow to admit change? The Church itself can do with change. Lots of it.

The whole world came to the boil over Egypt when Port Said was bombed by the British after Nasser nationalised the Suez Canal.[118] Anthony Eden was Prime Minister of England then. He had been a great Foreign Minister for his country. Up to that time he had yet to prove himself a good Prime Minister. I thought this was his last gamble and it was. He could have put the whole of Africa under his belt and retired on the laurels: "the greatest Prime Minister Britain ever had". As Foreign Minister Eden had created Nasser in his own image for the express purpose of removing King Farouk of Egypt. Nasser hid behind Neguib and together they removed Farouk. Ernest Bevin, the previous Foreign Minister in the Labour Government, told me earlier that while returning from a conference he had dined with Farouk, who made the formidable crack: "Soon there will be only five kings left in the world: The King of Spades, the King of Hearts, the King of Clubs, the King of Diamonds, and the King of England." Farouk was now gone. As Prime Minister-designate Eden must have thought that by the time he became Prime Minister Nasser would certainly be in power. Ruling Egypt. Therefore he would dance to his tune.

Nasser put Neguib under house arrest and took over the running of the country. Eden became Prime Minister of England. A "commesse" started in the Middle East, with Israel, the French, the Egyptians and the British.[119] The Russians, on the other hand, were just about to leave Budapest and the whole of Hungary. The Aswan High Dam was the root of the Egyptian trouble. It threatened to improve the prosperity of the Egyptians and the power of Nasser. Nasser was getting too strong in the whole area. The Egyptians were getting arms from Czechoslovakia. They needed arms to fight the Israeli. So the West refused to lend Nasser the money to build the Aswan High Dam. I suppose Nasser thought he had better retaliate where it hurt. He nationalized the Suez Canal.

As Eden had created Nasser he thought he could break him. But he made a mistake about the nose. He didn't bargain for the nose. It was a little bit too big. And defiant. I suppose Eden thought the only way to get at him was to bomb the towns and spread panic and alarm to such an extent that the people of Egypt would rise up against Nasser. But the people of Egypt had already recognised Nasser as a redeemer. Especially after he took over the Suez Canal in one swoop. But it looks as if the town of Port Said was bombed two days too soon. The Russians had already left Hungary. The bombing of Egypt seemed to have heralded the departure of the Russians and the uprising of the students in Hungary. Some took it as a signal. The Russians had not yet reached home. They merely turned back and drove on Budapest.[120]

The world stood helpless, unable to do anything. A few individuals did their best to save lives. This was laudable. But what about the mass slaughter that took place? In Egypt. In Hungary. Where was John Foster Dulles, the master of brinkmanship?[121] And the French were also involved. Could one of the French backroom boys be one of Dulles' schoolmates, from his days at the Sorbonne? A faint voice came from the United Nations, and it said, "Stop it". Somehow it seemed the voice of reason. There was another voice: that of the bankers in Switzerland. There was a run on the pound. The Hungarians continued to be slaughtered.

We did not have to wait very long for the report that Eden was ill. I was sure a doctor's certificate would be his resignation. Then he fetched up in a tiny West Indian island called Bequia, in the Grenadines, where there is peace and quiet. But I will tell you how he could have put Africa under his belt.

Suez was already taken. The Canal was captured. Cairo was a foregone conclusion. His forces could have run straight down to Khartoum. There, taken away the new constitution. Continued on to Uganda. The Kabaka (King) of Uganda was already in exile. All he had to do there was make a show of force. The British Government had already borrowed £250 million to make the Central African Federation work. The first £50 million was to improve the army so the Federation would work without a hitch. All he had to do there was turn to Kwame Nkrumah of Ghana and say, "Hand in the new Constitution I gave you." There might have been a run on the pound. Britain might have been called all sorts of bad names. But people forget quickly. All he had to do at that point was to say, "But look what I have! Almost the whole of Africa!" And this would have been Britain's Fourth Empire.

The Russians didn't stop shooting in Hungary until they were quite sure the doctor's certificate was placed before the Queen and Eden had resigned. Meanwhile John Foster Dulles sent his emissaries to buy up oil rights in most of the Arab States in which Britain had lost prestige. Somehow Dulles always looked to me like a dog that sucks eggs. Petrol rationing was reintroduced in England. Ships had to go round the Cape of Good Hope instead of through the Suez Canal. My personal reaction to the bombing of Egypt was very violent. I had just come out of the Underground at Notting Hill Gate. I bought an *Evening Standard*. There it was in bold black banners: PORT SAID BOMBED. The first man I met received a solid punch on the jaw. When he got up, quarrelling, shouting, "What d'you hit me for?", I showed him the headline in the paper. He too was concerned. He said, "Yes, but I'm on your side! I'm damn angry about it too." He was an Englishman. I apologised profusely. We went into the pub and had a drink. It only shows what these things can do to men's minds. War turns men into animals. Uncivilised animals. And the nauseating smells hang around long after it is over. Crick! Crack![122]

Early in 1948, when I enforced myself upon Hungary, the smell of the dead still pervaded certain parts of Budapest, the dead of the previous war. I wonder how long that of the new dead of the 1956 uprising will last.

I could not be in London for the premiere of *Fire Down Below*. I was in Norway filming *The Vikings* with Kirk Douglas and Tony Curtis. We lived in a yacht called *Brand Six* which once belonged to Barbara Hutton. *Brand Six* was to sail us to Dinard in France. As we were about to cast off a message came. The don, who had automatically inherited power and a new constitution, and had become Chief Minister in Trinidad, had arrived in London. He would like to see me urgently. His timing could not have been better.

I flew to him in London. He wanted to talk to me about the naval air base at Chaguaramas. I gave him all the information I had. A West Indian Federation was afoot. Trinidad was considered unsafe and dubious politically and therefore ruled out as the Federal capital by a fact-finding committee. This having appeared in a public statement, it was a foregone conclusion that the next time the West Indies met Trinidad would be chosen as the home of the Federal capital. And the don wished to take over the Chaguaramas base to form the Federal capital of the West Indies.[123]

I went to Dinard. Then back to London. Then to Dinard. On to Germany. To Munich. The don returned to the West Indies. His plans worked. Trinidad was given the Federal capital. But there were certain forces in Washington that would not think of giving up the base.

Eisenhower partially conceded it to the West Indies as a gift from America. That base can be used as a springboard for any attack the North Americans wish to make on South America. The United States of America is using up its natural resources at a fantastic rate. They look with longing eyes at the virgin territories in South America. Until the South Americans form themselves into a United States of South America, the threat will always remain. The granting of the base to Trinidad as the capital of the Federal West Indies would have virtually removed that threat. Again I must draw attention to the fact that Vice-President Nixon had to run for his life out of South America. Regardless of the Organisation of American States.

We completed the filming of the *Vikings* at the Bavaria Filmkunst in the studios at Geiselgasteg in Munich, West Germany. There I met Lutz Hengst and Helmuth Ringelmann. Helmuth was stepson to Dr. Erhard, the master and father of the West German economic recovery.

Munich gave me many insights into the German mentality. I visited the scenes where Hitler had his start — the Bierhaus putsch and the May Day shooting. A friend of mine owned the barber's shop where Hitler hid when the shooting started. I lived at the Mark Hotel, 13 Sennefeldstrasse. Herr von Mark and family looked after me well. I attended the opera with them and sampled the German "Kultur". *The Vikings* had everything to do with the five swans of German mythology. Wagner expressed this influence in his music. *Parsifal* shoots the swan. *The Ring* shows the fire and torment and torture which inspired the birth of the German people. Bismarck and Wagner were schoolmates. I understand they were both steeped in the teachings of Macchiavelli.

I witnessed the Oktoberfest when the whole of Munich is given over to beer-drinking in a field about 150 acres in area. There is a part I called the "recovery ward" where the drunks are piled up high to sleep off their beer.

I attended a remarkable performance of *Othello*. Ramon Vinay played the Moor. I cannot remember Desdemona's real name, but she was a giant in relation to Vinay. They both sang well. Verdi's music was never better served. The most moving scene was when Desdemona visited Othello in Cyprus. Music showed a great passage of time. The embodiment of the great love of two people. This part of the score runs about five minutes. The two people slowly walk to each other, weaving a spell of deep emotion in the audience. I must have been crying or sobbing aloud because when the lights went up for the end of the act all eyes seemed turned in my direction. I did not know the people sitting next to me. A woman in her German accent spoke in English and said, "You should be playing Othello." Ramon and his Desdemona took over thirty-five curtain calls that night. The steel safety-curtain came down. It was funny to see them climbing out of the steel door virtually hanging over the edge of the stage to take the curtain calls. The police eventually sent us home.

A great friendship grew up between Lutz, Helmuth and myself. We discussed the possibilities of importing coffee, cocoa and grapefruit from the West Indies. As my next film was to be *Virgin Islands*, I told them I would look into the matter on my trip to the West Indies.

As I had bought a car in Munich, I drove back to London, passing through Stuttgart, Frankfurt-am-Main, Mainz, Cologne, Brussels and Calais. Also Ghent. I saw some of the places where the terrible battles of the last war were fought. I saw the thousands of names inscribed on the Arch of Honour at Bruges. I was in time to witness the empty honour of a bugle call at six o'clock in the evening.

It was wonderful to be reunited with my family. A few days later I would be off again. As I had to cross American territory there was the snag of getting a visa. This time to go to a West Indian island. It was again refused. No reason given. But the film company wanted me. So they arranged for me to fly to Bermuda, wait there, then take a flight to Antigua. They would then send a charter plane to pick me up. To take me to Beef Island in the British Virgins.

After arriving in Bermuda I found I had to remain five *days* before getting a connection to Antigua. After putting out some feelers, I found a Standing Committee on Federation was meeting in Port of Spain with Norman Manley as its chairman. I just couldn't waste five days in Bermuda. I flew down to Trinidad, saw my sisters, then went and looked for Manley. We met at the Queen's Park Hotel and talked for five minutes. He told me he was looking forward to the Federation of the West Indies. That he would give his life to that end. Towards making the Federation a success. Norman Manley was expected to be the first Prime Minister of the Federation.[124]

I made a slow journey to Beef, covering the entire six and a half days. I stopped at Grenada, Barbados, St. Lucia, Martinique and Antigua. It was good to be reunited with Sydney Poitier. And make the acquaintance of John Cassavetes and his wife. Also Graham Tharpe, our producer. I didn't much care for the couple at whose place we stayed and so forgot their names. Also the island on which they lived.

After one month's filming in Marina Cay, I had four weeks before my next shots. I asked our producer to allow me to go home to Trinidad to do some business. He agreed. However, my main plan was to test American Immigration defences in the Virgin Islands and Puerto Rico. I travelled with the workers by ferry from Tortola in the British Virgin Islands to St. Thomas, US Virgin Islands. After breaking through the barrier I took time off to send a rude postcard to the American Consul who refused my visa in London. Then took the plane to San Juan, Puerto Rico.

They had a black book there with my name in it. I told the American Immigration Officer I only wanted to make connection with a plane to Trinidad, I did not intend to stay in American territory. He let me through. But his decision coincided with a strike of British West Indian Airways pilots. I settled into the airport hotel. As I had over $1,200 in American money I turned it all over to the hotel manager for safe keeping. News got around I was in San Juan. Despite the strike, there was a home-bound flight passing through San Juan the next morning. A seat was booked for me on that plane. If I missed that flight there could be no guarantee how long I would have to remain in Puerto Rico.

The Puerto Ricans had other ideas about my journey. Came the time for my departure the manager of the hotel could not be found any where in Puerto Rico. As I could not recover my money, the plane left for Trinidad without me. The police were called in, every possible security measure was taken to find my money. They all failed. When it was quite certain I had to stay in Puerto Rico, the manager turned up with a mass of apologies, regrets and anything to assuage my anger. "You like Puerto Rico, no?" "I like Puerto Rico, no!" "You see, Mr. Connor, we are showing the film on Thursday *Fire Down Below*. To raise money to send an underprivileged boy to school. To a good school. And we thought as you were here, well, we would make use of you. We will have you make a personal appearance to raise the money. So. You like Puerto Rico, no?"

"Well, in that case, I like Puerto Rico, yes."

"All right, boys, come in. He's going to stay with us." Five men entered from another room. One was an American. He said he was the press officer of the committee. He said, "I can go to town now. We have something to sell." They arranged for me to see the entire island and all that was being done to develop Puerto Rico. As it was a Puerto-American affair the whole proceedings of the concert were being done in English. The press officer wanted me to make an appearance before the film was shown and make a speech. He would like at least eight minutes. During that time I should say anything I wished. Perhaps explain about the people in the film. What I thought of Puerto Rico. Give my views on what I had seen there. If I did this, he said, the audience would look for me in the film.

"It is no accident that Pablo Casals has come to the land of his mother to live." This was the dramatic way I opened my speech. "It is no accident that Noel Coward and many other very famous artistes from America and England have come to live in the West Indies.[125] Because, as far as art is concerned, America and Europe have exhausted their creative inspiration." This was dynamite. Then: "You are doing a good thing. Sending a poor boy to a good school." I spoke about Rita Hayworth. How she arrived in the film, her first film for three years. A bit nervous. How she sailed through the part eventually, when she got going. I had the greatest respect for her as a woman, and as a lady. Anyone who can start off in life as a dancer and become a princess must have a lot upstairs. And I felt the bad newspaper reports about Rita Hayworth were wrong. Bob Mitchum got the idea of wearing a bar-striped T-shirt from a seaman he once knew. He said this chap had a permanent list to starboard. I thought Bob, wearing the shirt, made *his* permanent list to starboard even more permanent. Jack Lemmon, I said, was a gentleman. He went to Harvard. He has always been, and always will be, a gentleman. And that we would be hearing a lot more about him in the future in his career as a film star.

Then I spoke of the people of the West Indies. My people. "And you are my people too. Because Puerto Rico is in the West Indies. You will see them in the film."

My speech was more than the Americans bargained for but the Puerto Ricans loved it. The hotel manager was in, to let me have my bill before I departed for Ciudad Trujillo next day.[126] "To five days' stay in the Airport Hotel: No dollars and no cents. Paid, with thanks."

We flew over the thousand hills of the north-western corner of Puerto Rico. Then over sea, for ten minutes — and the sugar cane fields of San Domingo. We flew over more than a hundred miles of nothing but sugar cane and sugar cane, and yet more sugar cane. I spoke in the ear of a Jamaican woman sitting in front of me. "What would happen to this country if the price of sugar should fall?" And she said, "Sir, me no know what would happen to them children."

We landed in Ciudad Trujillo. I very much wanted to see a great exhibition on Pan-American education in the city. I went to St. Margaret's, the church built by the son of Christopher Columbus in memory of his father. I touched the casket in which the explorer's remains are stored. Then I went to see the city of Ciudad Trujillo.

At every street corner lottery tickets were being sold. Down town, near the wharf, the women were very sloppily dressed, the men groomed to match. I saw a priest and asked him what was wrong with the city, what was wrong with the people. He ran away. I went to the exhibition on education at 3 o'clock in the afternoon. Apart from the attendants I was the only person there to see what was being done about education in Santo Domingo. "Where are the people?" A young man said, "they came three days ago to pay their homage to Trujillo. After that, nobody comes."

The exhibition was housed in some magnificent buildings — the most modern of Western architecture. Apparently all the children born in Santo Domingo were the children of Papa Trujillo. They died for Trujillo. I blew my top at the airport. I didn't give a damn. I was leaving anyway, and didn't care if I never returned to that country.

I travelled with six Air Force men, who were going to Caracas to study flying with the Venezuelan Air Force. Up to that time the Trujillos had ruled Santo Domingo for 31 years. Even the highest mountain was called Trujillo. When one reaches such heights the fall can be painfully dramatic. My calling as an actor makes me interested in people and events. All that happens in life. So that I can hold up the mirror fearlessly and at least be a witness. Perhaps that is why St. Paul hated actors. He used to have them stoned to death.

The long route to Trinidad took me to Aruba, Curaçao and then to Caracas. While at this airport I thought of Simón Bolívar, the half-negro, who drove the Spanish Royalists out of the Americas. He was aided by men and money from Dessalines, Christophe and Pétion of Haiti. I thought how the wars of independence in South America were eventually won by Angostura bitters made by Dr. Siegert, a medical officer in the army of Simón Bolívar.[127] Most of all, I reflected on the oath taken by Simón Bolívar on Mount Aventine just outside Rome. Some historians call it a harangue. But history showed the result. Venezuela and the adjoining states have their troubles, most of them coming from the outside world. Jímenez was in power there, and the country was bristling with American aid. Despite the aid this was the city from which Nixon had to run his fastest. What a far cry from the days of Gomez when the country owed no one. Gomez was not an educated man. He was a bastard. But I would call him a benevolent dictator. He ran the country by military junta. He woke up one morning and it was explained to him that the country had a national debt of some $60 million. He sent for his military junta and had the country divided up into agriculture, customs and excise, mines, business, and so on. And Gomez took 25 per cent of all their takings. By 6:00 p.m. that day there was no national debt. He would deal with an average of two revolutions a year. But he lived to a ripe old age and died in his bed.[128]

On the strength of my short talk with Norman Manley I set up a film company: "Edric Connor (Films) Limited". I applied to the new Trinidad government for Pioneer Status, a tax holiday concession on profits and materials over five or ten years to allow the industry to prosper. I spent a few days at Peter Hill with my aunts, cousins and sisters and other relatives. The land had been prospected and oil found on it.

It might have been difficult for some people to get back to Beef. But not for me. The fact that I was able to get out meant the Immigration Officer did not do his job properly. I only had to threaten him with that and he let me in. I was now well known in San Juan. The Puerto Ricans would have made a stink in the press.

I returned to find Sydney Poitier on the verge of walking out on the job. He was hoping I would support him. He told me he had reason to believe the film company had run out of money. I couldn't join him in his ideas. I felt if the company had run out of money they would tell me. Until they did that, I was in a job. At the same time, he had been offered the lead in the film *Porgy and Bess*. He told me he turned down the offer because he thought the story "degenerate and degrading". "Sydney," I said, "If you don't play Porgy, I will." I wrote a letter to my Hollywood agent. I showed it to Sydney before posting it. I went so far as to tell Sydney how I would play Porgy. I didn't wish him to feel I would take the role behind his back if he turned it down. Sydney eventually played Porgy. He was tortured to a decision while sitting on my bed on a tiny island in the Virgin Islands at 3 o'clock in the morning.

I disc-jockeyed a programme of the opera for the BBC and produced it in an unusual way. Porgy was the star all right, but a pathetic little figure called Scipio, who did very little singing in the opera, was the one I made stand out. This little boy was having Catfish Row and its horrors impressed upon his young mind. To listeners he stood out prominently. I ended the programme by saying, "They tell me Catfish Row is in North Carolina. But I have seen Catfish Row on the banks of the Rhine, the Danube and the Thames. So cry, Porgy! Cry for Bess! Let us all cry for Bess! And Scipio!"

Soon after returning to London to spend some time with the children and my wife, I went to Munich to discuss further proposals on importing, and on a possible film with German backing to be made in Trinidad. As a result I sent the following telegram to the Minister of Trade and Commerce in Trinidad:

> If I take an order for two shiploads citrus fruit and one cocoa five or six thousand tonnage could we supply direct to Germany stop Will supply the ships stop Please quote prices and oblige by cable.
>
> -Edric Connor.

I also sent a prepaid reply. I stayed in Munich a whole week waiting for it. It didn't come. Then someone very high up in German economic circles told me, "You see. You people are not free." This was December 1957. I returned to London with my tail tucked between my legs.

The Minister wrote me a letter six months later. Talking about "laudable help to the West Indies" and a lot of nonsense. What I should have done was, take the German ships. Go to every one of the West Indian islands. Scoop out whatever there was to be found. Instead of being honest and above-board. I might do it yet. Trinidad grapefruit was dumped that year, 1958.

It is remarkable how time hangs heavy when one has suffered disappointment and a defeat. The days were long and the nights were cold. I drowned my sorrows in theatre. Then John Huston telephoned me from Paris. If he had wanted me to work for nothing I would have gone just the same. I was booked to play the role of Waitari in *Roots of Heaven* in the French Cameroons, French Equatorial Africa and the Congo.

The West Indian Federation was to be a fact on 22 or 23 April, 1958. When it was learned I would not be in London or even available to go to Trinidad for the inauguration of Federation, Oxford University Press asked me to make my contribution in an album of *Songs from Trinidad*. The book was completed in a fortnight. Then the haggling began with Alan Franks over what was to be in the preface. This preface was very frank and honest. Its theme was the "freedom of the spirit of man". If the letters we exchanged were published with the book it would have been a sensation.

Roots of Heaven deals with the preservation of game in Africa, particularly the biggest of all game, the elephant. Waitari, the African politician, is an ex-French Deputy. He had been to the Sorbonne, married a Frenchwoman, and had two lovely half-caste children. The night before leaving for Africa, Tony Richardson of the Royal Court asked me to play the lead in *Flesh to a Tiger*. Also to allow him to use some of my West Indian music. *Flesh to a Tiger* was written by a Jamaican, Barry Reckord. Unfortunately I couldn't play the "Shepherd" as I was going to play Waitari. But I could record the music in Paris next day.

I arrived in Paris and had a day and a half to spare. I was taken into a studio near Twentieth Century Fox where I reeled off 45 minutes of music and instructions on tape. I had this mailed to Tony. I then proceeded to seek out the haunts that Waitari might have had in Paris. I wanted to come to grips with this master-politician. I came to his early days at the Sorbonne and visited rooms in which he may have had his lectures. I sat through one of the lectures. But I still did not come to grips with the man. A girl was showing me around. I asked her to take me where he would eat. She took me up to University City miles from the Sorbonne. I slowly began to find Waitari. We went into this huge canteen where he had lunch. There were thousands of pupils there, people of all shades of beauty and ugliness. Talk about the wonderful French cooking! I will never forget the hogswill I had to eat in University City. Made mainly of potatoes and cauliflower. Cooked in a way that made the fifty French francs squirm at having to be paid over. I ate the mess and washed it down with a yellow apology for orange juice. For this I paid Fr. 10. I had to leave in a hurry to catch the plane. I had not given my verdict to the young lady. She asked, "Have you found Waitari yet?" I replied, "Yes. After eating that sort of food, Waitari had every right to become a rebel."

In Ubangi, one of our locations, I accidentally ran into the worst kind of slavery I have ever come across. Just on the outskirts of Ubangi some Pygmies are held as slaves, although it is illegal. They not only work for nothing; they have to feed themselves with whatever they get or find. No wonder they dig up their dead and eat them. The world must be steamrolled with education to stop these terrible things. Man must see himself in the eyes of other human beings. Man must live for truth and honesty. Die for it if necessary. Man must respect Nature. So that he will not shame the earth in which he may be buried.

We returned to Paris in due course to complete the film at Boulogne Studios. The Algerian war overspilled into Paris. Many evenings I found myself running along the Champs Elysées and Place de la Concorde, getting the sound of French riots. It is a high-pitched "Ping pong! Ping pong!", say F-sharp F. For me, cous cous was out. I was told to keep away from Algerian restaurants for fear I would be mistaken for an Algerian Muslim. In Paris I found a letter waiting for me from the Shakespeare Memorial Theatre at Stratford-upon-Avon. Inviting me to play the role of Gower in *Pericles*. To be produced by Tony Richardson. I had never done any Shakespeare, other than perhaps holding a spear at school, and the bit of *Othello* taught me by Frederick Ranalow. In fact I didn't even know Shakespeare wrote a play called *Pericles*. I asked the production manager to scour Paris and get me a copy of the complete works of Shakespeare. I found that Gower was Chorus. He would probably hold the stage all to himself. I sent a cable to Stratford-upon-Avon saying I would accept.

I got a long weekend off, flew home and found I couldn't enter my house because my wife had chicken pox. The house was quarantined. The children were all right. They had had their fair share of measles in the past. I lived at the Strand Hotel and communicated with my family by telephone. It would have been terrible if I had returned to Paris with chicken pox.

I returned to London three weeks later when the house was free for me to enter. Then, after all the years I had lived in Britain, I went to Stratford-upon-Avon for the first time. On several occasions I had been within a radius of five miles, but never actually there. I suppose if I had gone there before I would have been overawed at the possibility of appearing on the stage of its illustrious theatre and might very well have turned down the part.

I went to lunch with Patrick Donnell, the Assistant Director, and signed the contract. Then, later, to meet Glen Byam Shaw, the Director. I didn't want to know anything about the terms of the contract. All I asked Paddy was, "Tell me the snags". I signed the contract as it was. Michael Redgrave, at 50, was playing Hamlet. Richard Johnson was playing Romeo and was to play Pericles. He was also playing Sir Andrew Aguecheek. Patrick Wymark was playing Sir Toby Belch and was to play in *Pericles*. Geraldine McEwan and Dorothy Tutin were also there. Paul Hardwick and Ted de Sousa, Julian Glover, and a host of very nice people.

I went to Stratford with an open mind, feeling that if they did not find me good enough I would be thrown out. But I was determined to be good. This was to be a new approach to *Pericles*. Music was to be written by Roberto Gerhardt for half of the words normally spoken by

Gower. We had four weeks' rehearsal. Two weeks after we started those rehearsals the music was not completed. Roberto was trained by Schoenberg.[129] When the music was handed in, with its terrible accidentals and harmonies, I nearly went crazy. "Roberto! Why do this to me?" I asked for a day off from rehearsal, drove up to London and got my tape-recorder. Returned in time to find Roberto still at Stratford-upon-Avon. "Now, Roberto, record this. This music you have written for me." Roberto recorded his own music. With a lot of mistakes. After he left I played it back, with the score. Well, well, well. "If he himself cannot read his own music, I wonder what he expects me to do?" The Music Director and I got down to business. We recorded all the music for quality and accuracy. I then took the recorder and tape to my digs. I had it played at me from six till twelve every night. And absorbed it like bad propaganda. Had it played at me again from six till nine-thirty every morning. Until that music permeated every fibre of my being. I can tell you now, even ten years of brainwashing can't remove it.

Tony Richardson worked hard on me. I am very grateful. We understood each other. For instance, there was a fight taking place behind heavy gates. I was alone on stage; and the only person able to convey to the audience what was actually going on behind the heavy gates. Tony said, "I don't know how you're going to do this, Edric, how you're going to convey it. There's nothing I can tell you about it." "Shall I dance it, Tony?" "Yes. Dance. Do a dance. That is exactly what it needs."

The dance I worked out was pure Shango from Trinidad. Pauline Grant, the dance mistress, said after seeing it, "The only thing for you to do is hold your head up."

The fight was one of the great excitements in *Pericles*. I took all that the storytellers of Mayaro taught me to Stratford. I reflected that, as a boy, these men were preparing me for Stratford. And I did not know it. I believe I brought something new to the character of Gower. Normally he is played as a blackrobed scribe. A harbinger of death. Bemoaning loss. As I played him — a seaman representing all races and all ages — I gave him life by making him a super spiritualist medium. With power to materialise the subjects of the story into moving images so that they could be seen by the other seamen to whom I told the story on the deck of the ship.

Another innovation I made was to bring the audience into the show. I peopled the stage with imaginary sailors, also planted and pinpointed extra crew among the audience. Imaginary, of course. On several occasions some of the sailors, getting up from the deck to cross the stage, perhaps to tend a rope, would step aside from one of the imaginary sailors planted on the deck, they were so vividly planted in the imagination.

It was a happy company. If there was any discordant note, perhaps being the first Negro to appear there, I might have caused it. I must say, I learned a lot at Stratford. No one can go there without coming out a better actor.

One week before *Pericles* opened Paul Robeson was granted his passport and came back to England. It was only then that I learned from the *Daily Worker* that Paul Robeson had been offered the part of Gower and because he could not get his passport in time, I was given the role. To me this was quite shocking. I went to Glen Byam Shaw and asked whether he would like me to withdraw. I suppose I offended him. I am sorry. But I too have feelings to be considered. I come from the country districts of Trinidad. I come from the land, I am proud. Said Glen, "Withdraw? How can you think of that? You're doing a fine job. Carry on." And I left his office determined to give the performance of my life. To set a standard it would take years for the greatest actors in the world to equal. Instead of six hours' sleep at night I now slept for only three. I would show the whole darned lot of them what a second fiddle could do.

The day of the opening I was quite cool and calm. Television filmed me for the news. They asked if I felt nervous. No. But perhaps five minutes before Curtain Up the woes of all the Negroes of the world would weigh me down. Yes, they would weigh around my shoulders, and then I'd feel nervous, I presumed. But it is a good thing to feel nervous before a performance. It gives one a respect for standards and the desire to be as good as one's last performance. It happened exactly that way. It was awful, just before the curtain went up. It was excruciatingly awful. In quiet prayer, holding on to a piece of cord, I called for my mother and father, my grandfather, my brothers. I called for God and all the heavenly hosts to help me.

After I sang the first four bars and held my notes steady, I felt all right, and settled into the role. I received praise from all the press except the *Star* evening paper. The critic said he could not hear a single word from me, although he was only twelve rows from the stage. The leading critics were dotted all over the theatre. They heard. I thanked the *Star* for being there, but told him I thought he might have been twelve rows from the stage in another theatre. I had no reply from him. It doesn't matter any more. One paper said when I sang my voice was beautiful, but when I spoke they couldn't hear. Another said when I spoke my voice was beautiful, but when I sang they couldn't hear. One said he couldn't understand the words with my diction. But no one said I had any special accent.

Gower was alive. And this was the first successful production of *Pericles* in 300 years. I found out that Shakespeare wrote this adaptation of *Pericles* while he was in hospital and thinking about the after-life. This was the first of his three last plays, in which he dealt with the supernatural. The others are *The Tempest* and *The Winter's Tale*. I think I touched what Shakespeare wanted to say about some of the unseen forces that exist around us.

My 45th birthday was on 2nd August, 1958. And I was playing at Stratford. It was a Saturday and I had two performances. A matinee and the evening. Three busloads of friends came in from London to celebrate with me. I held a party for the company and staff. The management wanted me to make it just official staff and to prepare for 150 guests. But I quietly told the props and sceneshifters to bring their wives and friends. I told all the women who swept the theatre and did the scrubbing to bring their friends and their husbands. The cooks. Everybody. Bring all your friends! My wife and her relatives and friends came down early. I told them to cook for 400.

We had real rum from Trinidad. And rice from Trinidad. We made everything West Indian. We had a special bottle of Vat 19 and one of Orange Blossom for Michael Redgrave. I got the impression he liked it unadulterated. Boscoe Holder brought his dancers and singers and drummers. They gave a cabaret in the conference room. This lasted 45 minutes and was tremendous. The steel band boys came down and they played for dancing at the bar. In fact we took over the whole of the Shakespeare Memorial Theatre that night. Stratford-upon-Avon has not been the same since. I do not think it will ever recover from that party. It will be talked about for years to come.

I cannot remember with whom I cut my birthday cake. I think it was Googie Withers. The Italian chef made my cake and it was a gift from the Theatre. It had four and a half candles on it.

In the theatre in Britain there are many famous artistes who sometimes take newcomers under their experienced wings and guide them to the top. I never had such good fortune. I was never kissed by Noel Coward. Sir Laurence Olivier never came backstage to see me. Nevertheless I went backstage to congratulate him on his marvellous portrayal of the Moor in *Othello*. We discussed his make-up. I can only assume that it pays to be thrown into the professional theatre at the deep end. I got through vigorously and without any apparent harm. This happened at a time when Britain and the world were looking for new ideas and new cultural patterns. In my time there were "Discovery" programmes. I was lucky not to have been "discovered". Nobody ever discovered anybody. If you are good, you will certainly get to the top. You will certainly find someone coming forward to help. Kisses are good to a point. They are publicity. All publicity is good. However, one can be over-publicised. I have ten large scrapbooks of press cuttings. They have all come, unsolicited, from my friends, the critics, journalists, reviewers and other members of the Press.

Take all comments as helpful and be grateful that you are remembered. Work hard. Work late. Work until it hurts. You may not know who is sitting in the cheap seats, but they know when you are not giving everything. They are furthest away and hard to get. This part of the audience you have to fight and please. They applaud the loudest. They are the people who make you.

In February of that year (1958) I had been asked by Eric Fawcett to give a confidential report on all the Negro actors in Britain. He was expecting to produce *Green Pastures* later in the year, and wanted me to play De Lawd. When I returned from Africa and took over at the Shakespeare Memorial Theatre, he checked with the Theatre on my availability for the performance. He was given the all clear. He telephoned, asking me to attend at the BBC on 10th August (1958) to meet Marc Connolly, the author of *Green Pastures*. I duly attended, and Marc Connolly made me read the whole of De Lawd in his play. He couldn't find any flaws. I discovered he was forcing himself to find flaws in my performance. After an hour I took up my photographs and newspaper cuttings and left. Cordially.

A few days later I discovered that Marc Connolly brought a man with him from the United States and had him installed in London. No matter how well I may have read, he had brought his friend to play De Lawd. I had already played the role on stage and sound radio. The problem for the BBC and Connolly was getting a work permit for his friend. News got around that I was good enough for the Shakespeare Memorial Theatre, but somehow not for Connolly. The Negro artistes, while accepting the jobs, insisted they were not going to work with this American, who had been brought in through a back door. There was another American, John Bouie, loafing and poaching around London at the time. The BBC contracted Thomas Baptiste to play Gabriel. After he signed the contract, Connolly said he wanted John Bouie to play the role. Connolly began to play tough. He said if he couldn't get the artistes he wanted in his play, there was going to be no play. British Actors Equity, although representing artiste-members, were left wide open at this. They can get the Labour Department to refuse a permit. But they can do nothing to get a play put on against management or author determined to have a foreigner in a role. While I felt flattered at the action taken by the British Negro actors, I realised that it was not often sixty of them could get work at one and the same time. I chased them all to work — told them to go and show their real ability.

De Lawd was so insecure His angels walked all over Him. Gabriel's trumpet sounded very discordant notes. When Lucille Mapp, playing Cain's girl, vamped De Lawd, he stayed vamped.

The year 1958 was not only a dynamic year. It was very explosive too. The papers were full of the happenings at Little Rock. Some of them were even saying, "It couldn't happen here". Guns were blasting Quemoy from the mainland of China and the world was again on the brink of war. The *Sunday Dispatch* published a picture of Sir Oswald Mosley sunning himself in Capri.[130] A Negro was very badly beaten up at Shepherd's Bush by nine youths. The papers carried the news that Sunday morning. All the papers.

Notting Hill Gate, London, became a battlefield that evening. It was a pitched battle between Negroes and white Unionists and Empire Loyalists, Fascists and other hooligans. In the midst was a man from a prominent American newspaper.

For weeks we heard nothing more about Little Rock or China. The officers of the West Indies High Commission were very slow in doing anything to improve the situation at Notting Hill Gate.[131] Negroes were being gaoled for defending themselves. They were given heavy sentences. A couple of brothers were found with two empty milk bottles in their car. They were sentenced to six weeks in gaol for carrying dangerous weapons. Every night there was more rioting. Especially at the weekends. The publicity fanned the flames. Molotov cocktails were thrown into the homes of Negroes. Some of them were burnt out. But still it was much safer for them to be in their homes than on the streets.

There was a group of volunteers, many of them Jews. They gave vans and the use of their cars. We formed our own flying squad to get Negroes off the streets by taking them home in the vans and cars and protecting them if attacked. Then we begged the press not to give any publicity to riots. The whole affair quietened down.

Well. They said, "it couldn't happen here". It did. It was not easy to keep the people indoors, I can tell you. The men thought they were being herded into their homes to be burnt alive. They wanted to get out onto the streets with their knives. If we had not been firm in seeing they stayed indoors the gutters of Notting Hill Gate would have run with blood.

On 8th January, 1958, Norman Manley had withdrawn from the first prospective Premiership of the Federation of The West Indies. It is said that while he was away in Trinidad on a conference, his Jamaican militia was taken away without his knowledge and consent by the Colonial Office, to put down a general strike that had taken place in the Bahamas. I did not believe it. Although the Constitution of the Federation still left the leaders basically powerless, it needed a man like Manley to go in there and put it right.

Shortly after the Notting Hill Gate riots he and certain members of the Federation — West Indian leaders — came to London on a fact-finding mission. There was a meeting of responsible West Indians in London at the Howard Hotel. Privately I asked Manley why he gave up the Premiership. He told me there were domestic problems in his party and at the time he had grave fears for its future. I was not impressed. I saw it as the beginning of his decline. Even though he was Premier of Jamaica.

There was a remarkably violent meeting at Friends' House in Euston Road on a Sunday afternoon. With David Pitt and other West Indian leaders, Mr. Rogers, Labour MP for Notting Hill Gate, was also there to explain some nasty things he said about Negroes in the area.[132]

David Pitt opened the attack. He was my doctor. He knew I suffered from hypertension. But I was frightened for him. I thought he would burst a blood vessel. Norman Manley followed. More like Gandhi. Not even a Krishna Menon. The speech of a lawyer pleading a defence. But he told the West Indians to stay where they were and not to leave England. Don't go back home. Carl la Corbiniere, one of the Federal leaders, took up the song. "You just stay put, boys. Don't move. Don't come back." I am certain that none of the governments of the West Indies or the Federation would have lasted six months in power if the bulk of those West Indians had gone back home. So, "Stay put, boys. Don't come back. You are doing good for the West Indies by staying here."

It was comical to witness and I nearly laughed my head off at these lying, deceitful rantings. But it was when Rogers, MP, got up to speak that the anger of the West Indians was uncontrollable. The security forces were stretched to their limits to keep calm. If Mr. Rogers spoke I did not hear him. What emerged from this meeting? The spectre of the Immigration Bill. The spectre of the break-up of the Commonwealth. The spectre of the alarming failure of the Wilberforce programme.[133] Manley went to inspect some of the trouble spots at Notting Hill Gate. He, too, was manhandled.

Yes, 1958 was a terrible year.

I did my usual Christmas stint, singing to the white patients at St. Mary's Hospital, Paddington, and at old folks' homes. I continued to broadcast on television and sound radio as if nothing had happened. Now and then a friend would ask what I thought. I would say I wasn't interested in what happened at Notting Hill Gate. But I was interested in the lie told to us around 1954. When we tried to streamline the oil industry in Trinidad, we were told by the Colonial Office that we had only twelve years of oil left in the soil. Yes, I was interested in that lie. Because the next year, Trinidad Leaseholds Limited was sold to Texaco American for £65 million.[134] Texaco would not have bought those installations for that amount if there were only seven years of oil left. It all boils down to economics. If the British West Indies had been properly looked after by Britain, the West Indians would not have wanted to come to England. The West Indies were Britain's first empire. Then came Africa. Then India. Develop the territories and we wouldn't have come to Britain.

The year 1959 opened tamely in comparison, except that *The Defiant Ones* film was drawing interested crowds to see Sydney Poitier chained to Tony Curtis. They gave brilliant performances. I suppose the happenings of Notting Hill Gate prompted the British Film Academy to do something. Some little thing to show they did not approve of what their people had done at Notting Hill Gate. So they gave Sydney Poitier the Award for the Best Foreign Actor. They invited me to their annual dinner at the Savoy Hotel and asked me to accept the award on his behalf. They should have also given one to Tony Curtis.

We were at table with Sir Michael and Lady Balcon. Owing to this dinner someone suggested that I should apply to the BBC to be trained as a television producer. This I did, and surmounted the barriers one by one. Until, two days before the course started, I was told to get my Government's approval. Trinidad was nearly 5,000 miles away. The High Commissioner of the Federation and I were not on very good terms on account of the Notting Hill Gate affair. But I heard he was in Switzerland, and his deputy was my friend. I phoned him.

"Come on over," he said. I explained the situation, and he said, "I am in charge here now. I am the Commissioner. I want you to be a television producer." He wrote a very short note. The Head of the School was shocked when I put the Government approval on his desk two hours later. He had to take me.

Strange. At the end of the course he invited the students home for a drink. While I was talking to his wife he accused me of trying to seduce her. I was sorry for the poor woman. I stayed another five minutes, and left. Man, I had seen better faces over beer. If they can't get you on one charge, they try something else. When all else fails, they bring you in on a charge of Sex. Is this a sign of fear of the true Negro personality?

My period at Television School was uneventful. I think I brought something substantial to the class. It was the first time they had a singer and actor of films, theatre and television as a student. Each of us had to produce a passing-out programme. The news got around the Negro community that I was studying television and would need artistes for my programme. They telephoned, hammered on my door, and wrote letters. They all wanted to be in my programme. I planned it with Africa in mind. I wanted to surmount the barriers of language, so that education and theatre could go hand in hand.

I wrote my script for camera, sound and action. Light was foremost, of course. It was the simple story of a dream, realised less than five minutes after the dreamer woke up. A dream of love, compassion and the bringing forth of life. The only words, uttered by a disembodied voice, were, "Time shall be no more." There was dancing and singing, flying in an aircraft, and the vision of sunset over the clouds.

The programme was done on closed circuit. Shown at Broadcasting House, Television Centre, Alexandra Palace and Lime Grove, to different viewing panels. It was considered "sensational" and broke new ground for television. However, I have never been given a job as a television producer by the BBC or any television company.

Edric Connor and family in 1956 at Peter Hill, Mayaro,
Trinidad

The Connor family at Peter Hill, Mayaro

Teteron as it appeared on September 8, 1941 immediately
before evacuation

Watching personal effects go, evacuation of Chaguaramas

Jimmy Tardieu of Chaguaramas

House dismantled for removal, evacuation of Chaguaramas

Edric and Pearl Connor on their wedding day, London,
June 1948

Edric Connor as Dagoo in *Moby Dick*, 1954

Edric Connor as Gower in *Pericles*, 1958

Receiving Rita Hayworth in Trinidad, 1955

"Rita Hayworth receives me in Hollywood" (1963)

"Daddy" Worme and his boys. All rebels. A cathedral of
coconut trees in background (Mayaro, Trinidad)

Assessing the fishermen's nets, Mayaro

On taking the children home to Trinidad for the first time
(Geraldine and Peter Connor)

Edric Connor at St. Paul's Cathedral, London

Time to go Home

*M*y coverage of the MCC cricket tour of the West Indies in 1960 would fill a whole book. Yes, another book. There are many people at the BBC who would not like such a book to be written.

My major capture of the 1960 tour was the Trinidad Carnival. It was good to jump in a band. To dance in the streets. Especially when it came to showing my English colleagues how to do the Saga ting down Frederick Street.[135] "Off and on we hugged up anybody and joined in the steel band melody." The Carnival had developed enormously, without any special control. Just the good judgement of the people and their good taste.

I took my cameras to old St. Joseph Road at Laventille and filmed the Marabuntas making their costumes and designs and steel bands. The Marabuntas are called by that name because they are so-called social outcasts.[136] Bad men. I found them very good actors. They even refused my money when I offered them a drink. *They* saw the good I was doing for the Marabuntas.

I took my cameras to the oilfields and to Mayaro. To the Pitch Lake and Maracas Bay and over the fourteen miles of road I made the Americans build to replace the facility of Teteron Bay as the poor man's resort.[137] I filmed the Harbour with its sloops and yawls and sailing vessels as the sun came up at six and the chocolate was about to be boiled. Boys were selling papers, while the women in the red bodice called out "Oranges". I filmed the immortelles in bloom and the gay poui-trees caressing the hills. From Lady Chancellor Road, high above Government House, I filmed thirty cricket matches taking place at the same time in the Grand Savannah, the spectators moving from game to game according to its excitement. Ah, Trinidad, my dearly beloved Trinidad! With its creative people. Who gave me almost all I know about the drama and art and colour. Who gave me the colour and form of the Carnival inspired by its natural surroundings. The film was called *Carnival Fantastique*. The whole island is one vast theatre.

Normally when one receives a laboratory report on colour film, a lot of technical details of heat, colour and temperatures are cabled back to the producer-director. In this case, my laboratory report simply read: "Carnival Fantastic". Hence the title. It was one of two films I had shown at the Edinburgh Festival that year. It turned out to be the best film from the Commonwealth, and one of the 15 best films of the Festival. The other was called *Caribbean Honeymoon No.2*, dealing with British Guiana. It opened the Film Festival. It was the first time in the history of the Edinburgh Festival that any producer sent in two films and had them accepted and shown.

I left Trinidad a tired man, and took a week's rest in Jamaica. In Kingston. I cabled Manley asking him to see me. Because even then my application for pioneer status for film-making in Trinidad had not come through. I thought it might just be possible to get it in Jamaica. I also took a spare copy of the "Third Test Match, Jamaica" with a view to having it shown in Jamaica through one of the leading distributors on a percentage basis. I regret to say Manley roughed me up. I was so tired I cried to soothe my anger. Yet when we got to the door of his office and he was seeing me out, Manley was the sweetest character, and the most genteel on God's earth.

I left his office, went straight to a certain place, and stole all the plans they had been preparing for film-making in Jamaica. So we can say Norman Manley corrupted me. It was very simple. I made photostat copies at Barclay's Bank and replaced the originals. The film distributor was haggling. He wanted my film for nothing, perhaps thinking I would accept anything offered because of the BBC propaganda. I took my film away from him and back to London.

At the hotel in which I stayed lived a missionary. She had come down from America to "give aid to the peasants in the hills", she said. Not necessarily members of the Church, but just to give them monetary aid. I was very suspicious of this and probled a little deeper. Only to find that the fear of Castro, who had thrown out Batista in Cuba, prompted some Americans towards the feeling that the ideas that conquered Cuba would spread to the other West Indian Islands.[138] The Americans have a paranoid fear of Communism. I am sure that woman hardly knew that the people in the hills had never heard the word. Even if they had, they wouldn't know its meaning. They are more interested in the Ras Tafaris, a bearded sect that controls almost one third of the population of Jamaica. Some of them are attached to the Jehovah's Witnesses, who control another third of the population.[139] The other third are of various persuasions. I worked it out by a parallelogram. Jamaica was heading for a benign arrogance. God on one side, Castro on the other, and the devil in the middle.

Before my week ended the police found several caches of arms — cutlasses, hatchets and other missiles — in the vestry and storerooms of a certain local church. This must have been a shock to Manley and the middle class he was building with his so-called elite intelligentsia. The police found the place on the verge of a revolution. That it would have been bloody there is no doubt. I have always wondered what happened to the preacher, his followers and his sons. Were they executed? In spite of all the forces of communication, methods of stifling news are equally powerful. I have reason to believe there have been executions for treason.[140]

After the finding of this plot I decided not to fly straight back to London but to cover areas and islands near to Cuba. To trace the routes of the refugees from Cuba. With every revolution there are always refugees. I stayed a few days in Montego Bay. It was too affluent and therefore insecure for poor people on the run. I flew out to Nassau.

There was something uncanny about Nassau. I came down to the hallway of my hotel. A beautifully dressed woman stood up and made for the door at great speed. The receptionist called her back. She told me she thought I was a member of the Castroite group. One of the Bearded Ones. She was a refugee trying to get to the United States.

Many of these refugees, particularly the women, fleeing with all their money and jewels, are mistreated in Nassau. Men, white and coloured, hold them up to ransom and abuse their bodies. They put them in fear and take away their belongings with promises to get them into the mainland of America and so-called freedom. During the Haitian Revolution of 1791 the refugees went south: to Dominica, Guadeloupe, Martinique, St. Lucia, Grenada and Trinidad. They didn't dare to go to Antigua and Barbados. Simon Bolivar got aid from Pétion, Dessalines and Henri Christophe to wage his wars in South America. Now, with Castro taking over where Simon Bolivar left off, the refugees are going north, to America and Canada.

I flew back to London after having reconciled a few important points of history. My brains had been baked in the sun and it took me two weeks to catch the tempo of thought in the metropolis.

Although we had never met before, in February 1962 Canon Poole, of the new Coventry Cathedral, wrote asking me to meet him at a certain library in Dover Street, London. We were to discuss the consecration of Coventry Cathedral, also the dedication of the Cathedral to the arts.[141] The consecration was to be on the 21st May. The dedication, the 8th June. He was mainly interested in the dedication. He had to preach the sermon. I suggested orchestra, authors, actors, singers, dancers. The service to be done in four parts: the Creation, human needs, his sermon, and the closing ceremony.

I visited Coventry Cathedral three days before the consecration and found a service in progress. A special service for all the people who worked on the construction of the building — on the design and all the artistic elements. Sir Basil Spence, the architect, was there. I photographed him under "Gabriel and the Fallen Angel". This was one of the last pieces of sculpture done by my dear friend, Jacob Epstein. He used his son-in-law as the model for Gabriel. This young man is the brother of Lord Kilbracken, with whom I played in *Moby Dick*. Sir Basil posed patiently for me. He was concerned that I took him near the Devil. "Yes, I am taking you there because I am sure you have had a lot of problems to conquer." "And how!" was his reply. "It was hell. But it's done." The Cathedral had taken seven years to build. The Graham Sutherland tapestries, big as a tennis court, stood behind the altar at the far end of the nave. That is all I'll tell you about it. Go and see for yourself.

At Coventry I met a Jamaican joiner. He was the chief joiner — in control of all the woodwork done in the Cathedral. He was seconded to that job by a motorcar company in Coventry. This man had never been to a technical school but he had all the ancient skills of the master-craftsman.

I saw the consecration on television. The day we dedicated the Cathedral to the arts, Dame Edith Evans represented drama; the late Christopher Hassall, authors. Dame Ninette de Valois and her Royal Covent Garden Ballet represented the dance and I represented the Negro race and song. I had a trio of accompanists: Betty Lawrence, piano; Curly Clayton, guitar; and Brian Brocklehurst, bass. Curly and Brian came in as though they were lost urchins. I was glad they came that way. They looked more like wandering minstrels than musicians.

It was one of the happiest days of my life. We sat in front of a choirstall, Dame Edith on my right and Christopher Hassall on my left. The Cathedral was packed to capacity and more. Over 2,000 people were there. I felt I was on the threshold of a discovery, a great discovery. I began to ask questions, quietly. Then, as if on a screen, a large screen in front of me and just above the choirstall opposite, a figure began to form. Dimly at first; then slowly it sharpened. Inwardly I asked the questions: "Who am I? What is this? What's going on?" And a man appeared out of that figure. He was dressed in dark, flowing robes with white flowing sleeves. He wore no hat. It was a face I had seen before. Where? Where? It was the man I had seen at the airport at Cairo. The man who said, "You are walking upon old streets with new feet." I had also seen that face in an El Greco painting at Toledo. He was a beautiful man, aquiline in features. I quietly asked, "Please reveal more." Six temples changed in quick succession leaving the emblem of the staff and two snakes worn by doctors. Then slowly it faded away. It was time for me to go and recite "The Creation".

"And God stepped out of space, and He looked around and said 'I am lonely. I am going to make me a world.'"

After this poem, Dame Ninette's dancers, nine of them, came out on the altar and around the whole length of the Cathedral. They did Tschaikovsky's "Dance of the Muses". Christopher Hassall read Dylan Thomas's "Fern Hill". Dame Edith read an Old English poem about the Creation. Then I sang my songs of human needs. The human need for food, as expressed in a song from Brazil called "Dry Land". The human need for love, in a Negro wail called "Lef' Away". The human need for understanding, "Lost in Stars", from an adaptation of the book *Cry the Beloved Country*. Then the spiritual needs, from the "Glory Road" by Jacques Wolfe.

O the happiness of that day! As we sang the last hymn I asked one simple question, "Am I controlled by an outside force?" The answer was immediate. For two whole lines I could not sing a note. Then I spoke. "Thank you, God. Thank you." And my voice came back.

After the service was over the people were leaving. I went down to the vestry. As on all occasions of intense happiness I broke away into a quiet corner. The Provost must have discarded his duties. He was down in the vestry so quickly. He had come to say thank you. You could see he meant this because of the way his eyes shone. Then he said, "This Cathedral took seven years to build. For the last three years we have been here organising the consecration and these services of dedication. Over these past two weeks, up there on the altar and in the pulpit, I was not sure whether we had done the right thing — whether we should not have forgotten the rebuilding of the Cathedral — whether the age did not need cathedrals any more. But while you were up there, on the chancel and in front of the altar, saying the Creation and singing your songs, there were times when I wanted to shout, 'Hallelujah! This is it! Hallelujah! We were right!'"

I did not tell him of my experiences. Nor of the revelations. He was only the Provost. He would not have understood. Earlier I had been tortured in my search for truth. I was tortured until I flew to Paris. I found myself in a Roman Catholic church, rich with cloths of gold and lecterns. The wealth of the place was enormous. Overburdened with my thoughts, I asked to see the priest in charge. I suppose he thought I must have been some murderer or ex-convict who had come to confess to some fiendish deed. But I told him I had seen the splendours of the church. Could he guide me as to what I should do in order to be at peace with my soul? And the world in which we live? Tastes have become so shabby. The priest chased me out of his church. I must have been very distressed because an American priest came up to me and asked, "What is the matter, my son?' I told him what had happened. That priest sent me back to London. To a place in Soho Square. This convinced me that the church was in greater need of help than me. That it was possible I had something to give to the church. So the Provost would not have understood what I had to say. We broke off, and I remained to enjoy my happiness.

Earlier in the year Manley called a referendum in Jamaica. He lost. Particularly in the country districts. I remembered the missionary I met in my hotel in Kingston. I understand some of the peasants were told to vote against the Federation because if they had three cows, they would have to give one of them to make it work. After this loss for the ruling party a change of government was academic. With the subsequent secession of Jamaica from the Federation, there were nine units now left in the Federation. Trinidad, and the Little Eight.[142] A general election was called for in Trinidad. It is understood that Reginald Maudling, then Colonial Secretary in the British Government, was sent by Mr. Macmillan, the Prime Minister, with a briefcase full of good things to offer the Don to make federation work. It is further understood that the Don won the election and faced Mr. Maudling with a *fait accompli*. He too was faced with a *fait accompli* by his senior civil servants. They feared a dilution of their power in a Federation. "We want Independence!" The poor man could not discuss the matter any further. He simply had to return to his desk in Great Smith Street. Macmillan purged his Cabinet and kicked Maudling upstairs to become Chancellor of the

Exchequer. Trinidad was on the verge of its independence: Jamaica on 6th August, Trinidad on 31st August, 1962. Leaving a lot of Federal employees and Ministers on the very edge of redundancy.[143]

I had not seen our children for two years. They were sent home to Trinidad for their education – I wished them to have a sense of belonging and experience some of the scenes of their parents' childhood. I did not wish them to be misfits in later years. They were now coming home to London for their August holidays. We met them at the airport. Driving home in the car I asked Peter, "How are things in Trinidad?" His reply was indirect. "Only Independence, Independence, Independence. The papers are full of it. The radio's full of it. Only Independence. As if nothing else matters in the world but Independence." Then a flush of fire came from his eyes. "Daddy, the people want *work!*" My son was only seven and a half years old. He had seen the light. The sparks of his ancestors were lit in his soul. I drew him to me and he was trembling. He was not speaking about any one in particular. He was just speaking about a system.

Three days before the independence of Trinidad, the BBC asked me to do a short resumé of my work and experience up to Independence. My views on independence were very terse. "Independence … For me, independence has always been just a thought away."

On Independence Day I took my wife and children to Westminster Abbey for the religious ceremony. We were joined by Bob and Olive Pattison. I was put to sit in a cubicle at the back of the choir. It seemed to me the song, "I Vow to Thee, my Country", was sung in a pianissimo fashion by the choir so that my voice could soar over theirs as a solo. It really meant something to me, that day. When finished, we sat down. I looked across at Blake's bust by Jacob Epstein. For once I was not alone.

The Don came to London to attend the Prime Ministers' conference.[144] He found Britain in the throes of getting into the Common Market. The Little Eight were herded like forlorn lambs. He must have found out that these forlorn lambs could grow into angry bulls. It was most amazing, after the Prime Ministers' conference, to find the Don working with Edward Heath in Brussels to get Britain into the European Common Market. I suppose, to get in on the ground floor if possible. The Little Eight could be used by Britain to rival any industry or development Jamaica, Trinidad or British Guiana might attempt.

Maudling, as Chancellor of the Exchequer, could not lend Trinidad any money. He hadn't the mandate for it. Although they all worked furiously in Brussels, de Gaulle said "Non". There was a party held by the Trinidad High Commission at the Mayfair Hotel. My wife and I were invited. We were fully dressed. At the point of departure I could not bring myself to attend. It would have been against my conscience. I asked her to go ahead without me. But to tell a certain person that "things in Trinidad are so bad politically even the Prime Minister doesn't want to go home". I understand he got the message. Three days later he flew back to Trinidad.

Men afraid of power are dangerous. Even to themselves. We have some glaring examples of these in Trinidad and in some of the newly independent territories. Some of them seem to enjoy the fanciful titles of Minister of This and That but are terrified to sign a letter offering an increase to a clerk. The Federation of the West Indies broke up because of these men who hadn't the courage to say no. There had been a Federation of the West Indies before. That also collapsed. Almost a lifetime of work had gone into the preparation of this one. Pa Marryshow must have turned in his grave when the deed was done.[145]

The Constitution needed strengthening. We needed Manley in there to give it that strength. Without him the break-up was inevitable. I talked with Hugh Gaitskell about this just three months before he died. He said, "Believe me. My party didn't do it." The enormous size of the tragedy revealed itself glaringly. Hugh was not looking for my vote.[146]

Men are orbiting the earth at 18,000 mph. They are even on their way to the moon. We cannot think of the West Indies as an isolated region when we are thinking in terms of the world. If the British West Indies Federation had succeeded, Puerto Rico would have joined it. Then Martinique and Guadeloupe. And, who knows, we have now snuffed out the inspiration that the South American territories might have needed to bring about their own Federation of the United States of South America. The Chaguaramas Naval Air Base, which was to have been the Federal capital of the West Indies, is now a missile-tracking station.

It is said in certain quarters that the break-up of the West Indies Federation had to be so that it could be used as a precedent for the break-up of the Federation of Central Africa. To allow Nyasaland and Northern Rhodesia to go their own ways. If that be the case, then what a waste of time and money! What a waste of effort and people! Very, very few West Indians have ever been in the Central African territories. They have not seen the backwardness that British colonialism imposed there. The dismantling of that Federation would have come of its own accord in the same way as the independence of so many other British and French territories in Africa.

I was lecturing one evening down in Sussex. A call came through from Hollywood asking whether I would care to take part in a film. Of course I would. The only difficulty about the trip would be my American visa. I was quite prepared to test it. While waiting, another offer came for me to play in a Spanish film in North-West Africa. They seem to have wanted me very badly. The pressures were great. Telegrams were exchanged with Hollywood. I was told to wait. Then the film company sent a qualifying telegram and my passage via BOAC. I took the telegram to the American Embassy, Grosvenor Square. The investigations began all over again.

I went ahead calmly preparing for my trip. I was called to the Embassy. I was kept five hours that afternoon waiting for the visa. Before the passport was handed to me there was a long and searching discussion. A very affable Consul. He seemed a real human being, with a wife and children. He handed me the passport. Explained the designation, HI, which, he said, can be read as "Highly Important". He would show how highly important I was by being the first to bow and scrape to me. Then he asked whether I belonged to the Workers' Music Association. I began to search my mind. It took me back to 1944 when I started my career in England. I had received a letter from the Association asking me to be one of its Vice-Presidents. I looked at the list of Vice-Presidents that headed the letter and found among them Dr. Ralph Vaughan-Williams and Benjamin Britten. Two world-famous British composers. It had not taken me long to make up my mind. If the Workers' Music Association was good for Britten and Vaughan-Williams, it should be good for Edric Connor. I replied, accepting the Vice-Presidency. That was all the Americans had against me. The Consul said the Association was used as a Communist front. They were highly suspicious of anyone connected with it.[147] I grew so angry I began to tremble as if standing on a violent earthquake. I threw the passport against the wall of the office. If that was all the Americans had against me, I didn't care to go to America. Apparently this man had done a considerable amount of work to get me my visa. He now had to persuade me to accept it. He ended by saying, "Not all Americans are the same."

I left for Hollywood on Saturday morning, 1st June, 1963. Dave Horowitz, for the film company, and Mike Rosen, son of my agent, met me at the airport. They made me welcome and comfortable.

I went to America without a contract. The only contract I had was my return ticket. I had not seen the script. I knew the film was called *Four for Texas*. I was driven round to the Chateau Marmont on Sunset

Boulevard. Five minutes after I entered the hotel, as if my progress had been watched by television from the airport, the telephone rang and the secretary of the producer wanted to know my whereabouts. Where she could send me the script that day. I had to be at Wardrobe by 9 o'clock next morning and before the cameras around midday.

Dave collected the script and Mike drove me to his parents' home in Van Nuys. Shortly after, Mike took me on the Freeway. "You'll have to travel on this road every day to the studio so you might as well learn to drive on it," he said. All the vehicles were travelling hairsbreadth and dangerously, at high speed. After 90 minutes we returned to his home for dinner. I couldn't eat. It was my first trip to Hollywood. After my so-called dinner Mike again took me on to the Freeway. To teach me how to drive on this suicide strip at night. Life could be hard yet fleeting. After two hours of night driving I felt a match for anything there was in America. Quite ready to take on President Kennedy, if necessary.

At the studio Charley James was waiting for me at 9 o'clock to have me fitted out. They looked at me in make-up. I was OK. A natural. Then Dave collected me and took me to meet Bob Aldrich. I had seen him on television in London but we had never met before.[148]

He has such a delicate speaking voice I would like to hear him sing. Like John Huston, his birthday is one week after mine, 9th August. Most of my work was done with Dean Martin, Nick Dennis and Mike Muzurky. The processes of film-making are just the same as in England. They have greater facilities and, I suppose, a lot more money. They have been in the business well over 50 years. I allowed myself three weeks to find what made the place tick. During that time I concentrated on my work and whatever research I could do. Then I began to do guestings on sound radio and television.

My first guesting was on a sound radio disc-jockey programme which goes out from the Crescendo Restaurant. At 11:30 that evening I was on the air. Within ten minutes Rita Hayworth and Bob Schiffer and his wife came into the studio. I could see them from the fishbowl. Rita came right in, threw her arms around me, and kissed me solidly. She demanded to be put on the air. The D.J. was displeased. He tried to push her out. It was embarrassing. "Please. This is my friend. I am on the air with you, therefore it is my programme. I am the guest. Now Miss Hayworth is my guest. Ladies and gentlemen, I shall give Miss Rita Hayworth five minutes on my programme."

Rita went on and paid tribute to me. I could never have imagined she thought so highly of me. When we worked in Trinidad and Tobago she was very offhand and sometimes even rude. It was only then I knew what truly happened. She said so on the air. *Fire Down Below* was her first film for three years. During that time she was a fair target for the press and gossip columnists all over the world. The film company asked her not to be seen near to me. Not even to be kind to me. For fear we both would be made into another scandal. Then she ended her speech by saying, "They didn't want us to be photographed together except in the film itself. But when he has finished here and we go into the hall I am going to have a dozen pictures taken with him." I settled for one. And all these years I had thought she hated my guts.

She had had her friends at dinner and heard the programme. Heard me being announced on the air. Knowing the point from which the programme was being broadcast — apparently she had already finished dinner — she dragged her guests down to the Crescendo. Especially when she found out Bob Schiffer knew me. He was the chief make-up artiste on the film. Rita turned out not only to be a lady, but the princess I always admired her as. Many were the evenings she and her beautiful daughter, Yasmin, entertained me in their lovely home in Beverly Hills.

A remarkable person I met was Jonah Ruddy, representative of the *Daily Mail* and many other English papers. Jonah was a rebel. A man after my own heart. We would go out together on evenings debunking phonies. Jonah passed on less than a year after we met. From cancer.

My home from home was that of Larry Getz and Flora Mock and their two lovely daughters, Laurie and Kathy. Larry and Flora are two film directors trained at University College, Los Angeles. Two of the finest Americans I have ever met. They were introduced to me by Jonah Ruddy. They certainly showed me around. On the day I left Hollywood I did not get back to the Chateau until five in the morning — to pack and catch the plane at eight o'clock. They are rebels, too.

In the studio, Johnny Indrisano, ex-world-welterweight boxing championship contender, kept me fit for my fight scenes. He took me to a YMCA gym off Hollywood Boulevard on Saturdays and the studio gym on weekdays.

While I was in Hollywood Cassius Clay (later Muhammed Ali) was fighting Henry Cooper in England. The day before the fight, in an argument on the studio floor, I warned that Clay was wide open to a straight left or left hook. He would at least be knocked down. We took bets. I collected a lot of money next day. Johnny Indrisano had me meet Ted Post and his wonderful family. We spent many hours watching films of the career of that brute called Jack Dempsey. Neither Clay,

Liston nor Patterson would have had a ghost of a chance with him. He would have murdered them.[149]

There were times I ate at Schwab's, at Gigi's and at Villa Frascati. Doris Nieh, a very fine photographer, Chinese, took me around sometimes. We went together to Disneyland and the Hollywood Bowl. She took me up on the hills and tempted me. But I did not cast myself down. I would like to meet all these friends again.

I became very friendly with Maidie Norman, a brilliant Negro actress. We were together very often during my three months in Hollywood. Through Maidie I was able to see behind the facade of Negro life there. We attended a big ball at a Negro Doctors' Convention. There was a big Negro who sang a blues while we were dancing. I made the comment in her ear, "That's the trouble with the Blues. We don't know how to end them." I do not think she caught my meaning. I hardly saw anybody there that evening who was relaxed. Many of them were medical millionaires. We don't know how to end them.

I was entertained at the home of the Negro actress who played in the *Imitation of Life*, Juanita Moore. Present were about ten of the leading Negro actors in Hollywood. We had a frank discussion of our positions. They wanted to know how long I was staying. I put their minds at ease. "Only for this film." That night they nearly had a fight. One said he knew Canada Lee a lot better than the other.

It seems I must have made an impression. Most Negro actors cultivated a grey streak of hair, from the widow's peak in the middle of the head. What surprised the Negro community of Hollywood was the 16 mm copy of the film, *Carnival Fantastique,* which I took along with me. They could not imagine there were Negroes with such high theatrical standards in any other part of the world.

I was in Hollywood in time to see the famous Negro March on Washington. Although I was invited to go to Washington I declined. I was a guest of the country. I saw it on television. I was very much impressed with the organisation and glad to hear Martin Luther King tell the people to return home.[150] Not to lie down and think it was over, but to press the need for their freedom. The Black Muslims worried me. I am still to be convinced they are right. Oh, the need for Negro leadership in the United States.

Throughout Hollywood and in the studios I found a strong undercurrent of waste. Perhaps the outcome of the computer age. A job here for the Efficiency Experts. Everyone seemed concerned about civil rights. They pressed me for statements which, as a guest of the country,

I could not make. But I made observations. I found few in America called for punishment on those who let loose the dogs, turned on the hoses and used the electric cattle-prods. On Negroes. This frightened me. America has 165 million citizens of other races ...

However, I think I have been able to get near to a reason for this. Kennedy made great promises to the Negro. Over the last few years the American intellectuals have been toying with the philosophy and theory of violence in their writings. I presume that is the reason Kennedy invited them into the White House — in the hope that he would collectively draw their sting. We know Kennedy was not interested in violence in his own country — but violence in Vietnam, violence in the Congo. A few other places. The Bay of Pigs, for instance. Kennedy died violently. In his own country. It is one of the greatest tragedies of our time. It should concern each of us in this universe. It comes of the delinquency of the age and the paranoia of our times.[151]

The psychiatrists have wreaked mental havoc in Hollywood. Every individual is searching for a telltale stammer. The psychiatrists have made Hollywood a town of questions. They are the ones who are truly responsible for Method acting. But they have not told their patients Method acting simply prepares the student to learn to act. That is why Method actors overact so much. I could name a few of them.[152]

I attended a party at Beverly Hills at the home of a psychiatrist and, I believe, there were a lot of mad people there. For nothing I told him he could cure all those people in one evening. Just by making them give free movements to any of three types of drumming: African, West Indian, or Brazilian. That is all Hollywood needs as far as psychiatry is concerned.

Apart from Bob Aldrich, my two real bosses were Dean Martin and Frank Sinatra. I left a lot of unfinished business in Hollywood. But the three-month visa ended. I take great pleasure in keeping my end of a bargain.

I returned to London to some grave domestic problems.[153] Three weeks in Glasgow at the Citizen's Theatre, *The Physicists*, helped to relieve some of the strain. Another two weeks in the television play *The Avengers* helped further.

An instalment of *Espionage* for television was extremely satisfying. I was able to simulate a character who was legend and alive — Jomo Kenyatta — in a episode called "The Snows on Mount Kama". One of the most satisfying and worthwhile things I have done.[154]

Coventry called me again. The Rev. Simon Phipps, industrial chaplain, wanted to work on a new-style service. The first thing we did was cut out the sermon. Read the Bible, yes. But illustrate it with its counterpart in modern poetry and prose, music and song. With the congregation participating in the readings and the singing. Coventry Cathedral was my platform, on my birthday, 2nd August 1964. From here I say, "I do not believe any more. I *know*. Belief implies doubt. Knowledge rests on fact."

That morning we had a Communion Service with a violence unparalleled by any I have witnessed in the Church of England. A German girl partnered me. Coventry is my platform. From there I say there will be many uprisings in Africa. The Independence Movement has put many good men into power. But wherever you find the lion you also find the jackal. The jackals will not easily be moved. But the people will rise up and remove them. A United States of South America will develop, more for self-protection than anything else. The third World War, which may commence on Lobenguela's lands, will not be one of isms and powers. It will be the final struggle between good and evil. And will involve all races, creeds, nations and peoples.

It is time to go home now. The train is slowing down. It is time to go home. The land needs tending and I am head of the family. I must set an example. Yes, I have explored beyond the horizons of my ocean to the East. And dug deep beyond the mountains way out in the West. What have I found? People. More people. And fighting.

It is time to go home now. To plant some new coconut trees and oranges, mangoes and sapodillas. The peacocks have gone. I must get a brace to replace them. Ah yes, and some irises — the kind Hugh Gaitskell talked to me about. They should grow in our soil. Perhaps I shall prepare a special bed for them.

The train is slowing down, and the people are leaving. I must talk to them. To the children.

Listen to me, for a change! Somewhere in your imagination lies your ideal. Go forward to meet it with a song on your lips and a theme in your heart. It is like the horizon. A promise. Not a boundary. The more it eludes your grasp, the further you go into the vast Unknown. Do not be disheartened, because imagination is as vast as the universe itself. Pray, and work. Prayer links the mind of man with a greater Mind. Work overcomes limitations.

It is time for me to go home now.

Notes to the Autobiography

1. Agustin Barrios was a guitarist and composer from Paraguay, Andres Segovia a Spanish guitarist, Marian Anderson an African-American contralto.

2. The end of World War I, Armistice Day, was on November 11, 1918. Kaiser Wilhelm was the German emperor before and during the war, whom the victorious Allies held to be responsible for its outbreak and long continuation.

3. Parlatuvier was a remote village on the northern coast of Tobago (see map). In the early decades of the last century, people from the leeward villages like Moriah went there by boat to plant and tend crops. It was inaccessible by road to wheeled traffic well into the twentieth century.

4. An ajoupa is a small house, made of wattle and daub walls and a thatched roof, usually with palm leaves.

5. Or, in the Tobago vernacular, 'len' han'.

6. Connor gives a lively description of Spiritual or Shouter Baptist modes of worship, including 'catching the power' — falling into an ecstatic trance — and 'speaking in tongues', talking or shouting in an unknown language under the guidance of the Holy Spirit. 'Doption' (adoption) is a type of quick, forcible breathing which can hasten the trance state during a service.

7. The Warden was the chief administrative officer of a district (Ward or Ward Union) in Trinidad.

8. String bands, to accompany dances, were very common in the villages of Trinidad and Tobago at this period. The castillian, paseo and passé doble are traditional couple dances of Spanish or Venezuelan origin. The vie et quoix, or Vieille Croix (cross-wake), is a Catholic ceremony dedicated to telling the story of the crucifixion and resurrection of Christ, associated in Trinidad with the French Creole (patois) speaking rural folk.

9. Captain A.A. Cipriani and William Howard-Bishop were the main leaders of the Trinidad Workingmen's Association (see Introduction). Connor is probably recalling the 1925 elections for the Legislative Council (the first in Trinidad), when Cipriani was campaigning for the Port of Spain seat, which he won.

10. The first successful oil wells were drilled in the Guayaguayare area in Trinidad's 'deep south' region, in the early 1900s. See Introduction.

11. There was no paved road along Trinidad's east coast in the 1920s, during Connor's boyhood. The beach was the road and travel could be done (by foot or on horse, donkey or mule) only at low tide.

12. Austin and Vallee were popular American singers and songwriters; Al Jolson, born in Lithuania, was a Broadway entertainer; Paul Whiteman was the leader of a jazz band. They were all well known in the 1920s (and later).

13. In the 1920s and 1930s, several South African managers or supervisors were employed in the Trinidad oilfields. Their crude racism and brutal methods of 'handling' workers were one of the reasons for the oilfield strikes and riots of 1937 (see Introduction).

14.   Gordon Grant & Co., a large, locally owned firm, took over (often through foreclosure) many smaller cocoa estates in eastern and southeastern Trinidad during the cocoa boom years and just after (c.1900–1930).

15.   In Trinidad folklore, the *soucouyant* is an old woman who sheds her skin, travels as a ball of fire, and sucks people's blood at night; the *legahoo* or *lagahoo* is a person who takes the form of an animal at night.

16.   A 'crocos' or 'crocus' bag is a loosely woven brown jute sack.

17.   *Marchandes* are female vendors or hucksters; float and accra is a street food consisting of *acra*, a deep-fried saltfish and flour fritter, together with *float*, a deep-fried flat biscuit; Bajan cake is probably the same as 'bellyful', a heavy, sweet bun or cake made from pieces of stale cake.

18.   Cocoa contractors were peasants who planted and tended cocoa (or coconut) trees on a piece of land, in return for a fixed cash payment per tree from the landowner when the trees were ready to bear.

19.   The *Port of Spain Gazette* was founded in 1825, the *Trinidad Guardian* in 1917.

20.   Because of the poor road system, the establishment of cocoa and coconut estates along the eastern and southern coasts of Trinidad in the late 1800s and early 1900s was facilitated by government coastal steamers which served both coastal Trinidad communities and Tobago. After 1916 the SS *Belize* was the only coastal steamer. Small rowboats brought the cargo and passengers ashore, as the steamer had to anchor some distance offshore.

21.   Boiled chocolate or cocoa tea is a hot sweet drink made by boiling milk with ground 'cocoa sticks' or 'creole chocolate', hard sticks of processed cocoa flavoured with spices. Bul-jol is a dish made with salted fish, onions, tomatoes, pepper and oil. Souse is made with pig's feet marinated in vinegar or lime juice with pepper, onion and cucumber.

22.   Belair or belé is a graceful dance performed mostly by women in traditional Creole dress (see note 26); loosely it refers to any drum dance.

23.   A cuatro is a small, four-stringed guitar.

24.   In the early twentieth century, many small and medium landowners all over Trinidad lost their estates, often through foreclosure, to larger, generally white-owned firms which had extended credit on mortgage to them, especially in the boom years of cocoa (c.1880–1920).

25.   Watchicongs are cheap rubber-soled canvas shoes.

26.   The *douillette* is a long dress with a wide skirt and tight bodice with puffed sleeves, a traditional Creole costume for women in Trinidad brought there from the French West Indies, especially Martinique. The madras headscarf was a square plaid (tartan) cotton head-tie, usually worn with the *douillette*. The way it was tied was supposed to indicate the wearer's marital status or availability for courtship. Ma Laffy, at 50, was 'past it', not looking for a suitor.

27.   The lengthy account of emancipation and post-emancipation history in Trinidad which follows is a generally romanticized version of events. See Introduction.

28.   The Morant Bay Rebellion in Jamaica in 1865 was led by the black peasant Paul Bogle, and the mixed-race politician George William Gordon (both executed in the ferocious reprisals unleashed by the governor, Edward Eyre, formerly an explorer of Australia). It did not have a great impact on Trinidad.

29.   Family land — land owned by a kin group in common, descendants from the original purchaser in the 1800s who was often an ex-slave, which cannot be alienated, and to which all members of the descent group have customary access — was an important institution throughout the Caribbean. It helps to explain the existence, by the early 1900s, of black landowning families in places like Mayaro, some of them prosperous enough to educate their sons in Britain.

30.   Until the mid-twentieth century, most teachers in Trinidad entered the profession through the monitor or pupil-teacher system. A promising boy or girl in a primary school would become a pupil-teacher (monitor), teaching the smaller children while studying for teachers' certificate examinations under the headmaster/mistress. On passing the various examinations, the young person became a qualified teacher.

31.   The Royal Victoria Institute (RVI) and the Board for Industrial Training (BIT) at this period jointly administered training and classes for young apprentices in the various technical and craft skills. The recruits, like Connor, came from t0he upper forms of the primary schools. From 1907 the RVI/BIT awarded two or three 'trade bursaries' each year to boys aged 14 to 16 who came out top in special examinations.

32.   See note 31.

33.   At this time in Trinidad sums were expressed both in British pounds, shillings and pence, and in local dollars. The pound was worth $4.80 and 24 cents equalled one shilling (1/ –), eight pence (8d) equalled 16 cents.

34.   Mauby is a sweetened drink made from the bitter bark of a local tree.

35.   The Ozanam shelter, named after the nineteenth-century French social worker and founder of the St. Vincent de Paul Society, Frederick Ozanam, was established at Duncan Street, in a slum area of Port of Spain, as a cheap hostel for poor workers. Borstal is a British term for a reformatory, an institution for young offenders.

36.   Queen's Royal College, first founded in 1857, was Trinidad's leading grammar school for boys. At this period nearly all its pupils were upper or middle class, so the son of a black peasant family like Connor could have little expectation of going there. Its prestige, both academic and social, was very high. The City and Guilds Institute of London was a leading British technical examining body which certified technical and artisanal skills; these examinations were administered through the BIT from 1918, and local apprentices like Connor took them in Trinidad. The Stephens Gold Medal was awarded for excellent performance in these examinations; it was named for Bruce Stephens, a benefactor of the RVI/BIT.

37.   Whe whe is a gambling, 'numbers' game of Chinese origin, very popular in Trinidad. The depression, linked to the US Depression which began in 1929, had a profound impact on Trinidad; see Introduction.

38.   The pomerac is a fruit with a red or pink skin and white flesh, pear-shaped. *Pomme cythere* is the French Creole name for another edible fruit.

39.   V.S. Naipaul retold this famous Port of Spain legend in *Miguel Street* (1959), his first novel, with stories based on his childhood in Port of Spain during the war and postwar years; he calls the hero Man-Man.

40.   The Royal Victoria Institute, De Luxe cinema and Princes' Building, all in Port of Spain, were the best known venues for concerts and shows in the 1930s.

41.   Yehudi Menuhin was a famous American violinist, Mischa Elman a Russian-born American violinist, and Zinka Milanov a Croatian operatic soprano. See note 1 for Barrios and Segovia. Barrios was actually from Paraguay not Mexico.

42.   Here, in his typically understated way, Connor hints at the pervasive racism of Trinidad and Tobago society in the 1930s, which guaranteed that his picture (as a dark-skinned person) would be summarily rejected in favour of 'pretty' (light-skinned) individuals.

43.   Anansi stories are traditional African folktales about the adventures of the trickster, Anansi the spider, known throughout the Caribbean.

44.   All well-known film stars of the era.

45.   De Wilton Rogers was a pioneering Trinidadian novelist and playwright. Later he was a founding member of the People's National Movement, and wrote about the history of the party (see Introduction).

46.   Ten Commandments bare: that is, ten toes, barefooted.

47.   The Shouters Prohibition Ordinance was enacted in 1917, making the holding of public Shouter or Spiritual Baptist services illegal; it was repealed in 1951. Shango or Orisha devotees were also prosecuted under nineteenth-century anti-Obeah laws.

48.   Beryl McBurnie was the leading pioneer in researching, choreographing and performing traditional Trinidadian dance forms, beginning as a young woman in the late 1920s. In 1948 she founded the Little Carib Theatre in Port of Spain, where most of the prominent names in Trinidad dance worked. She died in 2000.

49.   These 'prophesies' look forward to the building of the Chaguaramas Naval Base during World War II, when the whole of the northwest peninsula of Trinidad was cleared of its residents, including the village of Mount Pleasant, and fishing in the surrounding seas was prohibited. See chapter three.

50.   Alupha Shekbewn and his Order of Melchisedek were one of several groups and individuals in Trinidad at this time, who protested the Italian invasion of Ethiopia in 1935, and who looked to Ethiopia and its ancient traditions and history as a symbol of race pride in the African Diaspora.

51.   Tubal Uriah 'Buzz' Butler, a Grenadian immigrant to Trinidad, was the major labour leader of the 1930s and 1940s; he led the hunger marches of 1934–

37, and the campaigns in the oil belt in the same years which culminated in the island-wide strikes and riots of 1937. See Introduction.

52. Sir Claude Hollis was governor of Trinidad and Tobago 1929–36, Sir Murchison Fletcher 1936–38.

53. For Charlie King and the events of June–July 1937, see Introduction. Volunteer forces, nearly all middle- or upper-class young men and many of them civil servants, were summoned to help the regular troops to repress the popular movement. Connor, whose sympathies would have been with the strikers and rioters, refused to 'volunteer' during the crisis.

54. Adrian Cola Rienzi, an Indo-Trinidadian lawyer and politician, was Butler's major trade union and political ally during this period, as well as his lawyer. For the Moyne Commission of 1938–39, see Introduction. Its chairman, Lord Moyne, was later assassinated by Jewish partisans in Cairo in 1944.

55. Walter Citrine, Secretary of the British Trades Union Council (TUC), was a member of the Commission. Its Report was written in 1939, but publication was delayed until 1945 so that its searing indictment of British colonialism in the Caribbean could not be used for German propaganda during World War II. However, a summary of its recommendations was issued in 1940, and some were implemented during the war years.

56. See Introduction for these men, all important figures in the political, cultural and literary world of Trinidad in the 1930s to 1950s.

57. Charles Lindberg, the famous American aviator, flew into Trinidad several times during the 1930s, opening up air routes for what became PANAM.

58. St Patrick floats were coastal barges plying between Port of Spain and the south-west coast of Trinidad (County of St. Patrick).

59. In the early 1940s, German U-boats (submarines) were extremely active in Caribbean waters, causing massive losses to Allied and neutral shipping.

60. For the US Bases in Trinidad, see Introduction.

61. Sam Brownes are rifles; chichi means pretentious, over-dressed, affected.

62. Here Connor is referring to events in the Sino-Japanese War, which began in 1937 when Japan invaded, and occupied, large parts of China.

63. In 1940, a British expeditionary force in France was evacuated from that country across the English Channel in an epic sea operation in May–June 1940, following the surrender of France to Nazi Germany.

64. The Spanish admiral, Apodoca, destroyed his own ships in the Gulf of Paria in February 1797, rather than allow them to be captured by the much larger British force which invaded and seized Trinidad. This force was commanded by General Ralph Abercromby, technically British Trinidad's first governor. Trinidad was formally ceded to Britain by the Treaty of Amiens in 1802. The famous British writer Charles Kingsley visited Trinidad in 1869–70 and published a book about the island, *At Last A Christmas in the West Indies*.

65. Erwin Rommell, a top German wartime general, was very successful in campaigns against the Allies in North Africa in 1941; Pearl Harbour in Hawaii

was bombed by Japanese forces on December 7, 1941, the event which finally brought the USA into the war as an ally of Britain.

66.   Trinidad had been, ever since the Venezuelan Wars of Independence in the early 1800s, a traditional base and haven for Venezuelan political exiles, often plotting to return. Juan Vincente Gomez was dictator of Venezuela from 1909 to his death in 1935.

67.   Winston Churchill, wartime Prime Minister of Britain (1940–45), was in power when the Bases or Lend Lease agreements were negotiated; see Introduction.

68.   The Tardieus were the most important family of land and boat owners in the northwest peninsula of Trinidad at the time of its evacuation. Members of this family are still seeking compensation for their wartime losses.

69.   Harold Simmons was a Saint Lucian pioneer folklorist, painter, writer and educator. See Introduction for Connor's reply in the *Trinidad Guardian*, March 5, 1943.

70.   See Introduction for more on Connor's lecture in July 1943, an important event which profoundly influenced many middle-class blacks; the text of the 'repeat' lecture delivered in December 1943 is included in this book as an appendix.

71.   The Tuskegee Institute in Alabama was founded by Booker T. Washington in 1881, to provide technical and practical education to African-Americans.

72.   Audrey Jeffers was an African-Trinidadian who founded the Coterie of Social Workers and was very active in social welfare work in the 1920s–50s. She was very race-conscious, and was an active politician, being the first woman of Trinidad and Tobago to be elected to a municipal corporation (that of Port of Spain, in 1936) and to sit in the colony's legislature (1946). Sir Bede Clifford was governor 1942–47.

73.   See notes 54 and 55 for the Moyne Commission and its report.

74.   Dora Ibberson, a British professional social worker, came to Trinidad in the early 1940s to set up and run the new Social Welfare department, as recommended by the Moyne Commission.

75.   See Introduction for the Trinidad and Tobago Youth Council (TTYC).

76.   Seabees: CBs, the Construction Brigade (engineers) of the US Army.

77.   The steel bands were emerging during World War II, but, because carnival was banned in 1942, 1943, 1944 and 1945, their existence was little known outside the working-class suburbs of Port of Spain where they were based. Only with the Carnival-like street celebrations held on VE Day (May 8, 1945) did their existence, and remarkable music, burst on the public consciousness. Created mainly by working-class young black men from Port of Spain, the early steel bands were generally disapproved of by the middle and upper classes, of all colours.

78.   Lennox Pierre was an African-Trinidadian lawyer, a strong supporter of local culture, and one of the few middle-class Trinidadians who supported the steel bands in their early days. He was active in the TTYC as a young man.

79.	For Paul Robeson, and his Council on African Affairs, see Introduction.
80.	D-Day, the Allied invasion of France, took place in June 1944; ships were crossing the Atlantic in preparation for this action early in 1944.
81.	The Colonial Centre was one of several hostels for colonial students in Britain, run on behalf of the Colonial Office at this time.
82.	Margery Perham was a well-known British academic, an expert on issues of colonial government and constitutional decolonization.
83.	Una Marson was a well-known Jamaican journalist, poet and feminist activist; she lived in London, and freelanced with the BBC in the 1940s.
84.	Margot Fonteyn (British) and Robert Helpmann (Australian) were famous ballet dancers of this period
85.	These were the infamous 'Doodlebugs' rocket bombs, deployed towards the end of the war (1944–45).
86.	The Shouters Prohibition Ordinance was in fact not repealed until 1951. For 'Pain Oer Ka Mange' — Connor's idiosyncratic spelling — see Introduction.
87.	Alfred Lunt and Lynn Fontaine were a beloved husband and wife team of stage actors, who flourished in the 1920s–50s.
88.	The Conservatives under Churchill were defeated, and the Labour Party under Clement Attlee won a landslide victory in elections held soon after the end of the war. Rationing and general austerity continued in Britain for several years after the war's end in 1945.
89.	Maxim's was a famous Paris restaurant; '*pissoirs*' are urinals (the British traditionally mocked public toilet facilities in France).
90.	For the TTYC, and the 1947 Prague World Youth Congress, see Introduction.
91.	Tomas Masaryk was a Czech politician who served as president of his country before World War II.
92.	Sir John Shaw was governor 1947–50.
93.	The Stokers' Dance is performed by 'sailors' in a carnival masquerade band, depicting coal stokers or firemen on steam ships; they hold long-handled shovel-like tools in front and do small, graceful, winding movements and steps. 'Tobo' or 'taba' foot is a condition of thickening of the skin on the sole of the foot, and the dance probably depicted the movements of someone afflicted with it.
94.	N.N. Nethersole was a close associate of Norman Manley of Jamaica. He was a lawyer, a trade union leader and a government minister in People's National Party (PNP) ministries under Manley. Theodore Sealy was a long term, and very influential, editor of the *Gleaner*, Jamaica's leading newspaper. Alexander Bustamante was the giant (along with his cousin Manley) of Jamaican political and labour movements between the late 1930s and his retirement in 1967. He founded the Jamaican Labour Party (JLP) and was the first Prime Minister of independent Jamaica (1962).
95.	The Fabian Society, first founded in 1884, was a group of left-wing British intellectuals, who believed in gradual, non-violent progress towards socialism.

It had always taken a keen interest in colonial issues, and its cheap publications were eagerly read by anti-colonial intellectuals in the 1930s and 1940s.

96.   Lobengula (the usual spelling) was king of the Matabele in the last few decades of the nineteenth century. His territory was in what became Rhodesia in southern Africa, now Zambia and Zimbabwe. His forces were defeated by Cecil Rhodes's agents in 1893, and he died the next year.

97.   The large influx of West Indian immigrants to post-war Britain is traditionally seen as starting with the arrival of the immigrant ship *Emperor Windrush* in 1948.

98.   Connor had clearly read Eric Williams's *Capitalism and Slavery* (1944), as this paragraph outlines one of the major themes of that book.

99.   Robeson, a Marxist activist, was persona non grata with the US government, and Connor's association with him was one factor which prevented his obtaining a US visa for several years. See Introduction.

100.   Ira Aldridge was an African-American who became famous in the middle decades of the nineteenth century as one of the very few black actors on the British stage.

101.   Zoltan and Alexander Korda were both well-known, Hungarian-born US film producers.

102.   The first mention of Connor's family is this reference to his daughter Geraldine (to whom, along with his son Peter, Connor dedicated his autobiography).

103.   For the visit by the Trinidad All Steel Percussion Orchestra (TASPO) to the Festival of Britain in 1951, see Introduction.

104.   The Lord Kitchener (Aldwyn Roberts) began his calypso career in 1943, and was still singing when he died in 2000; along with The Mighty Sparrow, he was Trinidad's most famous calypsonian of the second half of the last century. Boscoe Holder is a well-known Trinidadian dancer, choreographer and painter.

105.   This is the first mention of Pearl (Nunez) Connor, Connor's wife. See Introduction, and 'My Life with Edric Connor' by Pearl Connor-Mogotsi.

106.   Sam Wanamaker was an American actor and film director, and the person responsible for reconstructing the Shakespearean Globe Theatre in London.

107.   Elizabeth II's coronation was on June 2, 1953.

108.   The Rapallo Pact, in 1922, was an agreement between Weimar Germany and Lenin's USSR.

109.   The 'Fuzzywuzzies' were Hadendoa warriors from Sudan, who supported the nineteenth-century Mahdi in his rising against British/Egyptian control. General Charles Gordon was killed in Khartoum in January 1885, when the Mahdi's forces took the besieged city.

110.   Connor (with hindsight) is referring to the Suez Canal crisis in 1956, when Egyptian leader Gamal Nasser nationalized the canal.

111.   The Mau Mau rising against the British, mainly involving the Kikuyu people of Kenya and led by Jomo Kenyatta, was in full swing in 1953.

112.   John Huston was a famous American film producer.

113.   Connor refers to the period when sailing ships gradually gave way to coal-powered steamships, in the later decades of the nineteenth century, and when the skills associated with crewing sailing ships became largely obsolete.

114.   Max Schmeling was a great German boxer, who was famously defeated by the African-American champion Joe Louis.

115.   Connor's visit to Trinidad and Tobago was late in 1955. Under the 1950 constitution a measure of self-government had been granted, which was enlarged by the new constitution that came into effect in 1956. The trade union movement had also developed considerably since 1937.

116.   Bobol is Trinidadian vernacular for corruption.

117.   For the emergence of the 'don' (Eric Williams), and the formation of his People's National Movement (PNM) in January 1956, see Introduction. The PNM won power nine, not four, months after its founding in September 1956, and its victory at the elections was in fact very narrow (13 out of 24 elective seats in the legislature).

118.   In the following paragraphs, Connor describes the international crisis in 1956 over the nationalization of the Suez Canal by Nasser, the charismatic Egyptian president. It brought about the resignation of Anthony Eden, the British Prime Minister at the time.

119.   Commesse is Trinidad vernacular for a confused, noisy quarrel or disorder.

120.   Military forces of the USSR ruthlessly crushed an anti-Soviet popular rising in Hungary in 1956.

121.   Dulles was US Secretary of State in President Dwight Eisenhower's administration in 1956.

122.   Crick! Crack! is a traditional formula for ending a story in the Trinidad folklore tradition. The teller says Crick! and the audience answers Crack! It may be of African origin.

123.   The don, the new Chief Minister of Trinidad and Tobago under the 1956 constitution was, of course, Williams. For the Federation/Chaguaramas issue, see Introduction.

124.   Norman Manley, Premier of Jamaica, was active in the negotiations and meetings leading up to the formation of the Federation of The West Indies in1958, though, like Williams, he declined to leave office in his own country in order to lead the Federal government, despite very general expectations that he would be the first Prime Minister of The West Indies.

125.   Pablo Casals was a famous Spanish cellist who lived much of his life in Puerto Rico; Noel Coward was a British playwright who had a house in Jamaica.

126.   The capital of the Dominican Republic had been renamed Ciudad Trujillo after the dictator Rafael Trujillo, in power at the time of Connor's visit. After his assassination in 1961 the original name, Santo Domingo, was resumed (Connor uses San or Santo Domingo to refer to the country, properly the Dominican Republic).

127.   Though Simón Bolívar, the 'Liberator' who led the campaigns for independence from Spain in modern Venezuela, Colombia and Ecuador,

was almost certainly of mixed descent, Connor is being provocative in calling him a 'half-negro'; in his native Venezuela, he was, and is, considered to be a 'white' Creole. Dessalines, Christophe and Pétion were rulers of Haiti in the decades after Haitian independence (1804). It was Pétion who aided Bolivar. Dr J.G.B. Siegert, a German doctor, was involved in Bolívar's campaigns. His sons in 1875 transferred his firm, which manufactured the famous Angostura Bitters, from Venezuela to Trinidad, where it is still made.

128.   For Gomez, see note 66; Marcos Perez Jímenez was president of Venezuela when US Vice-President Richard Nixon made his ill-fated visit to Latin America in 1958.

129.   Arnold Schoenberg was a famous avant-garde composer from Austria.

130.   Little Rock, Arkansas, was the scene of serious race riots instigated by whites against the civil rights movement; in 1958, China and Taiwan engaged in military action in the Taiwan Straits over the island of Quemoy, off the south China coast; Mosley had been the leader of Britain's Fascists in the 1930s and 1940s.

131.   The West Indies High Commission was the diplomatic mission of the Federation of The West Indies to Britain.

132.   David Pitt was a Grenada-born doctor, who was active in Trinidad politics in the 1940s before emigrating to Britain in 1947. In London he did social work with West Indian immigrants and helped calm race tensions after the Notting Hill riots in 1958. As a member of the Labour Party he served in various positions on the London County Council/Greater London Council, and was made a Labour life peer, as Lord Pitt of Hampstead, in 1975.

133.   The Wilberforce Programme seems to have been a government project to improve relations between West Indian immigrants and the British society, named for the famous nineteenth-century abolitionist William Wilberforce.

134.   Actually Trinidad Leaseholds was sold to Texaco in 1956.

135.   'Saga ting' means to dance stylishly down Frederick Street, the main shopping street of Port of Spain, in the manner of the saga boys, fashionably dressed young Trinidadians boasting the latest styles in clothes, shoes, hair and dance steps.

136.   Maribunta is the Trinidad vernacular for a wasp; here it is the name of a steel band and its supporters who brought out a band for carnival, based in Laventille, a working-class, African-Trinidadian suburb of Port of Spain which was the main cradle of the steel band movement.

137.   Connor makes the rather unlikely claim that he was responsible for getting the wartime US forces to build the road from Port of Spain to Maracas Bay on the north coast, to replace Teteron Bay in the northwest peninsula which had been closed off to civilians when the Base was established (see chapter 3).

138.   Following his successful guerilla campaign against the dictator Fulgencio Batista, Fidel Castro took power in Cuba in January 1959.

139.   Connor certainly exaggerated when he claimed Rastafarians controlled almost one-third, and Jehovah's Witnesses another third, of Jamaica's population around 1960.

140. In 1959, Rev Claudius Henry, a 'messianic' leader, was charged with attempting a military takeover of the Jamaican government; he was jailed for six years for treason. His son and a small group of guerillas were later captured and sentenced to death. There is no evidence that Henry was linked to the Rastafarians.

141. Coventry Cathedral was destroyed by wartime bombing, and the new cathedral, completed in 1962, was seen as a symbol of Britain's postwar renaissance, especially in the arts.

142. The Little Eight refers to the eight smaller colonies, including Barbados, which made up the Federation.

143. See Introduction for events surrounding the Jamaican referendum (1961), the dissolution of the Federation (1962), and Jamaican and Trinidad and Tobago independence (August 1962).

144. The don is Eric Williams, then Prime Minister of independent Trinidad and Tobago, attending the Commonwealth Heads of Government Conference.

145. There had been earlier, limited federal schemes in the British West Indies, such as the Leeward Islands Federation, but the Federation of The West Indies (1958–62) was the only one linking all the British islands except the Bahamas (not British Guiana or British Honduras). T.A. Marryshow of Grenada dedicated much of his long political life to working towards a British Caribbean federation.

146. Hugh Gaitskell was the Labour Leader of the Opposition in Britain at the time of the Federation's dissolution.

147. See Introduction for Connor's connection with the Workers' Music Association, and its link to the US visa issue.

148. Robert (Bob) Aldrich was an American film director and producer.

149. Johnny Indrisano, Henry Cooper, Jack Dempsey, Sonny Liston, Floyd Patterson and Cassius Clay (later Muhammed Ali), were famous American boxers.

150. This was the famous 1963 March to Washington led by Martin Luther King.

151. The Vietnam War began during J.F. Kennedy's presidency (1961–63), and he was responsible for the US-sponsored invasion of Cuba, at the Bay of Pigs, in 1961. He was assassinated in November 1963.

152. Method acting derived from the teachings of Konstantin Stanislavski, and was popularized in the US by Lee Strasberg and others in the 1940s and 1950s. The actor tries to enter the personality of his/her character, to act as he/she would have.

153. Connor is alluding to the impending breakup of his marriage to Pearl Connor.

154. Jomo Kenyatta, leader of the anti-colonial resistance in Kenya, was president of independent Kenya from 1964 to his death in 1978.

Appendix I

Author's Note

Every year since 1950 I sang for the Middlesex Hospital Smoker Concert, which is in aid of their Cancer Research Fund. I did not sing in 1960 because I thought there was too much dishonesty about. My stand was vindicated when the Nobel Committee refused to give the Peace Prize. Nobody deserved it that year. Later Pope John in his Christmas Encyclical begged the world leaders, "For God's sake, be honest for a change".

There was a marked change where these two appeals mattered. I resumed singing. Immediately after my performance on October 27th, 1964, I had a coronary attack. The students of the Hospital took me into Latymer Ward for tests. The doctors ordered me complete bed-rest and in order to while away the time they gave me all the facilities I needed to record and write my recollections. I continued this while convalescing at their beautiful Convalescent Home at Clacton-on-Sea in Essex.

I want children to understand it. Self-justification is the sin of all autobiographies and this one is no exception. I have no other platform. Because I did not bend or break, my mother, father, and grandfather, are the only people who really know me. They are not here to explain.

I want to thank Dr. G.D. Hadley, Dr. A.J. Cameron and Dr. Everard for their vision, the Matrons and all the Sisters and Nurses of the two institutions for their kind care.

This is also "Daddy" Worme's book. I believe it is the one he would have liked to write.

-Edric Connor

Appendix II

My Life with Edric Connor

PEARL CONNOR-MOGOTSI

We lived in a rural area where there was no electricity, very bad roads (not tarred), and no telephones. My parents were known as Mother and Father to the whole village. They were never called Mr and Mrs Nunez, although because of Father's job, and because of the way he kept order and was always correct and a pillar of rectitude in the family, he was known as Mr Nunez. Ours was a communal type of life, where Mother and Father were the centre of this community, and Mother especially tried to assist individuals with problems.

Father took us to school by car, an old Austin 3239. Where we lived was outside of Port of Spain, where our schools were just five miles away, but to us children it seemed 500 miles. He took us every morning to school and was a great time-keeper. If we missed the call from the horn to come out to the car, we were left behind and had to be punished by Father upon his return. If you were late you never got away with it. He was a Victorian disciplinarian. You got licks whether you were a girl or a boy. When I was about 16 years old, I got a bicycle, and was allowed to ride to school. Such freedom!

Visitors were a great problem, under Father's supervision. If anyone visited us he would keep walking around the house and looking into the verandah, so that we could not get into any hanky panky. He never let us go out with strangers and he distrusted boyfriends. We always went for holidays to an old aunt, very boring, and we all wanted to get away from his control. Hence my brothers married very young and the girls were intent on escaping his regime. My older sister Lois married a Fleet Air Arm sailor and went to England, and my youngest sister married and stayed in Trinidad.

In 1947 I toured up the islands on behalf of the Trinidad Youth Movement promoting Federation, and visited St. Lucia, Antigua, Martinique, Guadeloupe and Dominica. Upon my return home I told my parents I wanted to go abroad to study journalism at Columbia University in America. But Father was advised by my Uncle Nat, who was a dentist in Harlem, that America was unsafe for a girl. I think that my uncle did not want the responsibility.

I was still in Trinidad in early 1948, when Edric Connor paid a flying visit home to keep in touch with his roots. He was hosted by Beryl McBurnie, our cultural icon and his great friend. Beryl asked Barney Maurice and myself to go around with him, and I took this opportunity to discuss my plans to go abroad to study. He suggested that I go to England, as there were many opportunities for education there. This was the first time that I ever met him. That is how I came to decide to go to London when the idea of America was wiped out by my uncle.

Father was quite happy because he thought England was a safe country. He did not know much about it. I travelled to England by ship, and landed at Bristol in the spring of 1948, with the idea of studying law. There was no question of flying at that time. People travelled by ship. This was some months before the Emperor Windrush *docked in Southampton, bringing hundreds of West Indian immigrants seeking work and education.*

The spring in England was very cold, but the landscape from the train windows was beautiful, like a multi-coloured carpet of wheat, rye, corn and other crops. We arrived at Paddington Station where Edric sent his secretary to meet me. She was an Englishwoman, and was quite kind and helpful. She took me to a hotel in Cromwell Road, where Edric came later that evening to meet me and take me out sight-seeing in central London, to see the lights at Piccadilly Circus. I had told him that my sister Lois was married to an Englishman and was living in Blackburn, Lancashire, and that I wanted to go to visit with her. He arranged for me to get a ticket to travel north in a few days' time.

My parents were glad that I would see my sister, who was freezing out in Blackburn, quite isolated. I did not know much about Blackburn and found the skies overcast, with 'dark satanic clouds' caused by the cotton industry and the mills. John Simpson, my sister's husband, was manager at a mill, and subsequently became Mayor of Blackburn. When I arrived in London he was just settling back into life after the navy, three years after the end of the war. My sister had one child, Susan, at that time. I wanted to check her out and see how she was getting on. At that time there were no coloured people in that town. She was isolated.

I was depressed by the situation I found, completely different to our life in Trinidad, and wanted to return to London as quickly as possible. Edric invited me to return to London and offered to put me up in his flat at Lancaster Gate, until I got organized. He also obtained information about universities and assisted me in planning how to get about to different places in London. In the interim, Edric and I began to know each other better, and to grow closer. I was a great admirer of his work and his commitment to our culture and liberation, and found him to be a kind and understanding person. He was concerned for me to get on with my studies and got his secretary to give me guidance in finding places and information. I met with an unexpected problem at London University where, in order to join the law faculty, I needed to have a qualification in Latin. So I registered with the Regent Street Polytechnic, which was quite near to Lancaster Gate, to take the University Entrance qualifications. The course was in Latin, Logic, History, and English. I qualified by the autumn of 1949, and registered at London University Law Faculty in 1950 for the LLB degree.

Within a short space of time I was able to find out about Edric's work and his career. He was a very well known broadcaster with the BBC, and had an early morning programme called Housewives' Choice, *in which the theme song was 'If I can help somebody as I pass along, then my living shall not be in vain'. This song epitomized most of his life, and the standards by which he lived.*

He was also promoting Trinidad and Caribbean culture at every opportunity, by singing our folk songs and performing them whenever he could. He was an expert on our folk dances, which he taught me. (Father never allowed us too near the native culture. He wanted us to have a good English education and to emulate the British way of life.) For the first time I heard from Edric about calypsos, Carnival, the dances and songs. Beryl had taught us a bit, but Edric was an expert himself, and I thought he was on the same wicket as I was, just the right person for me. There were only a few black and Caribbean people in London at that time. I knew of no other Trinidadian except for an old family friend, Frank Singuineau, who was an actor. One felt isolated and in need of close friendships.

Edric had come to the UK initially, in 1943, to study engineering on a scholarship from the Victoria Institute, and was based in Dagenham, Essex. However he took his portfolio to the BBC, with introductions from his friends, Irene Nicholson and Lord Montague, who had been involved in making a film in Trinidad during the previous year. He was immediately taken up, as his material was original and he could perform the songs himself. He eventually gave up engineering altogether.

Within three months of my arrival, Edric asked me to marry him. When we decided to get married I wrote to my parents, who were quite surprised because that was not on the cards when I left home. I did not even know Edric very well, only as a celebrity of Trinidad & Tobago. He came from a totally different background to mine. In a way I felt isolated, as there were so few of us in London. So when he proposed to get married, I thought that I was of an age to marry and he was quite a suitable person. It was like an arranged marriage, and I decided he was the right person for me, as we had so many interests in common.

We were married at the Registry Office in Harrow Road (London), in June 1948, and my sister and her husband were witnesses. Then we went off on honeymoon to Eastbourne, where I had my first taste of racism in England, because the hotel told us there had been no booking and there was no room. You can imagine how upset I was. However, Edric contacted his agent who had made the booking, and after much coming and going, the manager came out and apologized profusely. Then we were given a room. That was one of the worst nights of my life, and I could not wait to leave the next morning and return to London. That was the first bad omen.

When Edric first came to England he stayed with friends, so he was in a protected environment. He had never been turned away before. I was part of his first experience of overt prejudice. He was very popular and well known, yet these people were not prepared to put him up in their posh hotel. This incident coloured my outlook for most of my life in England. I could not understand his having a white secretary, white agent and white friends. I did not realize that he had to work with the people who were here.

I became more involved with our Caribbean culture, which was also Edric's main interest, and this made me more interested in him. He taught me things I did not know about Trinidad and about the American bases where had worked. I only knew about them because of the incidents on the streets of Port of Spain, but it was by working for them that he got the money to leave for England. He told me about his parents. His father was a shoemaker in Mayaro, but was also a small farmer. He had three sisters, whom I only met when we visited Trinidad for the filming of Fire Down Below *in 1956, with Geraldine and Peter, our children. When he went there to film* Fire Down Below *with Robert Mitchum, Rita Hayworth and Jack Lemmon, we took the opportunity for me with the children to join him. My first return visit home in 1956 after nine years. Edric played the role of Jimmy Jean, a local boat captain. He made friends with all the cast, especially Rita Hayworth, who was welcomed by Beryl McBurnie at the Little Carib Theatre. He was given the Freedom of the Cities of Port of Spain and San Fernando, which was a great privilege for him and boosted his morale. As a result of all this acclaim, a small park in Mayaro, the village where he was born, was named after him. This had a lot of meaning for the local people, and his family, who lived at Peter Hill in Mayaro.*

It was his ideas and his friends that influenced me most in my relationship with him. He was a nationalistic black man who understood black people's talent and ability. Paul Robeson was his hero, and one of our most distinguished visitors. Edric met him at Paddington Station when he arrived in London in 1949, at the time when his (United States) Government was about to take away his passport. I was very new in England and thought tea would be the thing, so I bought a new tea set to commemorate the visit. He and Edric talked intently about the situation in which Paul found himself and had little time for tea. Paul had to leave us for another appointment after about two hours.

Edric believed in the liberation of our people and all other people of colour in the world. I only found out about Marcus Garvey when I went to the Polytechnic and University, and began mixing with politicized people from other Caribbean islands and Africa, and those living in Notting Hill Gate, which was a centre of Caribbean settlement. Garvey's wife was also resident there and was involved in many of the activities of our community. We met most of the Caribbean writers like Andrew Salkey, V.S. Naipaul, C.L.R. James, Jan Carew, George Lamming and Sam Selvon, all of them writing about our people, and later broadcasting plays and talks on the Caribbean Service of the BBC.

I began working in the political field as a young student. I had letters from Beryl McBurnie introducing me to George Padmore. He was still living in London at that time, working with Nkrumah of Ghana as his advisor. I met David Pitt again here in London where he had come in 1947 with his wife Dorothy and two children to practise as a doctor. I had worked with him in the WIN (West Indian National) party in Trinidad, representing youth, so the connection continued. He was very close to C.L.R. James, our foremost intellectual. Many activists were in London trying to get the Colonial Office to liberate their countries. Edric was working closely with this movement, with representatives from Kenya, Ghana, Nigeria, Jamaica and others. Jomo Kenyatta, Tom Mboya, Kwame Nkrumah, Dr Azikiwe, Seretse Khama, Norman Manley and Albert Gomes were all coming in and out of England to the Colonial Office. Edric was a central permanent figure in London, with a very high profile, mainly because of his work with the BBC (the voice of Britain), and our home, a flat at 27 Lancaster Gate, London W2, was a central meeting place. There were no embassies or other centres to accommodate our people in those years.

Edric was also a sportsman, and played cricket on Sundays in country villages with many of the English team, including the brothers Alec and Joe Bedser, who were his friends. I attended many matches with him. It was a pleasurable pastime, outside of the tensions of the theatre. He was also a lover of football, and was friendly with Matt Busby. He wrote a calypso for Manchester United, which was revived recently on the terraces. When the plane carrying the team to Munich crashed he was in contact with Busby, offering condolences and help.

Edric suffered a setback when we were first married and he wanted to sing in opera. The music critics here could not envisage someone they called a calypso singer singing in opera. So he could not get a chance to demonstrate his ability. He studied opera by listening to Caruso records and practised until he knew many operas by heart. But there was no chance in the rarified atmosphere of these specialists for him to succeed. Consequently, when he got an offer to go to Hungary to sing the role of Amanasro in the opera Aida, *he leapt at the chance, and at the height of the cold war travelled to Hungary. This turned out to be another blow to his career, because he was blacklisted and considered a communist, which he was not. He was simply a black man originally from the colonies trying to sing opera, and getting no chance to do so in England. Times have changed since then. He walked a very thin line trying to boost his career and make his name. He got no money for the job, but he did receive a beautiful suede fur-lined coat and hat, making him look like a Russian bear. He was quite happy about having gone to Hungary, underestimating the damage it would do him. He did not realize that we who lived in the West were not allowed to break that curtain open until the powers that be said so. In addition it was the time when Paul Robeson was being scourged and demonized and attacked by the press. Edric was compared with Robeson because he was the only high-profile black singer/actor on the UK scene. They were both black men of African origin, so they put them in the same bag.*

I worked with him on his collection of Songs from Trinidad *for the* Oxford University Press, *and his collection of* West Indian Spirituals and Folk Tunes *for Boosey & Hawkes, music publishers. I helped to organize his two albums with ARGO Records,* Songs from Jamaica *and* Songs from Trinidad, *recorded with the Jamaican quartet The Southlanders.*

He performed in concert at Wigmore Hall, and other famous venues, but this work was not lucrative. When he was invited to take acting parts, and perform in musical drama, he fitted into this very successfully. He played Jim in Georgia Story, *and Abe in* Summer Song *(the Dvorak musical), on London's West End. His great opportunity came when he was invited to play Gower in* Pericles, *directed by Tony Richardson in 1958 at the Theatre Royal, Stratford-upon-Avon. That year I took our two children to Stratford to join Edric for the first night of* Pericles, *and arranged for a team of Caribbean singers and dancers under the direction of Boscoe Holder to perform at the first night party in the little theatre backstage. I provided a Caribbean meal for the whole company, which was a great success.*

I had registered for the LLB at London University in 1950. In my second year I became pregnant and in March 1952, I had my daughter, Geraldine. I had to discontinue my studies and become a housewife. When Geraldine was one year old I had a great shock. We had a birthday party for her, and I had gone to take some of the children home. When I returned I found Edric collapsed on the bed. He had had a heart attack. This was my first knowledge of his illness, which dogged him for most of his life, and affected my life as well.

By 1954 we moved to Compayne Gardens, awaiting the move to our house at Crediton Hill in Hampstead. I was again pregnant. Edric was away filming Moby Dick *and only returned in time for the birth of our son Peter on 24th January 1955.*

It was in 1956 that Edric got the idea that I could set up a theatre agency to represent non-Caucasian artists from all over the world. We called it the Edric Connor Agency, and upon my return to London in late 1956 I began working on setting this up. We provided a much needed service for Third World artistes, and it thrived and became very well known, filling a gap in the casting of plays and films. Edric's name was the main attraction to these artistes, who all knew of him. I was still an unknown factor, the backroom girl.

Edric was all this time working on his own career. He took part in many films. His roles included John Kumalo in Cry the Beloved Country *with Canada Lee and Sidney Poitier, Chief Ushingo in* West of Zanzibar *(at the height of the Mau Mau disturbances) in Kenya, Sandpiper in* The Vikings, *Captain Jason in* Virgin Islands, *Waitari in* The Roots of Heaven *(Equatorial Africa), Balthazar in* King of Kings.

In 1960 he contracted to film the MCC cricket tour of the West Indies for the BBC. This covered a period of five months. During this time I was his 'runner', collecting the films from the airport and delivering them to the BBC. He also produced seven short films at this time. Of these, Carnival Fantastique *and* Caribbean Honeymoon No. 2 *were accepted and shown at the 1960 Edinburgh International Film Festival.* Carnival Fantastique *was judged best film from the Commonwealth, and was amongst the fifteen best films from all countries. A great achievement for Edric. Again I was responsible for taking these films to the Festival because Edric was in a play at the Royal Court Theatre in London, co-starring with Rex Harrison in* August For the People. *Later in 1960 we arranged to get distribution of* Carnival Fantastique *at the Cameo Cinema, Oxford Circus, for a four-month run, and national distribution.*

By October 1960 we were invited to the Independence Celebrations in Nigeria by Dr Azikiwe, the first President of independent Nigeria. At that time our great friend Ben Enwonwu, the distinguished sculptor, suggested that Edric should make a film celebrating the occasion. He was eventually commissioned to do so. He stayed back in Lagos to do the reccee, and I returned to London to look after our business. After coming back to London to prepare for the film, he booked his cameraman, and wrote the script for the film, named Bound for Lagos.

Subsequently, a series of events followed which affected his work on the film. First his cameraman fell ill with conjunctivitis, and had to return to London, to be replaced with someone whom Edric did not know. He was then plagued daily by demands from the extras for 'dash', a form of tips in Nigeria. He had never experienced anything like this before. Then many other things began to go wrong and he eventually fled from Lagos to Kano, in Northern Nigeria, where our friends Merle and Edick Michaelski lived. They had married at our home in London before going to Kano in 1957, where Edick practised medicine. They put Edric up for a few days, after which he flew back to London.

The tragedy for him was that he was working alone without much support, because of budget considerations. There was no one to separate him from the demanding mobs. He left his transit van, cameras and other equipment behind, only taking the films with him. I knew that things were not right when he returned to London. He seemed to be in a deep depression, and I thought that he had been bitten by the tsetse fly, because he slept for many hours in the few days after his return. There was little I could do, as I had no hand in the planning of the film. I was able to assist him with some Nigerian artistes to complete filming in the studio.

In the 1950s ours was an open house, where we entertained the West Indies Cricket Team, which won the Ashes in 1950. The heroes were Frank Worrell, Clyde Walcott and Everton Weekes. But two cricketers who enjoyed celebrity via the calypsonian Lord Kitchener were Ramadin and Valentine. We were also involved with two recipients of the Nobel Peace Prize: Chief Luthuli when he was in London in transit to Sweden, and Dr. Martin Luther

King, who was brought by Claudia Jones, editor of the West Indian Gazette, *to a meeting with us and David Pitt (later Lord Pitt), before going on to Sweden to receive the Nobel Peace Prize. We hosted the West Indian leaders during their intensive lobbying with the Colonial Office. Amongst them were Sir Grantley Adams of Barbados, Norman Manley of Jamaica, 'Odo' Burnham of Guyana, and Errol Barrow from Barbados, as well as Dr Eric Williams of Trinidad and Tobago.*

Over all these years the Agency thrived, and added personal management to our portfolio. Between 1957 and 1963, we developed careers of many black artistes who became well known, like Joan Armatrading, Patti Boulay, Rudolph Walker, Nina Baden-Semper, Carmen Munroe and Ramjohn Holder.

But by 1958 there was tension building up in our home, where Edric resented the growing intrusion of the Agency in our life. I had sent our children home to my parents when Geraldine was eight and Peter five years old. I had found it very difficult to take care of them on my own. (Edric was often away working, and did not understand my dilemma, and the problems I had with au pairs and housekeepers). The Agency had grown so large that it demanded my full-time attention. In the interim we went to Nigeria for Independence in 1960 and he was given the commission to film the event. But that also created problems, as explained earlier. He was becoming more and more frustrated. Added to all this he was refused entry into the United States on several occasions, and lost much lucrative work, because of his connection with Paul Robeson. This was not public knowledge. Further, he had a recurring heart problem which made us very unsettled. I felt that I had to pull up my shoestrings and make the Agency profitable. About this time I was invited to take part in Lindsay Anderson's film Oh Lucky Man, *playing the role of Mrs. Gandhi. The film won an award at the Cannes Film Festival.*

Although I brought the children back to London in 1960, I had no arrangement to keep them here, particularly as they had progressed so much in their education. So I sent them back to Trinidad. Then, because we were not going home for Independence in 1962, we brought the children to celebrate with us in London. I thought another few years at home in the West Indies could only benefit them, so back they went to my parents in September 1962. In 1963 Edric was again invited to go to America to make the film Four For Texas *with Frank Sinatra and Dean Martin. This time he got a visa, and set off in the summer of 1963 for Hollywood. He was hosted by Rita Hayworth who gave him much support.*

His career had gone full circle, from music and singing to drama and acting on stage, in concert, at Wigmore Hall, and the Moss Empire Music Hall circuit, though the most remunerative were films. He had a lasting connection with The Players Theatre under the Arches in the Strand, where he appeared weekly whenever he was in London. I also became a habitué of this theatre. He represented American blacks in Britain, and sang spirituals and songs like 'Ole Man River'.

He brought the first steel band to England for the Festival of Britain in 1950. The band was called TASPO, Trinidad All Steel Percussion Orchestra, under the direction of his friend Griffiths. When they arrived the customs were confounded, never having seen musical instruments made of steel drums. This band was not conventional. One of the instrumentalists who was excelling at that time was Ellie Mannette (now Professor Mannette) in the USA. He does not mention Edric's name, but Edric arranged for him to get a scholarship with the Birmingham Symphony Orchestra, which changed his life. This was the kind of thing that Edric was always doing, giving a helping hand to others.

He was committed to all things West Indian, and this was what made me committed to him, in whom I saw my own aspirations realized. Edric was a great nationalist. He believed in the independence of our country and the life of our people. Consequently, as soon as he felt that his feet were firmly planted on the ground, he formed his own film company, Edric Connor Films Ltd, to make documentaries about the West Indies and the test cricket series. So interested was he in Trinidad that he bought a cinema in San Juan, and refurbished it completely, arranging to send down prestigious films like Ingmar Bergman's The Seventh Seal *and* Black Orpheus, *featuring Marpessa Dawn. He left the cinema in the hands of an Indian associate. The cinema was closed down. Edric then got involved in a brick factory, which was supposed to benefit from the new building industry. This also went broke.*

His efforts to work on projects in Trinidad were ill fated. Most of the things he wanted to do fell apart because they were left in the hands of strangers, while he was abroad in the UK. The only option was for us to go back to Trinidad to live, which was impossible because of his work here. The film company thrived for a while, and it was through this company that he got the commission to film in Nigeria after Independence. The British Film Institute backed him to make his groundbreaking documentary Carnival Fantastique, *about the emergence of the newest form of musical instrument, the 'steel pan', and also to film Carnival for public consumption. He managed to get distribution for the film, which was shown at the Edinburgh Festival and in London's West End cinema, the Cameo at Regent Street, for six months. A real achievement for a newcomer to the film industry.*

However, after he met Robeson in 1949 and brought him to our home, he was tarred with the same brush. But he was not a communist, simply a nationalist involved in the future of Trinidad and the West Indies. Soon after his welcoming of Robeson, his work with the BBC began to dwindle, and he was victimized. Although he was a very good actor he was not able to get a visa to go to America, until 1963, when he made his last film.

In Edric's day a black actor was 'A Raisin in the Sun'. Now the young ones are going to drama school and making progress, but it has taken a long time. Edric paid the price for his conviction and belief in the liberation of black people. Our close friend Claudia Jones was also involved in the upliftment and liberation of our people. Now the West is kissing the Russians whilst we look on, still on the outside. Being called names.

The Edric Connor Agency grew and developed because there was such a need for it. There was no representation for black and coloured people. I was inspired because it was a pioneering job, and two Jamaican brothers, Barry and Lloyd Reckord, were bulwarks of my efforts, one a writer, the other an actor. We decided to set up workshops to give actors some experience; Edric was there as a backdrop and I was running the show. He was advising me until I got to know the ropes and the people; he was the founder of the Agency.

But we had a terrible background of struggle, which damaged our relationship. When Edric returned from America in December 1963, he wanted me to close down the Agency, but I was adamant that too much had gone into building it up to stop. We clashed over this decision. He disliked my working with men, for whom there was more work than for women. It was very difficult. In addition, most of his wages from America went to the taxman, leaving him very short of funds again. He was sort of desperate, and I was no consolation, seeing the work I was doing as a lifesaver.

By 1964, we decided to separate and I moved out of our home in Crediton Hill to a flat in Paddington, where I could continue running the Agency. I then decided to found the Negro Theatre Workshop, and we were selected to represent Britain in the First World Festival of Black and African Arts, in Dakar, Senegal, in 1966. I organized some twenty artists to perform the St. Luke Passion, *which we called* The Dark Disciples, *to be staged in a cathedral at Easter time. It was a resounding success. In 1977 I went with the Trinidad contingent to Lagos, Nigeria, for the Second World Festival of Black and African Arts. I attended the colloquium, speaking on the media in Africa.*

Edric suffered a fatal stroke and died in October 1968. He was living in Abercorn Place, St. John's Wood, and his cousin Fitz Henry was staying with him. Late on the night of 6th October, I had a phone call from Fitz, telling me that Edric had collapsed and was taken by ambulance to the St. John and Elizabeth Hospital, in St. John's Wood. This was like a hospice, run by nuns, not the place for a neurological case. The next morning I went down and found Edric in a coma. I rang up David Pitt, asking what we should do, and he suggested that Edric be moved to the National Hospital for Neurology, at Queen's Square, London. However it was already too late to do anything. He never recovered from the stroke and died on the 16th October, 1968.

I arranged for his funeral with Rev John Dover-Wellman, our local vicar. This was arranged at his Church, Emmanuel, West Hampstead. He gave Edric a great send-off in a packed church, with two bishops attending. George Lamming gave the eulogy. I then had to arrange to take Edric's body back to Trinidad for burial, as that was his wish. He had two funerals: one in Hampstead, London, and the second at the Anglican Cathedral in Port of Spain, Trinidad. Among the bearers of his coffin were Derek Walcott, a great admirer, and Lennox Pierre, his close friend.

I tried to do my best to give him the send-off he deserved, although we were separated. There was too much in our past together to do otherwise. I was very saddened by his untimely death at the age of 55 (1913–1968). I recognized the tremendous struggle his life had been, and the toll it had taken in the end.

Appendix III

Lecture on West Indian
Folk Music (1943)
By Edric E. Connor

Ladies and Gentlemen,

A most important task befalls me this evening; that of lecturing to you on West Indian Folk Music, a subject so great in magnitude, significance and importance that I fear it cannot be adequately expounded in one short evening. I shall endeavour to be as practical as possible so that at least the elementary phases of West Indian Folk Music can be grasped. I say elementary because there are certain forms of West Indian Music which relate to certain customs which call for specific Rhythms and Musical patterns.

I want to say at this stage that there has been so little known of West Indian Music that you may find me at times clarifying some of my findings by referring to Histories.

The good fortune was mine to be born in a family that retained, up till a few years ago, much of its old Customs. My childhood was spent in the beautiful countryside at Mayaro, where each individual knew the other and life was just the making of Music, most of the time.

Having done some research work in West Indian Folklore, I shall endeavour to present to you this evening some of the things I greatly enjoyed while carrying out my investigations. The fact that my experiences were enjoyable must not in any way hide the fact that I encountered innumerable difficulties and more than once fell in the hands of the Police. It is nevertheless most gratifying to be able to demonstrate here some of my findings as evidence in the case for West Indian Music, for West Indian Culture, and I shall consider myself sufficiently compensated if I could arouse and hold your interest during the moments at my disposal.

Over a period of 300 years, millions of Negroes were uprooted from their homes as free and happy men and transplanted in the West Indies as unhappy slaves. These slaves are definitely responsible and should be eulogized for the music they brought and developed in these parts. These were people who enjoyed a very high standard of liberty and prosperity in their homeland even in captivity, because in the early days slaves in Africa enjoyed more equity than free peoples of most of the foreign powers. Their troubles began with the Trans-Atlantic Slave Trade. The differences here must be explained. In Africa a headman's slave was given land to work and he paid a yearly ground rent of rice, palm oil, and fowls to his master. In the West Indies the slave was a beast of burden and the fact that he reacted to such treatment, with song, is positive proof of his highly cultured and civilized mind, a mind tempered by a civilization older and superior in many ways to the one that caused his bondage.

His customs and religion were always dear to him because they were natural. When he trod the earth, he walked with his God who was everywhere — in the trees, in the air, the dust, the water he drank and the very food he ate. One cannot see why he should be forced to divorce his customs and general folklore. One may be tempted to think it is a further means of domination, which actually destroyed his very conscience. Yet it is deplored that there is a dearth of regional folklore in the West Indies.

West Indian Folklore can be classified under six heads: Songs, Dances, Tales, Games, Proverbs and Customs. In order that I may adequately present the subject of the evening, it will be necessary for me to touch at least five of the six phases — that is, Songs, Dances, Tales, Games and Customs.

GAMES

Our Games are numerous and varied. Some are pleasant and light and fanciful while others demand exceptional talent and skill. I have introduced games into this lecture because most of them are musical. The musical games range from the re-enacting of Slave catching, to Stick fighting and Damier. Most musical games are played at Wakes and moonlit nights, by children and grown ups alike.

Presentation Ting Tang,   (General)
Koke Oko   (Trinidad)
Bay Sez La Reins   (Trinidad)
Bai Banan   (Grenada)
In My Own Native Land   (Trinidad)
Roogoo Roogoo Roogoo Zook

FOLK TALES

In our Folk Tales we discover the genius of their composers. Of all the Nancy Stories I have heard, there are an exceptional few without music of any sort. The composers have been able to interweave mood, atmosphere and music into most marvellous forms. The characters of most, Lappin, Tou Couma, Compere Shouval, Compere Tigre, Bra Nancy, Madame Cow, Beau Lion, Ti Chat Macaque, Morocoy, Galappe, and a host of other characters too numerous to mention, have furnished us with so much music that I can visualize a veritable bacchanal of songs if they were all used the same evening.

I may mention here that as a child, and even now at my age, I can still visualize the grand Ball thrown by Beau Lion. There was Madame Coshon with a beautiful smile on her face and dancing gaily with Compere Lappin to the music of Bra Nancy's Orchestra.

VOOM KA VOOM KA VOO BAM BAM

There are also sad stories; tragic to the very supporting tunes. It is to be observed wherever the tales deal with characters of the wilderness they are gay, light and happy, but when they are built around human beings they are always tragic. Outline Folktale: *Lim Lim Lim.*

DANCES

Our Dances are numerous. Many are extinct in these parts, but quite a few have survived the test of Modern tunes. It is regrettable that Legislation has been so strong against them. The fact is, this brand of West Indian Folklore is destroyed by false Public Opinion — opinion of a subject it knows little or nothing about, and in many cases never heard of. I proved it a couple of years ago. Of twenty-five persons only one understood the name Bilnap to be connected with a sort of dance which he had never seen. The other twenty-four never even heard the name. Yet, certain prominent members of the Community abhor it, and that's how the evil propaganda is perpetuated.

There is this answer I can arrive at as a possible reason for this sophisticated reaction against the Bongo. It respects no class. It is contagious. You hear it, you move in its direction and without previous knowledge of its steps, you jump into the ring and dance until you are exhausted. Then you suddenly catch yourself and say, "Hello, I must have been dancing".The next move is to hurry away and recapture your lost pride.

Before, getting down to the dances, the Music and the Orchestra which supplies same must be gone into. All dances are based on Rhythm, and Rhythm, like the offspring of Africa, has a definite affinity to the drum and anything akin to drumming.

A unique original West Indian Orchestra would contain 3 drums, 1 Shack-shack [Chac-chac], a Conch Shell and a Bottle and Spoon or anything that could give a ringing sound, but certain dances call for certain combinations of instruments.

DANCES (INSTRUMENTS)

Calinda	1 drum (Martinique Cutter)(Tambour Bamboo)
Belle	2 drums, Foulé and Cutter
Limbo	Any amount of voices and clapping of hands
Bongo	10 or 12 pieces of sticks played rhythmically by five or six men
Shango	3 drums, Amilay, Congo and Mama
Doption	Any amount of voices and clapping of hands
Reel Dance	3 drums, Tambourine, Congo and Mama
Asseter	3 Drums, Chac-chac, Ogen
Beguine	Ballroom Instruments
Meringue	Ballroom Instruments
Rada	3 drums, Bula, Seconde Maman Chac-chac, Ogan

I can go on as though there is no end to the list.

THE CALINDA

It is out of the Calinda tunes and Spiritual that we derive our now famous Calypsos. The Calinda is a form of Pussy foot sand dance, which is more or less contrary to the rhythm of the drum accompaniment.

Ding Ding Wai Wai is about the oldest Calinda tune known and its influence on the Calypso is still evident. This tune is historic, being traced to the days of slavery. It also figured prominently in the Canboulay Riots [sic] of 1881 and about 1925 it was revived to campaign the Hon. A.A. Cipriani to the Legislature.

To 1834 and later *Ding Ding Wai Wai*
1881 *Hound Dog arrange*
1925 *Who you votin[g] for – Cipriani*
[no date] *Michel dances Calinda*

BELE DANCE

The Bele Dance is known throughout the West Indies except Barbados. The name is from the French Bel air. It is quite possible that it comes from the Bele tribe on the Sanaga River, West Africa.

I would rather have you see this dance than listen to my explanation of it.

Maria Oh, Way ha (Grenada)
Sweet Man Do Re (Trinidad)
Go Way Jestina (Trinidad)

LIMBO

This can be easily classified as a game, but the Rhythm used is so unique and the movements required demand so much skill and technique that I cannot but classify it as a dance.

Limbo, Limbo like me

BONGO

As mentioned before, the Bongo is a dance which I consider contagious. The instruments which supply the music and rhythm are 10 or 12 pieces of stick played by 5 or 6 men and any amount of voices. The music is furnished by beating the sticks rhythmically, known as Kwe Kwa. The dance serves a dual purpose of competition:

(1) Emulation by intricacy or movements
(2) The effect of mirrored halves.

The Kwe Kwa rhythm is accompanied by an abstract groaning and grunting from the dancers. These sounds replace those of drums.

It is most unfortunate that this artistic and prominent bit of West Indian originality should be suppressed. Ladies and Gentlemen, it gives me great pleasure to present to you the Bongo demonstrated by Evacuees from the North Western peninsula.

Ladies and Gentlemen, that is Class. That's originality. That's Folklore. That is the spirit of Trinidad — a spirit that moves one's very soul. Maybe if our Legislators, our Magistrates, Priests and Policemen were to see it as you have in its true perspective, I am confident that they would readily release the sanctions imposed against it.

SHANGO DANCE

The dance concerns religious rites. It is the ritual indicative of the mimetic past of a people. It endeavours to express the subconscious reactions to a life history of the race. It is one of the Soul surviving affinities between the Afro-West Indians and the West African Negro. While the dance is still practiced by a few Trinidadians, I regret to say that the rites at present are somewhat confused and I expect the custom as a whole to become extinct within the next twenty years provided something is not done to avert the catastrophe. However, Grenada, Martinique, Haiti and a few other small islands are waging a losing battle against other religions and national prejudices. The fact is a method of substitution is being carried out — a system deliberately leading the people away from their African Gods to the Christian saints.

For example:

Ogun	is now supposed to be	St. Michael
Ajajah or Ayelah	is now supposed to be	St. Michael
Shango	is now supposed to be	St. John
Imanjah	is now supposed to be	St. Ann
Oshun	is now supposed to be	St. Philomen
Oyer	is now supposed to be	St. Catherine
Osan	is now supposed to be	St. Francis
Bon Zewon	is now supposed to be	St. Jerome
Abatala	is now supposed to be	St. Bartholomew
Ashareke	is now supposed to be	St. Benedict
Dada Mazeokoe	is now supposed to be	St. Anthony

The Shango Dance is much like the Orisha or Yoruba Dance. The difference lies in their religious rites. However, unlike the Shango certain forms of the Orisha dance are done with the shoulders, knees and hands, in a sitting posture.

Three drums are used to beat out the rhythm for the dance. Amiley, Congo and Mama (in Haiti they are known as Rada drums), Bebe or Bula, Tambour seconde, and Manan. During the ceremonies, it is not unusual to find the drummers hypnotized by their own drumming. I have experienced this myself —The effect is pleasantly paralyzing. This custom is resorted to in times of trouble, sickness or thanksgiving, when a greater and unseen power is called upon for deliverance and succour. It always involves the sacrifice of goats or fowls.

SONGS AND CUSTOMS

I have combined these sections because we cannot adequately discuss one without referring to the other. Our songs, particularly those of Trinidad, are derived from certain Customs which have furnished interesting History. Associations of the poorer classes, throughout the West Indies, have developed Co-operative systems which result in the most simple and stable form of Economics one can expect to find. There are also Religious Associations whose power has been felt and recognized. The recognition in this case did not go to the doctrine taught, but to the Unity afforded by their Religion.

These associations have given us Music in the form of War Songs which discourage fear. Work songs which lighten Labour, Lullaby ha[u]nts which invoke and Spirituals which deal with Generation, and Future Life after Sorrow and Death through the trials of this world.

The War Songs are typical Calinda tunes. It is out of these War Songs — Calinda, tunes associated with the Sprituals, Games or songs etc. — that we derive our now famous Calypso and other West Indian Music similar to the Calypso but called by different names, in different islands of the West Indies. To explain these Songs, I must recall the custom during Slavery when Conch Shells, horns and bottles were blown to call the slaves of neighbouring estates to put out cane fires. This custom gave rise to the term Canboulay.

Canboulay came to denote a torch-light procession which was very much enjoyed by slaves and masters alike. The spirited singing, dancing and marching through the adjoining estates was always welcome and one can well imagine the number of estate fires there must have been in those days.

We will again consider *"Ding Ding Wai Wai"* — one of the songs of that period. Pay careful attention to the words:

Hoolay La Woozay, Moonyay Moin
Ding Ding Wai Wai (Repeat)

This is the very verse preserved and it is quite clean. It shows no sign of a banal sequence. Demonstrate *"Man Man Tirez"*. This takes us back where we left off — the Canboulay.

On Thursday 31st July 1834 at midnight, the atmosphere throughout the West Indies was very tense — a tension passively constitutional and spiritually painful as tears of joy were shed by the slaves when they were officially declared free. In Trinidad, the psychological pain quickly gave way to revelry and Canboulay processions outstandingly marked the celebrations on 1st August 1834. I am glad I was able to get the name of at least one ex-slave. He was known as Mariguin. It is handed down that he was a small wiry man who was a born king. On his death bed some years after the abolition he composed and sang *"La mort Mariguin fais Gren Moune ca Haley"*.

As time went by Canboulay took on enormous proportions and about 1849 it was shifted by law from the celebration of Emancipation Day to the Carnival which is a European fete. Whereas before the slaves marched from estate to estate for social purposes or to put out fires, now these free people marched through the streets from district to district for purpose of competition, which involved stick playing and kaiso-singing. Therefore the brutal rivalry in freedom is obvious. Canboulay continued this way until the riot of 1881.

It was totally suppressed by law in 1884. Nevertheless the spirit of competition continued to exist. Stick playing was allowed in enclosed areas and drum beating necessitated a formal licence by law. From then on songs of a more bellicose nature were modified to a sort of martial music to facilitate marching.

I think it fitting that we should always retain memories of Mariguin, Albert Gregoire who died last December, Alphonso Junction, Freddie Mungo, Peter Agant, Candy Boucan the king of Me Minor in Tambour Bamboo, George Inniss, Robert Miler and James Brice who at the age of 95 is still alive and kicking. Those are old stick warriors and singers of our war songs. They assisted in moulding West Indian music.

From L.O. Pierre: Text of Lecture-recital entitled "An Evening of West Indian Folk Songs and Dances" delivered by Edric Connor at the Princes Building, Port of Spain, on 2 December 1943. [Lennox Pierre attended the lecture]